"The Harvard University Graduate School of Design is about to select a new dean, erect a new building, and modify its programs. This reorientation of the School is an opportunity to respond to the changing role and demands of environmental design."

"Preface," *Connection* (Winter/Spring 1968).

Platform 12: How About Now? Harvard University Graduate School of Design

Table of Contents

129–164

"With a predicted world population of 7 billion by the year 2000, what architectural firm is geared to handle the real problems of our times? [. . .] Retooling is an extravagance to be reserved for an occasion that absolutely demands it. The significance of crisis is that it indicates that the time for retooling has arrived. Assuming that crisis is a necessary precondition for the emergence of new theories, how do the affected parties respond?"

"Considering the immense volume of 20th-century building, how much can we be truly proud of as architecture? Fume-ridden traffic and pedestrian-hating highways provide the soulless generators of large-scale planning. Across the land from the coasts, bulldozers munch hungrily on the beautiful marshlands and mountains. Admit that in all planning theory, little has been accomplished in preserving the planet's resources."

. . . **A conversation with GSD students in January, February, and March** . . .

165–200

"One is not certain what the architecture is. Is the place for bicycles architecture? Is a tree growing on a building architecture? Are the painted duct work and exposed mechanical unit architecture? Is the unit bare for functional reasons? For aesthetic reasons? The planes of interpretation always appear in a new light, and just as one thinks he has grasped the essence, it slips away and reappears in another place, mocking attempts at definition as timeless or immediate. Architecture, at best the result of process and situation, is ambivalent."

"Perhaps you don't realize the significance of your official answer to the question, 'What does it mean to be an architect?'"

201–236

"Where then would you place 'history' in the education of an architect?" [. . .] "There has been a lot of talk lately about the New Economy, new modes of production, and virtual reality. How much are these things 'new beginning'? How are we to interpret all this?"

"This publication is an attempt to do just that—to seek the formation of a number of prevalent tendencies, and coherences, among the many that currently operate within the School. Therefore it represents a specific set of choices, a point of view. It takes a stance. But in configuring its inclusiveness it has also had to leave out things, to edit. All for the sake of constructing the clarity of an archeology, one that according to Foucault's schema manifests a history of its conditions of possibility."

. . . **A conversation with GSD students in April and May** . . .

237–256

"Every time you don't publish something, you are being a critic. Yet you don't share that judgment. That negative determination happens without comment, in the click of a trash button. What I'd like to hear about is what happens in your head between the look and that judgmental click. Why this and not that?"

Conclusion

"How About Now?"

257–292

Appendix

Letter from the Dean

> *Engagé* is the past participle of the French verb *engager*, meaning "to engage." The French have used *engagé* since the 19th century to describe socially or politically active people. The term became particularly fashionable in the wake of World War II, when French writers, artists, and intellectuals felt it was increasingly important for them to take a stand on political or social issues and represent their attitudes in their art. By 1946, English speakers had adopted the word for their own politically relevant writing or art, and within a short time, "engagé" was being used generally for any passionate commitment to a cause.
> —*Merriam-Webster Dictionary*, s.v. "engage"

Beginning with its first issue some 12 years ago, the task of *Platform* has always been to produce a collection of the previous year's work of the Harvard University Graduate School of Design (GSD) from a particular perspective, and through that process to enhance and contribute to the School's future projects. The concepts of the "Index," "Still Life," "Live Feed," and "Setting the Table" have provided some of the recent approaches to the presentation of the work of the Harvard GSD. This issue of *Platform* continues that remit, yet for the three student editors, Carrie Bly, Isabella Frontado, and Natasha Hicks, as well as for me personally, it also signals a change.

As the last *Platform* for which I have the privilege of writing an introduction, it marks the culmination of an unrivaled opportunity to help shape one of the world's leading design academies. The idea of a project in an intentional state of constant transformation, evident in previous years, is here augmented by a sense, not only of reflection, but of anticipation of new directions and possibilities. In that regard, this edition of *Platform* represents a transition, moving from the critical consideration of the School's recent achievements to its potential future areas of attention under the leadership of a new dean.

That is also why the tone and focus of this issue is thought of and constructed as a series of "conversations" with the reader. These conversations are analogous to those that take place within the Harvard GSD on the role and responsibility of design within contemporary societies.

One of the key lessons of the past decade for me has been linked to the necessity of situating design within a broader global, environmental, social, political, and cultural context. This is one of the prerequisites for the greater effectiveness of our profession, and one that goes hand in hand with the need for collaboration with other disciplines.

At the same time, it is imperative that we do not relinquish the key responsibility of design, which is to imagine, configure, and construct artifacts of intelligence and beauty. How do we create situations that will transform the lives of the inhabitants and beneficiaries of our spatial imagination? Engaging with that question has always been central to our practice, and will no doubt continue to be so into the future.

Mohsen Mostafavi
Dean and Alexander and Victoria Wiley
Professor of Design

Letter from the Editors

Seventy-eight years ago, a group of 10 Harvard University Graduate School of Design students called for a reevaluation of design education and the work produced through it. In a letter to the dean, *An Opinion on Architecture* (1941), they proposed several areas for change, including: connecting pedagogy with professional practice; inviting visiting lecturers; increasing collaboration between the landscape and architecture programs; and developing a forum for students to discuss their shared experiences.

Out of these proposals, the students highlighted the need for a publication—a periodical that would "state the principles on which modern design is conceived" and "stimulate architects in the United States" through a review of their work. This first student publication, *TASK*, produced six issues from 1941 to 1945, and served as a forum to discuss the rapidly changing needs of a society and the ways that design could respond to those needs. *TASK* was not the last in this pursuit. From publications like *Connection*, produced in the 1960s, *for'm* in the '70s and '80s, and *APPENDX: Culture/Theory/Praxis* in the '90s, to the contemporary *Open Letters* and *Veri Very Vary*, students at the GSD have consistently sought to process their intellectual inheritance in order to evaluate their position as designers within and beyond the school.

This imperative need for conversations on the principles and values driving design, and for a place to share these conversations publicly, is the lineage that *Platform* 12 both arises from and reasserts today. Like many years past, this last year has again brought students, faculty, staff, and invited guests together to talk about a particularly critical moment. From major shifts at the GSD such as the changing deanship, to the tensions of global, national, and state politics surrounding issues such as migration and climate change, today, a desire for conversations continues to permeate and stimulate life at the GSD.

Platform 12: *How About Now?* offers a selection of student work from the 2018–2019 academic year in the context of a conversation framed by questions. These questions ask us to articulate where we stand, and in turn invite us to take a position that reveals the subjectivity of our own perspectives, suggesting that we must approach design from multiple angles and avenues.

In recognition of the institutional history that has shaped GSD coursework and conversations around design, each section of this book begins and ends with a question borrowed from an archival GSD student publication (1941–present). While these questions were formed in specific historical moments, when recontextualized in *How About Now?* they build on the conversations unfolding over time between students, faculty, and invited guests. With these questions we seek to recognize the influence of institutional and disciplinary history, the evolving considerations of such questions in the work we produce today, and the current conditions those considerations are channeled through.

To invite the reader into discussions produced this year in studios, lectures, seminars, workshops, and independent projects, *How About Now?* places a question, rather than a title, as an entry point into each project. Each question is formed through either a student's abstract or the professor's course syllabus, reflecting the unfolding of important relationships between students and faculty. With these questions we seek to draw out the aims of the work and encourage conversations to take place between these projects.

In our review of past student publications and the work of this school year, we found a multitude of positions on design's engagement with social, political, formal, and pedagogical issues. *How About Now?* presents conversations containing substantial, subtle, and at times silent distinctions between the questions, values, and positions present in each work. It is our position that projects critically engaging with design agendas—for whom and for what are we designing?—reveal the agency of designers and our potential to work together to build a better future.

The tradition of students' critical engagement with design agendas is not limited to curricular work. Like students of the past, GSD students of 2018–2019 went above and beyond to engage with the social, political, and pedagogical domains of design through their work in extracurricular groups and organizations.

Student group work is documented here as four unbound inserts and framed as conversations, formal and informal, with the student community.

As editors, we are proud to be part of a past and current student body interrogating the challenges and complexities of inherited design agendas. With this book, we seek to bring attention back to the medium of student publications as a necessary forum for questions and conversations around the principles and values that drive design work. Since the *Platform* series recently joined this lineage, we close this volume with a proposal of our own—one that promotes a design education urging fluency in social, political, formal, and pedagogical conversations, as these conversations have arisen and transformed over time, as they converge around questions of values, and as they ask again and again, *How About Now?*

Carrie Bly
Isabella Caterina Frontado
Natasha Hicks
Editors

GSD NEWS

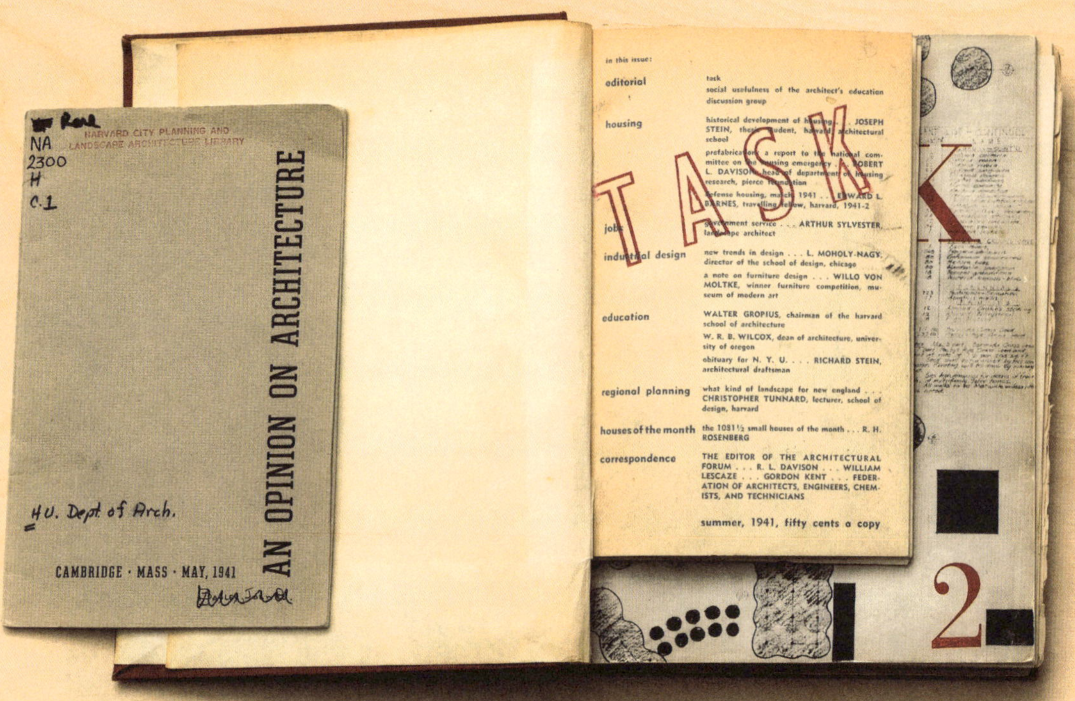

An Opinion on Architecture
Bruno Zevi, et al. (Cambridge; MA: The Century Press, 1941).

An Opinion on Architecture was a critique of architectural education and practice published in 1941 by Harvard GSD students Bruno Zevi, John Bayley, Robert Hays Rosenberg, John Taylor Moore, Warren Radford, Frank Tresedor, Arthur Cheang, William Joseph, Dahong Wang, and T. J. Willo, and addressed to Dean Joseph Hudnut. The students perceived their education to be "unclear from a social point of view" (too detached from the world), "unclear from an aesthetic point of view" (modern architecture had become nothing more than a style), "inadequate from an engineering and construction point of view" (lack of relation between construction and design courses), "insufficient from a professional point of view" (no relation with building practice), and "insufficient in terms of collaboration" (with allied design disciplines). This self-criticism emerged out of their commitment to social consciousness, which they believed rooted the modern movement they ascribed to, and was essential to the survival of democratic thought (particularly in the context of war devastation). They encouraged collaboration across departments, and proposed changes in curriculum, open juries, public lectures, and the creation of a student publication.

TASK: A Magazine for the Younger Generation in Architecture
Years active: 1941–1945; 1948; frequency: irregular; number of issues: 7; format: print journal

TASK, the first student journal publication at the GSD, was produced in Robinson Hall by students of the GSD, MIT, and Smith College. It was an immediate response to *An Opinion on Architecture*, and first went to print in the summer of 1941. The editorial statement reads: "We believe that the architectural schools and the profession do not sufficiently reflect society's needs; nor train the student and the young architect in the principle of collective work. That is why we are publishing this magazine [. . .] it is to be the expression of students who realize that architects today are either unaware of the rapidly changing needs of society or are unable to answer them." The first issue's editors were Eunice Hall (Smith College), Judith Turner (MIT), and Warren Radford, Robert Hays Rosenberg, Richard Snibbe, John Bayley, and George Metzger (all GSD). Six issues were published between 1941 and 1945; and a single postwar issue (number 7/8) was published in 1948.

1936
Harvard GSD is established; Joseph Hudnut is installed as GSD Dean; Walter Gropius arrives a year later.

1941
"[*TASK*] will be a means of achieving clarity of ideas, and forms of organized action, so that our work [...] will answer the requirements of society" –*TASK*, no. 1.

1942
Women are admitted to the GSD. "The woman-architect should, on getting work, ask for: 1. Equal Pay, 2. No Segregation, and 3. Equal Opportunity for advancement." –*TASK*, no. 4.

1943
"The war has blasted the architect's world. [...] Again he has been reminded that he is part of a society. The necessity for reevaluation and sharp adjustment confronts him." –*TASK*, no. 4.

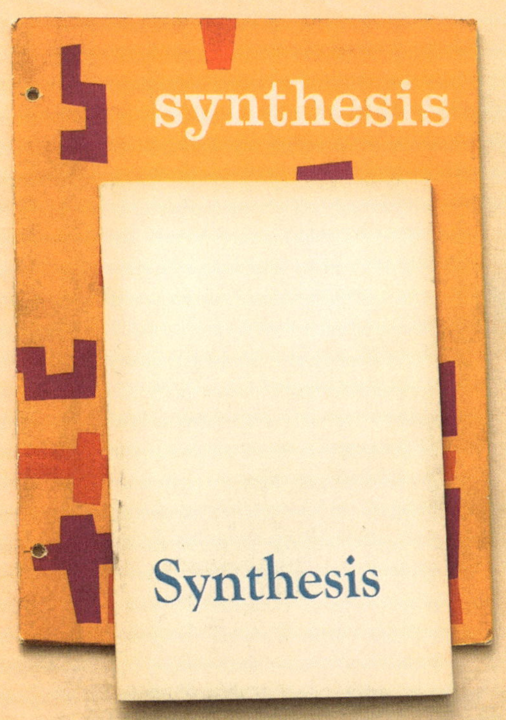

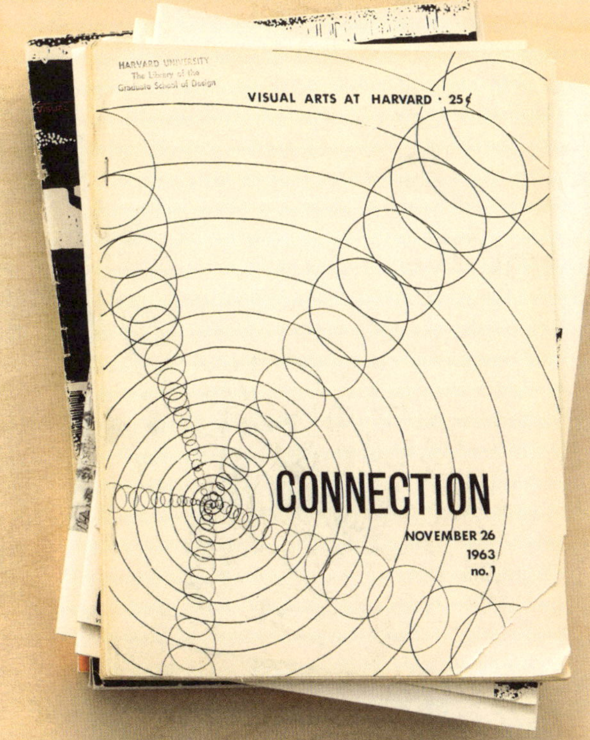

Synthesis
Years active: 1957–1958; frequency: yearly; number of issues: 2; format: print journal

Synthesis was published during the deanship of Josep Lluís Sert, and after Jaqueline Tyrwhitt had joined the GSD in 1955, in what was then the Department of City and Regional Planning. The two worked closely together to foster further collaboration among the three disciplines (architecture, landscape architecture, and urban planning) taught at the School. It is within this line of thought that *Synthesis* appeared in 1957, and dedicated to the topic of urban design (courses leading to degrees in urban design were first announced in 1959, and then established in the academic year 1960–1961). Published by students of the School, the editorial statement of the first issue echoes the urgency of collaboration: "The intent of *Synthesis* is to provide a platform for student views and work. The editorial policy has been to combine contributions from students and professionals from the many fields represented in the three departments of the GSD." The second issue, in a larger format, was revisited as a pilot project for the expression of student opinion, and the editorial emphasis shifted exclusively to student work that was developed outside the academic curriculum.

Connection: Visual Arts at Harvard
Years active: 1963–1969; frequency: relatively regular, 2–4 issues per year: 1963 (2), 1964 (6), 1965 (4), 1966 (4), 1967 (4), 1968 (2), 1969 (2); number of issues: 24; format: mimeographed journal (nos. 1–4); print journal (no. 5 onward)

Connection, published by graduate students of the GSD, provided a forum for individuals from the School of Design, the Department of Fine Arts, and the Visual Arts Center. The mimeographed first issue states the intent: ". . . to cut across barriers within the field of the visual arts, and to find out if the graduate student is, in fact, alive." Charles Jencks was the editor of the first 11 issues, and the driving force behind an ambitious biweekly publishing schedule for this 1960s journal. A special edition by Alex Tzonis delivers visual documentation of the April 1969 riots and confrontations at Harvard between students and police. The editorial statement articulates, "Four years after a prominent architectural historian declared (during a symposium at Yale) that ours were times of mild manifestos, and that revolutions were over, revolts and confrontations are a common phenomenon in both cities and universities." The back cover shows the photograph of a student, in her Marimekko pants, thrown to the floor, dragged and surrounded by police armed with batons. This was the last issue.

1953
Josep Lluis Sert is installed as GSD Dean.

1957
"It is the problem of the conscious, artistic design of the urban environment requiring a specialized training for which no curriculum has yet been established."
–*Synthesis*, no. 1.

1965
"What about computers? [...] They may assist our understanding of form. [...] We have instigated a pilot course this year at the GSD to study the potentialities"
–*Connection* (April 1965).

1966
"Which war shall we escalate–the war in Vietnam or the war on poverty, slums, poor housing, and urban problems?" –*Connection* (December 1966).

for'm
Years active: 1979–1982; frequency: relatively regular, 1–2 issues per year; number of issues: 5 (November 1979; April 1980; November 1980; April 1981; May 1982); format: xeroxed leaflet (fold and clip)

A full decade after the last issue of *Connection*, *for'm* appeared. The title derived from the fact that it was published by the architecture students' forum. In the form of a fold-and-clip leaflet, the editorial did not go beyond stating a broad invitation for participation and no prescriptive definition as to content. It was, "The idea of a publication as a vehicle for student expression. [. . .] The more variety that we get in the form of student contributions, the better." Surveys include favorite architects (Louis Kahn, Frank Lloyd Wright, I. M. Pei, Richard Meier, Palladio), least favorite (Philip Johnson, Peter Eisenman, Edward Durrell Stone, Robert A. M. Stern). Lectures are defined as "theirs" (the School's: Frank Gehry) and "ours" (the Forum's: Philip Johnson). Interviews include those with John Hejduk, Jorge Silvetti, and Harry Cobb. The publication includes architectural competition results. The one consistent feature across issues: a final coloring page.

The Harvard Architecture Review
Years active: 1980–1998; frequency: irregular: v.1 (1980), v.2 (1981), v.3 (1984), v.4 (1984), v.5 (1986), v.6 (1987), v.7 (1989), v.8 (1992), v.9 (1993), v.10 (1998); number of issues: 10; format: published print journal

The Harvard Architecture Review (HAR) was launched in 1980. A student-initiated and student-run publication, it was published by MIT Press and was open to the interests of its (changing) student editorial staff. Contributors are plenty, and generally comprise practicing architects or academics with insight into the selected topic, which are expressed in scholarly essays rather than opinion pieces. With Gerald McCue as dean and Harry Cobb as chair of architecture, it reflected the views of practicing architects and scholars that understood design as research. The *Review* was a topical publication, each issue with a single theme: (v1) "Beyond the Modern Movement"; (v2) "Urban Architecture"; (v3) "Autonomous Architecture"; (v4) "Monumentality and the City"; (v5) "Precedent and Invention"; (v6) "Patronage"; (v7) "The Making of Architecture"; (v8) "In Between: To and From Architecture"; (v9) "Toward a Journal of Architectural Research"; (v10) "Civitas: What is City?" In this last issue, now under Dean Peter Rowe, the study of the design disciplines reaches beyond the physical environment to embrace the social and political aspects of practice.

1968
"This is an election year. This is an assassination year. This is a riot year. This was a year of the regulated poor people's march, the conviction of many spocks and coffins." –*Connection* (Summer 1968).

1969
Maurice D. Kilbridge is installed as GSD Dean. "What we are observing in the attitudes of the students is more than 'a trivial issue of morality.'" –*Connection* (Spring 1969).

1972
The GSD moves from Robinson Hall on the Harvard Quad to Gund Hall on Quincy Street.

1979
"In fact, the United States is no longer Western Europe, if it ever was. [...] Our urban areas, where much architecture happens, are enriched from many cultures." –*for'm*, no. 1 (November 1979).

re/alignment
Years active: 1992–1994; frequency: irregular; number of issues: 3 (November 1992, May 1993, January 1994); format: print journal

re/alignment is the first journal published by and for students of the landscape architecture program at the GSD, and coalesces Heidi Hohmann, Jean Cavanaugh, and Barry Abrams as editors. Signaling to Virginia Woolf's "communication is health" idea, the first editorial statement reads: "*re/alignment* will try to shatter the enervating silence of the profession [. . .] landscape architecture needs a crucible for developing voices, a publication that fosters written exchange between members of our field and other design professions. To this end, *re/alignment* hopes to advance an eclectic discussion between practitioners, academics, and students. [. . .] we must reexamine our past and rethink our present." A new beginning envisioned. Of long-lasting value are interviews with Garret Eckbo (by Deborah Gerhard) and Dan Kiley (by Jane Amidon); and a redesign by Paula Meijerink of Franklin Park (the 19th-century park by Frederick Law Olmsted) in response to the question, "What should the park of the 21st century be like?"

Studio Work and *Studio Works*
Years active: *Studio Work*: AY1986–1987, 1987–1988, 1989–1990; *Studio Works*: AY1992–1993 through 2005–2007; frequency: yearly; number of issues: first iteration, 3; second iteration, 12; format: print serial (changes format); and online (later issues)

Studio Works is a GSD publication whose lineage differs from other GSD-student-generated journals. In 1986, to celebrate the 50th anniversary of the GSD, *Student Work 1985–1986* was published under Dean Gerald McCue as a representative (albeit not complete) catalog documenting and celebrating the spirit of the School. Renamed *Studio Work*, it continued for three successive academic years as a journal that "traced the evolution of design education in the GSD studios" through a selection of drawings and models from core, option studios, and thesis projects. In 1993, after a three-year hiatus, the publication was reissued as *Studio Works* 1 (note the plural) in a new and revised edition under Dean Peter Rowe, with Linda Pollak as main faculty editor for the first issue, and Jane Amidon, Nathan Cherry, Noam Maitless, and Craig Verzone as student editors from the different academic departments. Like its predecessor, the content of *Studio Works* was the work and life of GSD studios.

1980
Gerald McCue is installed as GSD Dean; urban planning relocates to the Kennedy School. "How is one to incorporate history once again as a legitimate source of inspiration?" –*HAR*, no. 1 (Spring 1980).

1982
"But the grading issues, by uniting the student body, however briefly, also raised some related questions. Does the GSD need a student council?" –*for'm*, no. 5 (May 1982).

1984
"The large body of theoretical writing has been successful in creating an intellectual context for the architecture. At the same time, however, it tends to mask the inability of the architects to enter the political sphere." –*HAR*, no. 6 (Winter 1984).

1992
Peter Rowe is installed as GSD Dean. "What will we do with Detroit, with coastal fishing towns, with rural agricultural communities shriveling on the Great Plains?" –*re/alignment* (May 1992).

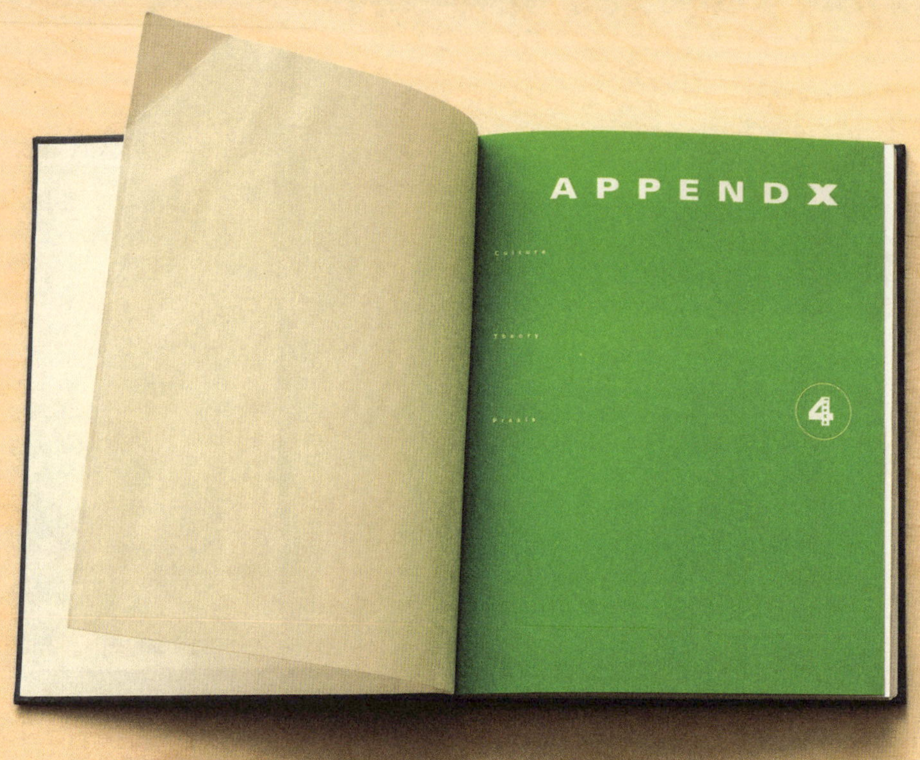

Appendx: Culture/Theory/Praxis
Years active: 1993, 1994, 1996, 1999; frequency: irregular; number of issues: 4; format: print journal

Appendx was published by editors Darell W. Fields (Harvard PhD student), Kevin L. Fuller (designer), Milton S. F. Curry (Arizona State assistant professor), and sponsored institutionally by Arizona State University and the GSD. The opening "Black Manifesto" is seminal in defining the voice of *Appendx*. Recognizing that a diversity of positions and lived experiences at the intersections of race, class, ethnicity, and gender are not represented in the field, the editors claim: "We began looking for a space of resistance and rigorous critique [. . .] from which new possibilities for the discipline could emerge. We found no such place, and began to make one from scratch [. . .] Needed is a journal that will provide a place to redefine scholarship as an inclusive, rather than exclusive, endeavor." As such, the journal is structured by categories that embrace worlds of knowledge, and change in order of appearance within each issue. "Syntax" is about practice; "Verbatim" is about theory, and both "Precinct" and "Adjacency" are about culture (either a well-defined familiar or a rather unexplored context respectively).

1993
"As for questions posed by representatives of other disciplines, the most frequently asked was, "What does architecture have to do with literature?"
–*Appendx*, vol. 2.

1994
"We decided that what was needed was a forum to show 'that which is not shown' [...] For many students, important work is done outside the design studio." –*isthmus*, vol. 1, no. 1.

1996
"Now, visibly upset with me and my response he asked, 'What does your blackness have to do with architecture?' I answered, giving him a more specific example, 'Ask your Mama.'"
–*Appendx*, vol. 3.

1998
"The GSD as we presently know it is the result of successive influences."
–*Studio Works* 5.

GAMUT magazine

February/March 1999
Volume 1, Number 1

Fit to Print

1 Representation
1 Planning
2 Editorial
2 GIS Symposium
6 BigDig.com
6 City gardens under siege
7 Exhibit review
8 Gallery

Calendar

Conferences
3/4 - 3/6 *New Urban Realities: Conference on the New Urbanism and Cities*, Gund Hall
3/12 - 3/13 *Fifth Annual Harvard GSD Asia Pacific Design Conference*, Gund Hall

Exhibits
Thru 4/4 *Industrial Monuments: Photography by Phillip Jones*, Fuller Museum of Art
Thru 4/11 *Building Representation: Photography and Architecture. Contemporary Interactions*, Fogg Art Museum
Thru 2/19 *Recollecting a Culture: Photography and the Evolution of a socialist Aesthetic in East Germany*, Photographic Resource Center, Boston
2/1 - 2/26 *Natural Forms: Mixed Media*, Nancy Houfek, Loeb House, Cambridge
2/6 - 2/27 *Articles of Faith: Lawn Marys & Front Yard Saints*, Somerville Public Library
2/1 - 2/19 *Photographs of the Sierra Nevada*, Matthew Hollingworth, Wiesner Student Art Gallery, 2nd floor Student Ctr., Harvard

continued on page 3

Welcome back. photo: staff

Image and Imagination

Like most people, I was more than a little surprised at this year's ASLA Awards (*Landscape Architecture*, November 1998). More troubling, however, than the fact that more than half went to just two offices was the exceptionally poor nature of the photography: the images managed to show both too little and too much of the place. Page after page of pretty, well-composed photographs in Southern California sunshine, completely devoid of the people who are purported to haunt their splendid spaces left the reader in serious doubt about the value of this photography

Image, page 3

Germany Re-visited

In January, Professor Carl Steinitz's "Alternative Futures for the Dessau-Worlitz Gartenreich" studio, conducted in collaboration with German landscape architecture students representing the Anhalt University of Applied Sciences and the Technische Fachochshule Berlin, presented the results of the studio project to a public audience in both Berlin and Dessau. At both presentations, the Studio's choice of using the Web and various other computer simulation technologies spurred much lengthy debate. Dr. Thomas Weiss, Director of the

Worlitz, page 4

isthmus
Years active: 1994; frequency: none; number of issues: 1; format: print journal

isthmus, a journal edited by student Mark Strong, states that it was started and entirely run by students from the GSD with the purpose, "to bring to sight written and visual projects undertaken by students that are not strictly architecture. Such work has not been exhibited, published, or viewed through traditional publications [. . .] *isthmus* can provide some food for discussion among students about design's relation to culture and theory." In providing a forum to show "that which is not shown," the first and only issue of *isthmus* includes material from art installations and essays to histories of the published canon of modernism ("Can Our Cities Survive?" compared to "The Heart of the City"), and discussions on colonialism and nationalism in India. The essays bring to the fore work and research done in parallel to studio projects. It is more of a compendium of works than a curated collection driven by an editorial statement.

Gamut
Years active: 1999, 2000–2001; frequency: irregular; number of issues: first iteration, 3 (February–March 1999, March–April 1999, Summer 1999); second iteration, 2 (Spring 2000, Spring 2001); format: print, fold, clip; revised design: print journal.

Gamut is a publication produced and managed by students at the GSD. It has two iterations: one, a black-and-white print, fold, and clip newsletter (Andrew Gutterman, editor); and the second, a printed square-format bicolored journal (Andrew Gutterman and Anand Krishnan, editors). If the first iteration compared the GSD to a prison given the lack of "contact with a larger reality," *Gamut* hopes to provide enjoyment to those who live within the GSD's walls. The second iteration, a year later, is a relaunch in which *Gamut* offers a new, possibly sustainable, model for student publications: a short three-column editorial by each student editor (thus offering a diversity of perspectives in each issue) and short single-page essays. A refreshingly light section, with portraits of students, faculty, and staff, offer one-sentence commentary in response to a simple question coming from the "donut" (a playful approach to gathering content that will be picked up by later GSD student publications).

1999
"Has perhaps too much emphasis been placed recently on the tools of change, rather than the values they symbolize?" –*Gamut*, vol. 1, no. 2.

2000
"If technology has redefined our definition of place, then ecology has provided us the means to imagine our work as a thread in a larger fabric. What exactly is the larger fabric?" –*Gamut*, no. 1.

2003
Alan Altshuler is installed as GSD Dean.

2008
Mohsen Mostafavi is installed as GSD Dean.

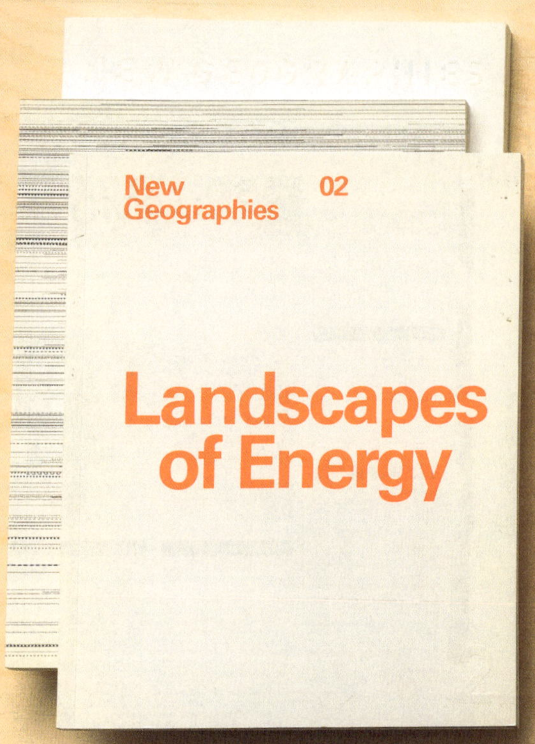

New Geographies
Years active: 2008–present; frequency: yearly; number of issues: 10 to date; format: published journal

New Geographies was founded, and continues to be produced, by GSD doctoral candidates with support from the Aga Khan Program at the GSD (at the time of the first issue directed by Hashim Sarkis) and additional grant funding sought after by the students themselves. The opening issue of *New Geographies* states that the journal emerged out of the realization that in an era of increasing globalization there was "the need to create a platform for repositioning the agency of design within new scales of context." With the advantage of a well-framed intellectual project, the editors examine the emergence of the geographic as a paradigm that shifts and expands the agency of design. Following the model of *The Harvard Architecture Review*, each issue of the journal is topical and has rotating student editors. 0: "Design, Agency, Territory"; 1: "After Zero"; 2: "Landscapes of Energy"; 3: "Urbanisms of Color"; 4: "Scales of the Earth"; 5: "The Mediterranean"; 6: "Grounding Metabolism"; 7: "Geographies of Information"; 8: "Island"; 9: "Posthuman"; 10: "Fallow".

Platform
Years active: 2008–present; frequency: yearly; number of issues: 12; format: printed serial

Platform is a GSD publication in the lineage of *Studio Works*. However, in the first issue's introduction, "An Archaeology of the Present," Dean Mohsen Mostafavi shifts the focus of the publication from merely documenting the work in the trays and the evolution of design to sampling the broader research and academic life of the School. *Platform* goes beyond studio work and thesis projects to lectures, exhibitions, events, research labs. For the first 10 installments the publication was given to selected junior faculty members, who were asked to take an editorial stance and make sense of it all. As Dean Mostafavi wrote in the first volume: "to seek the formation of a number of prevalent tendencies, and coherences, among the many that operate within the school." Beginning with the eleventh installment, the editorial voice of *Platform* was given to students; Esther Bang, Lane Raffaldini Rubin, and Enrique Aureng Silva took on this task with *Setting the Table*. Editors of the twelfth volume, Carrie Bly, Isabella Caterina Frontado, and Natasha Hicks, delve into past and recent GSD history in a year of upheavals (at all scales) to find commonalities and ask what is it about design education and practice that engages us: what are we individually and collectively committed to?

2009
"What are the social, political, and spatial implications of the next mode of energy, and how can design practices partake in shaping a more just urbanization?" —*New Geographies*, no. 2.

2013
"We wanted to pry open the gap between the stilted obfuscation of Academic English and the sloppy narcissism of Internetspeak." —*Open Letters*, issue no. 00 (October 3, 2013).

2014
"Are we now the cut-and-paste generation?" —*Very Vary Veri*, vol. 1.

2015
"The problem, though, is that this particular model of practice is becoming increasingly difficult for all of us to sustain in current social, cultural, and economic conditions." —*Very Vary Veri*, vol. 2.

Open Letters
Years active: 2013–present; frequency: biweekly; number of Issues: 74 to date; format: print/fold broadsheet

Open Letters is a student publication defined as "a biweekly experiment that tests the epistolary form as a device for generating public conversations about architecture and design." Its founding editor-in-chief, Chelsea Spencer was inspired by a letter from Mack Scogin to Benedetta Tagliabue published in *Harvard Design Magazine* in 2012 and decided to start what may have seemed a small project (to explore the epistolary form), but was ultimately driven by big ambitions (generate public conversation related to architecture, landscape architecture, urbanism, and design). New issues of the student-run publication have been consistently released every other Friday during the academic year for the last seven years (thanks to an efficient model of rotating students, copy-folding and web publishing, and distribution at the donut and online). Letters are written by and to individual people (students, faculty, and staff alike), to organizations and institutions, and to buildings, landscapes, or cities. There have been love letters, anonymous letters, curriculum proposal letters, letters of admiration, letters of discontent, and others published from the archives.

Very Vary Veri
Years active: 2014, 2015, 2017; frequency: yearly; number of issues: 3 to date; format: print journal

Very Vary Veri is a student-edited journal that proposes an interdisciplinary, inclusive, and critical platform searching for "diverse perspectives on design from law, finance, government, real estate, public health, education, and beyond." An individual student edits each issue. In the first issue, editor Simon Battisti calls for critically assessing the fundamental: "In a big world of extremes, the moderate can be radical." Etien Santiago's editorial in the second issue calls on a reassessment of history and the activity of learning: "these parallel [student publications] though non-official accounts of the larger conditions in which the canons of design disciplines were created, remain vital today." The third issue, edited by Ali Karimi, looks into how the condition of "intellectual relocation" has impacted practice given differing contexts of displacement. "The history of the 20th century is one of exile [. . .] As we confront a 21st century marked by refugee crises, changing national boundaries, and debates over immigration, it is time to reframe the discussion by approaching exile as the most important condition of the 20th century and a major one for the century to come."

2016
"In these past four decades, the depoliticization of life—and therefore architecture—has occurred at a much quicker pace than anyone could've anticipated" –*Open Letters*, issue no. 42, (November 4, 2016).

2017
"Network technologies and digital platforms invite the public to participate in the process of collective creation. What effect will this new media have on the way cities evolve?"
–*HRED*, no. 6.

2018
A plan to expand Gund Hall is announced by Dean Mohsen Mostafavi.

2019
Sarah Whiting is installed as GSD Dean.

The student publications shown on these pages are a selection of works that were published by and for GSD students. Additional publications, including ongoing works, include but are not limited to:

Trays: a student journal of the GSD
Years active: 2008; format: online journal

Harvard Real Estate Review (HRED)
Years active: 2010–present; frequency: yearly, irregular: Fall 2010, 2012–2013, 2013–2014, 2015, 2016, 2017, 2018; number of issues: 7 to date; format: online journal

MASKS the Journal: Journal of Dissimulation in Art | Architecture | Design
Years active: 2015–2016, 2016–2017, 2017–2018; frequency: yearly; number of issues: 3 to date; format: online journal, published on demand

Process: Journal of the GSD Design Research Forum
Years active: 2016–present; frequency: irregular (March 2016, April 2016); number of issues: 2 to date; format: leaflet on newsprint

OBLI\QUE
Years active: 2016–present; frequency: yearly; number of issues: 2 to date; format: online journal, published on demand

Test Print
Years active: 2018–present; number of issues: 2 to date; format: photocopied and stapled

WiD Bibliography
Years active: 2019–present; number of issues: 1 to date); format: PDF, limited edition print, compendium

UD:ID
Years active: 2018–present; format: online blog

Journal descriptions, volume and issue information provided by Inés Zalduendo (MArch '95), Special Collections Archivist, Frances Loeb Library, from "GSD Student Publications: A History from the Archives," 2017 (unpublished).

"But architectural education is potentially the most important single element in the future of the profession. [. . .] Are our schools equipping us to design within the framework of existing limitations—social, legal, financial, and technical? Are we being prepared to see this framework as a whole and help it develop along the lines which develop more enlightened planning?"

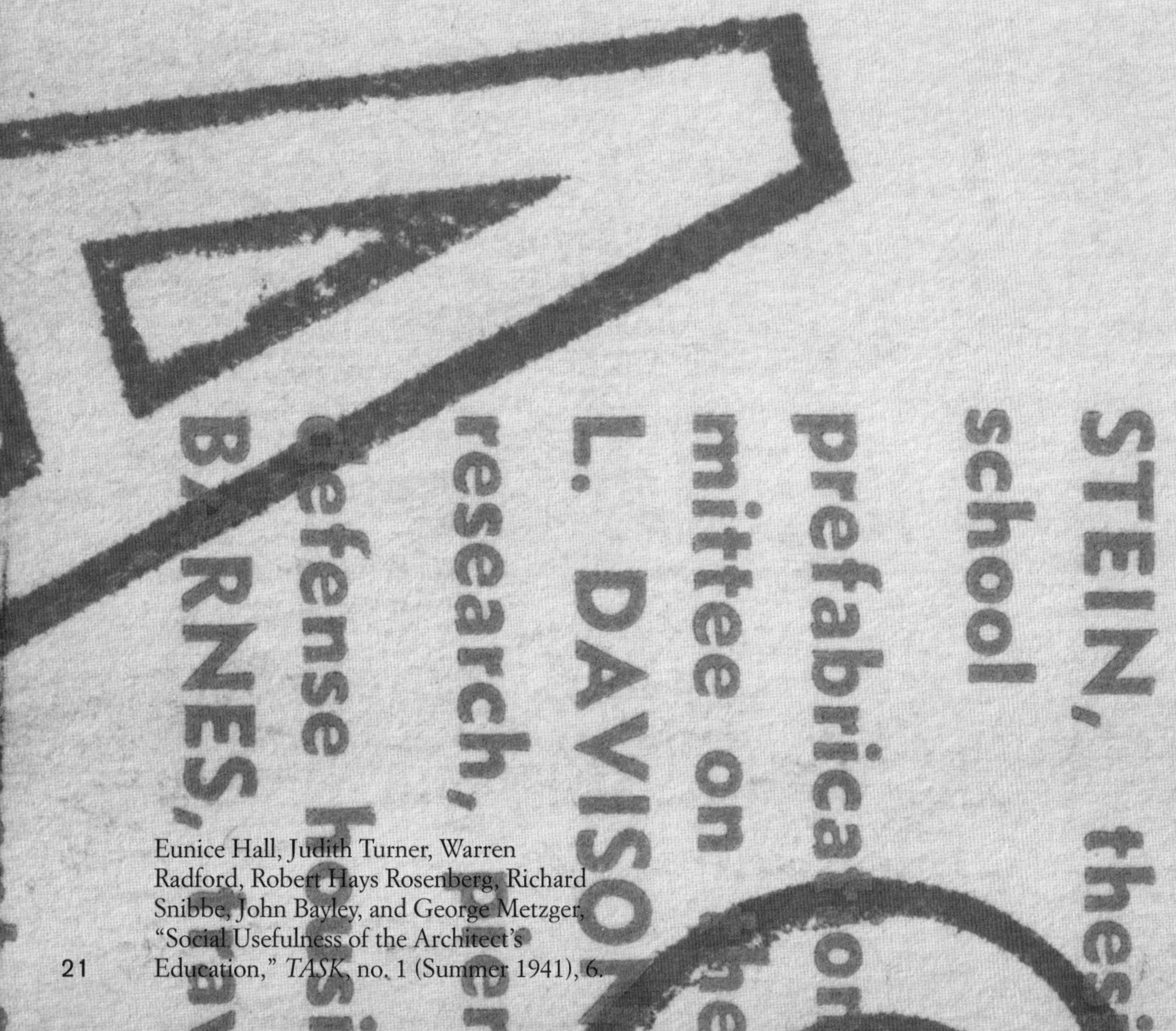

Eunice Hall, Judith Turner, Warren Radford, Robert Hays Rosenberg, Richard Snibbe, John Bayley, and George Metzger, "Social Usefulness of the Architect's Education," *TASK*, no. 1 (Summer 1941), 6.

What are the foundations of design education?

First-Year Core Studios: First Semester Architecture Core: Project; Landscape Architecture I: First Semester Core Studio; First Semester Core Urban Planning Studio; Elements of Urban Design; Collaborative Design Engineering Studio I (with the Harvard John A. Paulson School of Engineering and Applied Sciences); Second Semester Architecture Core: Situate; Landscape Architecture II: Second Semester Core Studio; and Second Semester Core Urban Planning Studio

Studio space in Gund Hall.

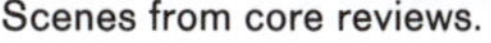

Scenes from core reviews.

First Semester Architecture Core: Project

How can relationships between the visual, experiential, and conceptual aspects of architecture be explored?

1–2
Danmo Fu (MArch I)
Instructor: Jenny French
Project: Jump Cut

3
Isabel Chun (MArch I)
Instructor: Jenny French
Project: Jump Cut

4
Luke Warren (MArch I)
Instructor: Lisa Haber-Thomson
Project: Hidden Room

5
Rachel Coulomb (MArch I)
Instructor: Jenny French
Project: Site/Building Reciprocity

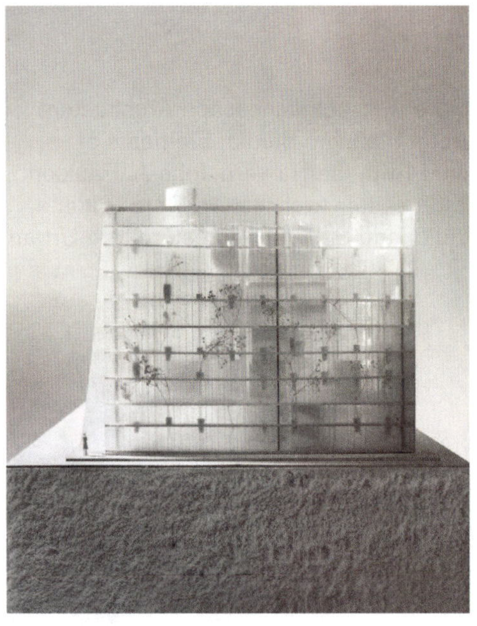

1

2

3

4

5

6

Landscape Architecture I: First Semester Core Studio

How can we explore the relationship between the material, experiential, and political aspects of landscape architecture?

6
Diana Guo (MLA I)
Instructor: Jungyoon Kim
Project: Riverfront Park

7, 9
Joanne Li (MLA I)
Instructor: Jungyoon Kim
Project: Riverfront Park

8
Eric Van Dreason (MLA I)
Instructor: Danielle Choi
Project: Courtyard

7

8

9

To Mayor Marty Walsh:

I, __________, am a concerned resident of South Boston writing to you today about the recently proposed BPDA redevelopment plan for Dorchester Ave. This plan does not do enough to ensure the prosperity and welfare of the residents of Southie. I am a supporter of the Opportunity Network People's Plan for South Boston, which includes proposals for the following:

1. Adoption of new IPOD (Unity IPOD) over Dot Ave
2. Creation of a Unity and Justice Fund
3. Fund participatory budgeting program for racial justice

I believe that these initiatives are necessary to create a Southie that supports and lifts up all of us, rather than the select few. I support the People's Plan!

Sincerely,
(Sign & Print Name)

Address:

10

First Semester Core Urban Planning Studio

How do planners make spatial arrangements to address issues at different scales?

10–11
Anne Lin (MUP),
Sydney Fang (MUP),
Emily Duma (MUP)
Instructor: Toni L. Griffin
Project: The People's Plan for South Boston

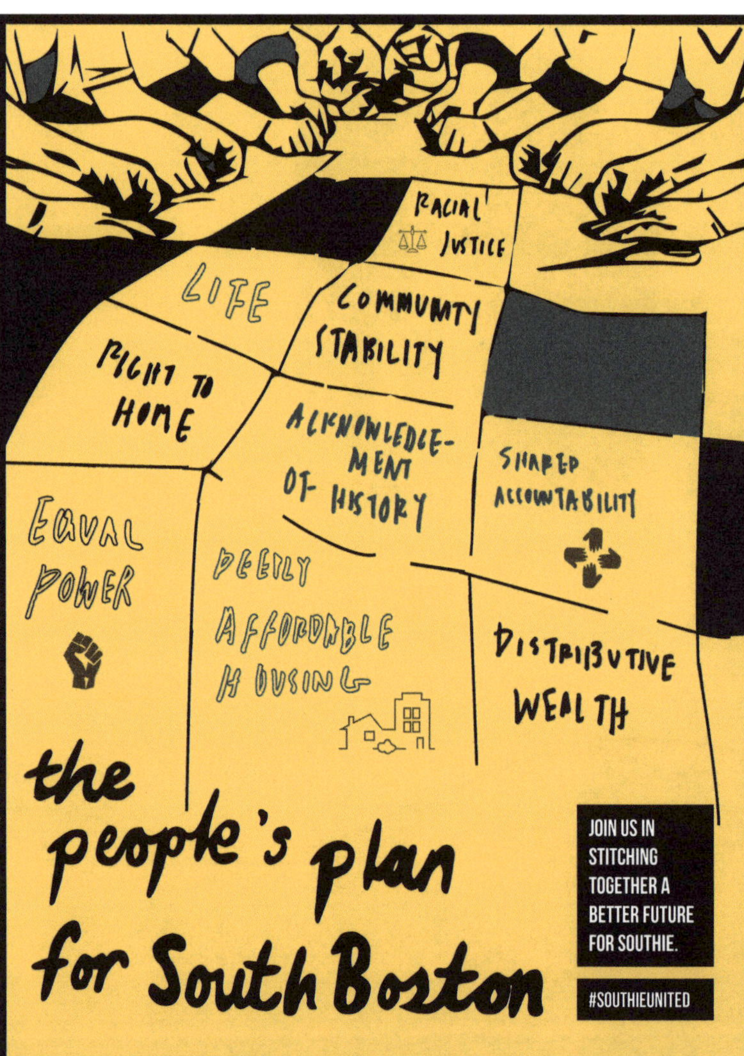

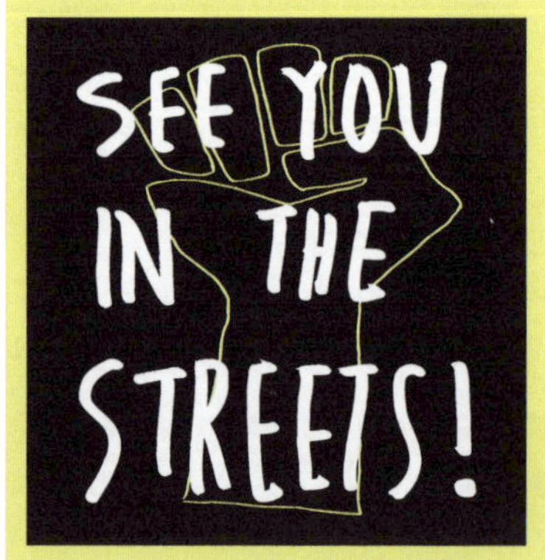

11

Elements of Urban Design Studio

To what extent can or should new development connect to and negotiate between existing and adjacent communities with the broader city, as well as region-wide ecological infrastructures?

16–19
Boxiang Yu (MLAUD) and Cindy Xiao (MAUD)
Instructor: Rahul Mehrotra
Project: Exercise 03—East Boston

16

17

18

19

Collaborative Design Engineering Studio II (with SEAS)

How can design address issues of mobility and be ready for market implementation?

12–15
Hane Roh (MDE), Mitsue Guerrero Monsalve (MDE), Yash Bhutada (MDE), Togo Kida (MDE)
Instructor: Jock Herron

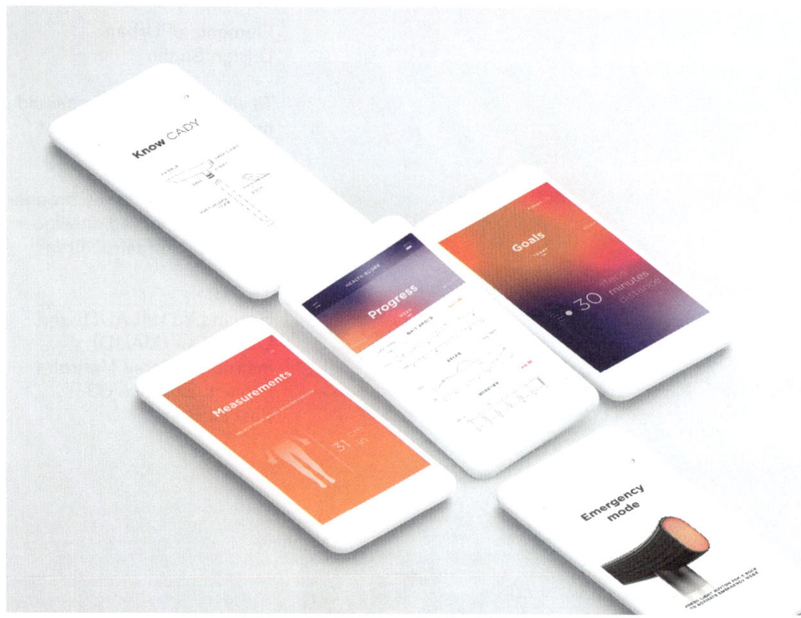

12

13

14

15

Second Semester
Architecture Core: Situate

How might architecture and building form draw on site and program?

20–21
Qin Ye Chen (MArch I)
Instructor: Megan Panzano
Project: Spatial Array

22
Diandra Rendradjaja (MArch I)
Instructor: Sean Canty
Project: Film Studio

23–24
Rachel Coulomb (MArch I)
Instructor: Michelle Chang
Project: Campus Club

20

21

22

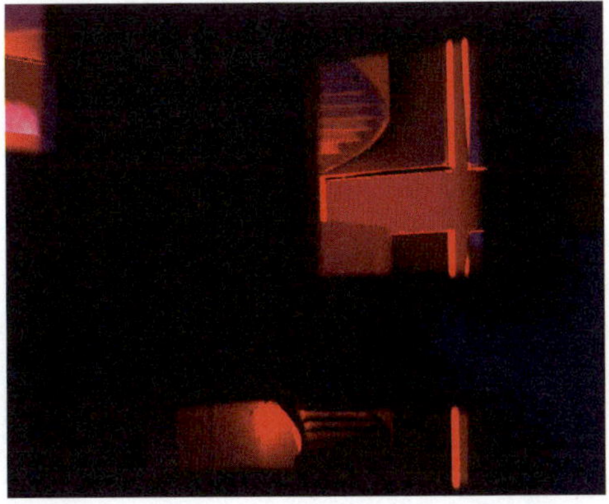

23

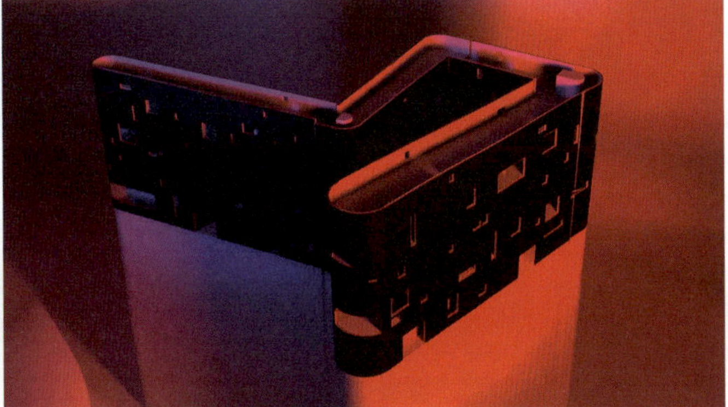

24

Landscape Architecture II: Second Semester Core Studio

Using Franklin Park as a site for intervention, how can landscape be positioned as a dynamic threshold?

25, 26
Sarah Li (MLA I)
Instructor: Craig Douglas
Project: Franklin Park

27
Dominic Riolo (MLA I)
Instructor: Paola Sturla
Project: Franklin Park

28
Angela Moreno-Long (MLA I)
Instructor: Emily Wettstein
Project: Franklin Park

25

26

27

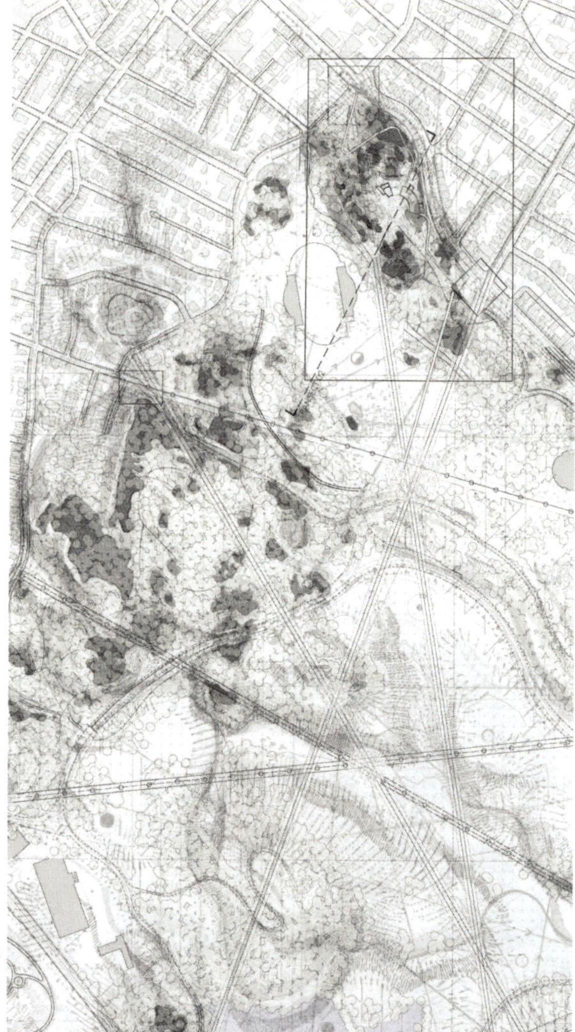

28

Second Semester Core Urban Planning Studio

How can the planning process reflect, mediate, and highlight community values, public goals, and private markets?

29, 31
Nevena Pilipovic-Wengler (MUP) and Sydney Fang (MUP)
Instructor: Dan D'Oca
Project: Homegrown Lowell

30, 32
Cynthia Deng (MUP, MArch I) and Anne Lin (MUP)
Instructor: Dan D'Oca
Project: Acre Canalway Commons

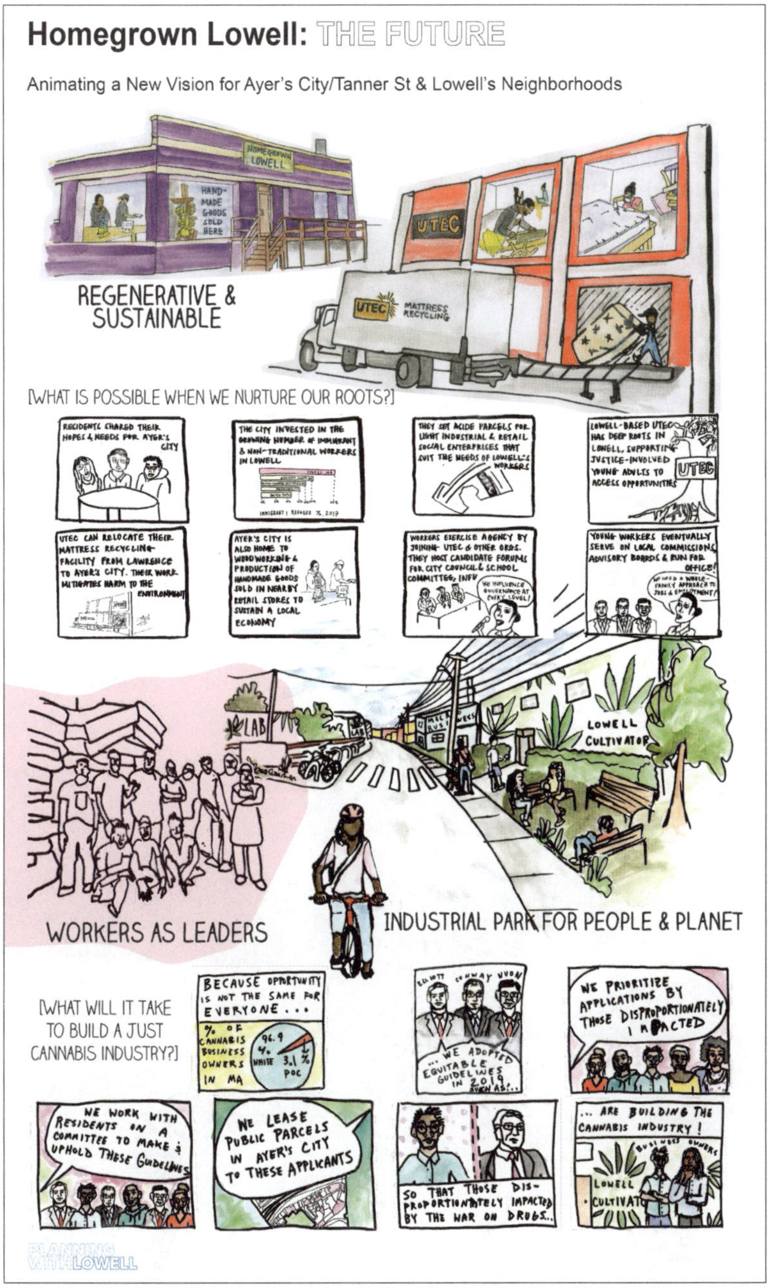

Homegrown Lowell: THE FUTURE

Animating a New Vision for Ayer's City/Tanner St & Lowell's Neighborhoods

HOMEGROWN LOWELL
HAND-MADE GOODS SOLD HERE
UTEC
UTEC MATTRESS RECYCLING
REGENERATIVE & SUSTAINABLE

[WHAT IS POSSIBLE WHEN WE NURTURE OUR ROOTS?]

RESIDENTS SHARED THEIR HOPES & NEEDS FOR AYER'S CITY
THE CITY INVESTED IN THE GROWING NUMBER OF IMMIGRANT & NON-TRADITIONAL WORKERS IN LOWELL
IMMIGRANT ; REFUGEE %, 2017
THEY SET ASIDE PARCELS FOR LIGHT INDUSTRIAL & RETAIL SOCIAL ENTERPRISES THAT SUIT THE NEEDS OF LOWELL'S WORKERS
LOWELL-BASED UTEC HAS DEEP ROOTS IN LOWELL, SUPPORTING JUSTICE-INVOLVED YOUNG ADULTS TO ACCESS OPPORTUNITIES
UTEC
UTEC CAN RELOCATE THEIR MATTRESS RECYCLING FACILITY FROM LAWRENCE TO AYER'S CITY. THEIR WORK MITIGATES HARM TO THE ENVIRONMENT
AYER'S CITY IS ALSO HOME TO WOODWORKING & PRODUCTION OF HANDMADE GOODS SOLD IN NEARBY RETAIL STORES TO SUSTAIN A LOCAL ECONOMY
WORKERS EXERCISE AGENCY BY JOINING UTEC & OTHER ORGS. THEY HOST CANDIDATE FORUMS FOR CITY COUNCIL & SCHOOL COMMITTEE, INFU
WE INFLUENCE GOVERNANCE AT EVERY LEVEL!
YOUNG WORKERS EVENTUALLY SERVE ON LOCAL COMMISSIONS, ADVISORY BOARDS & RUN FOR OFFICE!

LAB
LOWELL CULTIVATOR
WORKERS AS LEADERS
INDUSTRIAL PARK FOR PEOPLE & PLANET

[WHAT WILL IT TAKE TO BUILD A JUST CANNABIS INDUSTRY?]

BECAUSE OPPORTUNITY IS NOT THE SAME FOR EVERYONE . . .
% OF CANNABIS BUSINESS OWNERS IN MA
96.9 % WHITE
3.1 % POC
ELLIOTT CONWAY NUON
... WE ADOPTED EQUITABLE GUIDELINES IN 2019, SUCH AS:..
WE PRIORITIZE APPLICATIONS BY THOSE DISPROPORTIONATELY IMPACTED
WE WORK WITH RESIDENTS ON A COMMITTEE TO MAKE & UPHOLD THESE GUIDELINES
WE LEASE PUBLIC PARCELS IN AYER'S CITY TO THESE APPLICANTS
SO THAT THOSE DISPROPORTIONATELY IMPACTED BY THE WAR ON DRUGS..
... ARE BUILDING THE CANNABIS INDUSTRY!
BUSINESS OWNERS
LOWELL CULTIVAT

PLANNING WITH LOWELL

29

30

31

32

How do we explore the relationships between technology, materials, and the agency of design thinking?

Selected Visual and Material Science Courses: Materials; Graphic/Volume Conflations; Interface Design: Integrating Material Perceptions

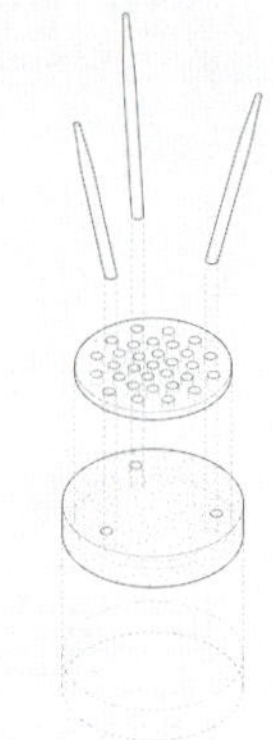

1

Materials
Instructor: Jonathan Grinham

How do we classify stuff? How do we build with stuff? What are the energy, health, and societal implications of stuff?

1–2
Luke Warren (MArch I), Aditi Agarwal (MDes EE), Hangsoo Jeong (MArch I), Victoria Lopez Cabeza (MDes EE)
Project: Mycelium Stool

2

Graphic/Volume Conflations
Instructor: Viola Ago

How do we explore the relationships between advanced technology and the agency of more conventional design thinking in a fabrication-heavy project setting?

3–7
Estelle Yoon (MArch I)
Project: Halftone Blur

3

4

5

6

7

8

Interface Design: Integrating Material Perceptions
Instructor: Sawako Kaijima

How do we combine material interests of architecture and engineering at the scale of material properties?

8–9
Hiroki Kawashima (MAUD),
Xinyi Zhou (MLA I),
Qiaoqi Dai (MLA I),
Xingyue Huang (MLA I)
Project: Gradational Reciprocity

9

10

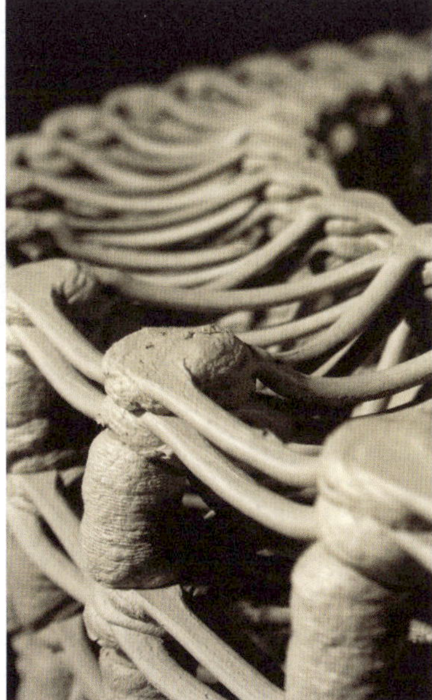
11

Independent Study
Advisor: Martin Bechthold
Project: From SPT to RST

How can spatial printing technologies (SPT) be improved to incorporate real-time information?

10–14
Hyeonji Im (MDes Tech), Sulaiman Alothman (MDes Tech), Francisco Jung (MDes Tech)

12

13

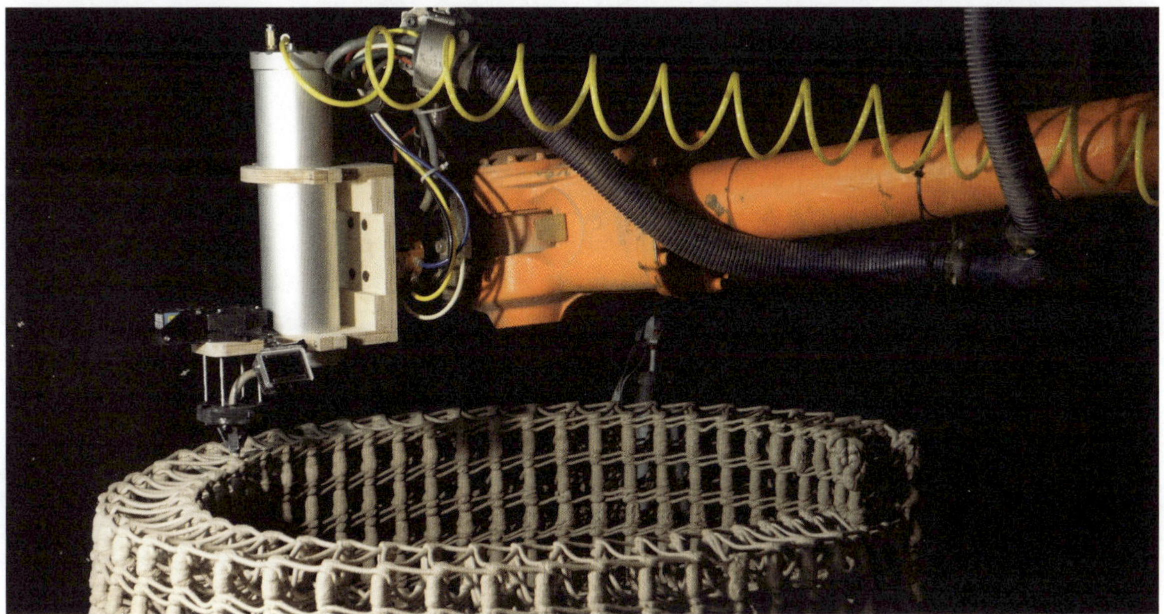
14

How can relationships between discourse and representation be explored through the process of making?

Kanchan Wali-Richardson (MLA I)
Landscape Representation I
Instructor: Emily Wettstein

How can history be used to explore and expand design discourse?

Olivia Howard (MArch I), Caleb Negash (MArch I), Isaac Pollan (MArch I), Luke Warren (MArch I)
Buildings, Texts, and Contexts I
Instructors: Erika Naginski and K. Michael Hays

monadfest_o 2018

Written and Performed by Cherry Fung, Olivia Howard, Caleb Negash, Isaac Pollan, Fiona Riley, Jack Rodat, Edda Steingrimsdottir, Breanne (bree) Taylor, Luke Warren, Yiou Wang, and Paul Wood

The monads begin behind gold curtain. They begin to agitate to the curtain, creating a bodiless continually moving material. DJ Monad Jack arrives on the podium with noise cancelling earmuffs operating as headphones. (The baroque embraces opposites). Handel's Harpsichord suite no.7 in G minor (Dubstep Remix) begins to play. The monads emerge from underneath the gold curtain and move in undulations around the stage.

MONAD YIOU: The Monad is nothing else than a simple substance.

MONADS: SIMPLE SUBSTANCE!

Monads condense themselves.

MONAD CALEB: The Monad can begin only through creation and end only through annihilation.

MONADS: ANNIHILATION!

Monads do their best to explode themselves.

MONAD EDDA: Each Monad is subject to change, and change is continuous in each.

MONADS: CONTINUOUS IN EACH!

Monads send a motion smoothly through their entire bodies.

MONAD FIONA: Men act in like manner as animals.

MONADS: ANIMALS!

Monads perform their understanding of certain speciated fauna.

MONAD FIONA: Platonic forms fold but never reach the formal element of the fold.

MONADS: THE FOLD!

Monads begin to fold themselves.

MONAD CHERRY: Folds upon folds

MONADS: FOLDS UPON FOLDS!

Monads begin to fold themselves upon each other.

MONAD BREE: Stuff

MONADS: STUFF! (stuff, Stuff. Stuff!)

Monads move in explosive staccatos.

MONAD LUKE: Coils of matter, the folds of the soul

MONADS: FOLDS OF THE SOUL. folds of the soul. folds of the soul.

Monads begin to tie themselves in a knot to become one amorphous,

"Hi Monadfesto Team, can you please share your abstract and research questions with us?"

Important Research Questions: Just what is it about the Baroque that gets us out of the bed in the morning . . . and why is the Renaissance so very lame in comparison? Is the presentation of process particularly illuminating as a final product? How does this reframe our understanding of temporality? How many Monads does it take to screw in a light bulb? Can one recreate traditional/canonical architectural periods of thought through new forms of media? Is style and sensibility cyclical?

History
Lecture
Performance
Representation

"For me, the issue more than ever is this: how can we, as people who are committed to thinking our way through this posthuman convergence—how can we, who are in this together but are not one and the same, develop a set of values, attributes, and terminologies whereby we can think differently but together about the challenges, the contradictions, the exhilaration, and the exhaustion of the fourth Industrial Revolution and the sixth extinction in a materially embedded way—becoming in and with the world? Because, guys, we only have one world."

Rosi Braidotti, "Posthuman Knowledge," Lecture,
March 12, 2019

What does a collective project look like? Is individual authorship important? What does an inventory of architecture reveal?

Natural Monument
Instructors: Mauricio Pezo and Sofia von Ellrichshausen

By “basic” we mean a primary level of complexity for discreet and ubiquitous elements (e.g., those 1:1, 1:2, 2:3, or 3:4 ratio fenestrations one might find in any unpretentious provincial settlement).

By “remote” we mean the extreme edge of sublime settings along the Chilean National Park system (perhaps assuming “every paradise is a lost one”).

By “format” we mean a spatial character without particular size; in this case, the five formats derived from a rectangular volume: the dice, the plate, the block, the strip, and the tower.

By “seclusion” we imply a physical detachment from the urban life without losing communication (therefore influence) with its culture.

It would be deceiving to claim a return to nature since there has never been a real departure from it. Buildings complete nature as much as nature finishes buildings (and ultimately erodes and ruins them). Through a self-referential definition of architectonic format, by means of rather basic walls, floors, roofs, and openings on them, the studio explores this fundamental form of reciprocity: a series of cottages for remote locations will be understood as articulation devices to mediate from one nature to another—from a conditioned confinement for a voluntarily secluded couple to an emancipated and vulnerable wild domain.

All in all, after overcoming the myth of the idyllic garden, the heavenly countryside filled with fruits and flowers became the land for agricultural production overlapped with an original need for pure enjoyment, for the sheer pleasure of unpolluted nature. And perhaps between that labor and that leisure time, there is another time: a loose one (lost and lax at once), a temporal space not only for procrastinating at work but also for serendipity and contemplation in solitude. Once more, the paradox is simple: nature is unintentional; artifacts are not.

Our main concern is the paradoxical bridge between our own subjectivity and that of the architectonic object, and vice versa. Following our Naïve Intention program, the studio speculates on the apparent contradiction between intentionality and chance, rationality and futility, prediction and circumstance. Based on given constraints, every student will elaborate an inventory of architectonic propositions. A selection of them are later developed in pairs through handmade models, drawings, and paintings. The central aim of our exploration is not so much to focus on the specific phenomena and their causes but in their potential to be translated into a work of architecture: into a synthetic (even ascetic) object, a unitary and self-centered structure that basically refers to itself.

Through a collective representational approach, how can drawing reveal the complexities of a landscape?

RHIZOSPHERE
Instructor: Teresa Galí-Izard

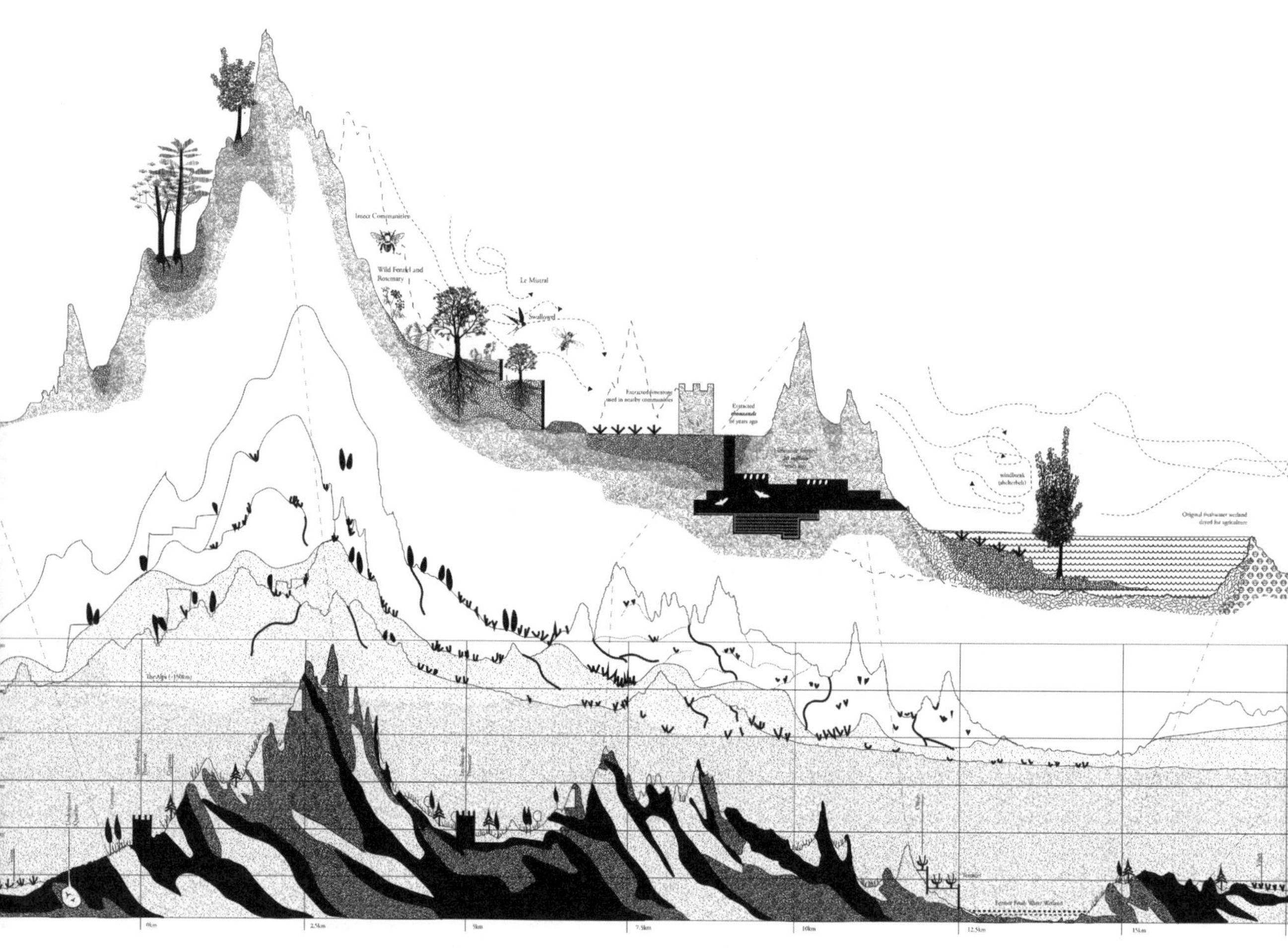

1

Through a systematic representational approach and restrictive unique lens, this studio unveiled the complexity of the site through a collective shared language. Using black-and-white line drawing as a common ground for different sources of knowledge such as geological maps, data from climate, field observations, scientific articles, and abstract diagrams, the studio discovered, through drawing, new relationships. Drawing revealed the potential of La Camargue, France, with the careful consideration that each drawn line revealed rich information. This eventual unfolding of relationships formed the basis of future proposals.

Agriculture
Landform
Plants
Option Studio
Representation

1, 5–6
Melissa Naranjo (MLA I AP)

2, 7
Danica Liongson (MLA I, MDes ULE)

3–4
Charity Cheung (MLA I AP)

2

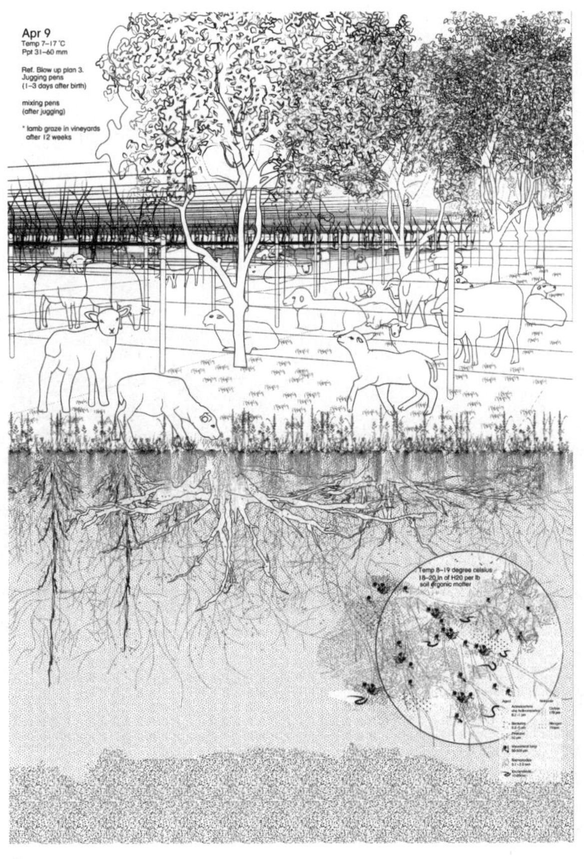

4

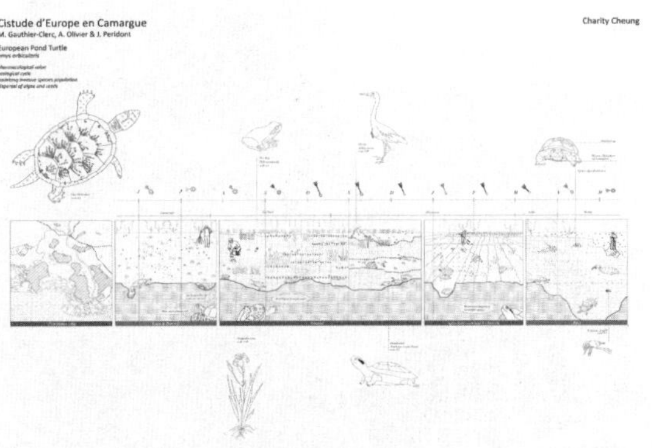

3

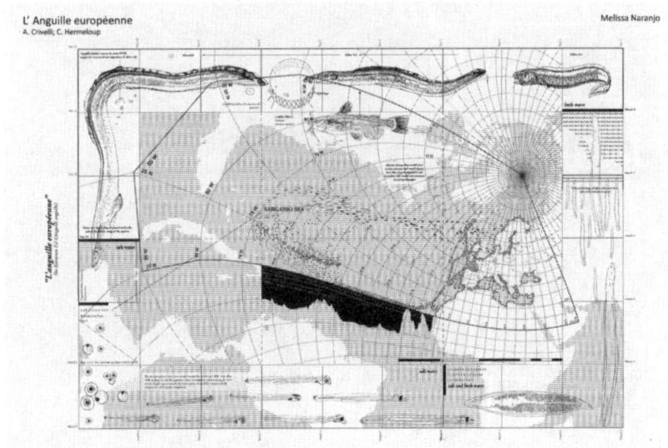

5

6

7

How can two different methods of approaching a site inform contemporary urban challenges?

Multiple Miamis (Option Studio) and
Multiple Miamis: Infrastructure, Affordability, Identity, and the Public (Seminar)
Instructors: Chris Reed and Sean Canty (Option Studio); and Lily Song (Seminar)

1

Funded by the Knight Foundation, and using Miami as an urban laboratory, these two courses, a project-based seminar and an option studio, are each part of a series of courses that seek to address contemporary urban dilemmas facing many American cities and explore opportunities for transformative urban design and planning interventions. The seminar explores how urban planning and design can promote affordable housing, retail, and services, public mobility and access, and sustainable and resilient infrastructure systems in more inclusive and equitable terms; the option studio explores questions of how design can address issues of inequity, race, affordability, and resilience in the context of the contemporary American city. Both explore these questions through different methods of analysis, and each provides a different understanding of site.

Option Studio
Representation
Seminar
Social Equity
Urbanism

Implementation Strategy

It will take time and patience to develop a network of cooperatives backed by health care, requiring the cooperation of a diversity of stakeholders, agreement on a vision for economic democracy, and market studies to determine the best businesses to pursue locally. A demonstration project such as the home care cooperative can prove the viability of this model in Miami. There is potential for these cooperative businesses to grow beyond health care to serve the other large anchor institutions that top Miami's employment charts—the education and government sectors. A framework of cooperatives centered around the service sector and care labor could reframe other industries in Miami, from tourism and entertainment to community policing.

The process for implementing such a framework includes:

1. Identifying founding partners and working with them to establish the mission and theory of change for the cooperative organization.
2. Conducting feasibility analysis for businesses, avoiding those with high fixed costs.
3. Obtaining start-up funding from foundations and governments.
4. Modeling a demonstration project such as a home care cooperative.
5. Suggesting local policies supporting worker cooperatives and other minority and women-owned businesses.
6. Establishing certification programs that recognize the skills learned by prospective worker-owners, potentially including high school students.
7. Attracting further investment from private sources.
8. Expanding businesses and client industries.

1
Ting Liang (MLA I AP, MAUD) and Zishen Wen (MLA I AP) for the "Multiple Miamis" option studio
Instructors: Chris Reed and Sean Canty

2
Muniba Ahmad (MUP) and Syed Ali (MUP) for the "Multiple Miamis" seminar
Instructor: Lily Song

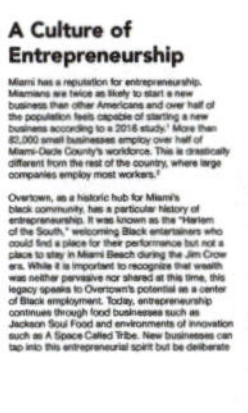

2

What is your personal architecture?

Hee Young Pyun (MArch II)
FAMILY
Instructors: Mack Scogin and Helen Han

Blurring the
boundaries between—
recollecting and forgetting
bird and friend
place and space
time and timeless
inmate and passerby
nest and sanatorium
sensory and illusionary
tide and fly
interior and exterior
chirping and talking
nursing and surfing
land and island
shelter and freedom
wheelchair and wing
now and then
birdwatching and crying
path and destination
solitary and collective
research and meditation
migration and stillness
water and earth
living and dying
feathery and cloudy
causeway and beach
story and mythology
seeing and missing
stranger and family
newcomer and leftover
infancy and senility
ornithology and pathology
ocean and sky
memory and dream
you and me!

Each student had to select a site and was assigned their own program by the instructors. The site is Nahant Beach in Massachusetts, and the program is the CORS—the Center for Ornithological Research and Sanatorium.

A place becomes memories, and memories become dreams. This process of place—memory—dream is reversed, as our dreams give meaning to our memory, and memory gives meaning to a place. We cannot share our memory, but we can share the moments. And our memories of the place accumulated over time become a place itself. Rather than looking for the origin of memory, we believe in memory constantly on the move.

What are the shifting ways in which architects imagine "the subject" and treat the people who interact with their work?

Izzy Kornblatt (MDes CC)
Architecture in Early Modern England
Instructor: Erika Naginski

Robert Venturi's celebration of 18th-century English architects John Vanbrugh and Nicholas Hawksmoor in *Complexity and Contradiction in Architecture* (1966) implies that their daring embrace of the picturesque continues to offer important lessons to the 20th-century architect. Not enough has been said about Venturi's attention to Vanbrugh and Hawksmoor. Beyond formal techniques, what did these architects, and the picturesque, have to offer to Venturi and his partner Denise Scott Brown?

To answer this question, this paper looks to Castle Howard, where Vanbrugh and Hawksmoor first pioneered a new mode of generating architectural narrative. Here, on the property of wealthy estate owner Lord Carlisle in North Yorkshire, England, the two architects composed an eclectic array of monuments throughout a vast, rolling landscape of hills and forests—all to tell a story about Lord Carlisle's conception of himself and his family. Their method of composing images to be seen by the visitor as she/he moves through space became known as the picturesque, and as Neil Levine argues, this narrative mode marks a turning point in Western architectural history.[1]

With the picturesque, Vanbrugh and Hawksmoor rejected prescriptive circulation routes normalized in classical architectures. In such prescriptive circulation, views of architectural elements can be broken down into hierarchical composition (where each design element both in plan and in elevation has a clear position with regard to the others). The picturesque, on the other hand, allows a single style to be represented among many, allowing the architect to craft a narrative in which each style embodies a particular set of meanings. For example, the Temple at Castle Howard, which offered the Carlisle family a place to enjoy the grounds, mimics Palladio's Villa Rotonda: the Villa Rotonda was an appropriate symbol of leisure as it was known to be Palladio's only villa designed purely for entertainment (rather than the administration of agriculture). In a similar manner, the Mausoleum adopted the form of the ancient Tomb of Caecilia Metella outside Rome, announcing itself as a place of worship and resting place for the estate owner's remains. No less referential, the Pyramid monumentalized the beginning of the Carlisle family line. The crafting of elaborate narratives with these elements calls upon the architectural subject, the beholder of the view, to actively use their background knowledge and interpretative thinking. "At Castle Howard," Levine writes, "a widely dispersed grouping of three seemingly unrelated structures [the monuments] . . . establishes distant focal points in the expansive landscape to create a spatial nexus in which the beholder must assume a new subjective stance and thus a much more personal and active role in the determination of meaning."[2]

This mode of mobilizing historical styles, pioneered by Hawksmoor and Vanbrugh, became central to the Beaux-Arts architectural tradition over the subsequent two centuries. Eventually, it became a target for early-20th-century modernists challenging the forms and social responsibility of architecture. These modernists asserted that such historical eclecticism represented decadence and a failure to capture the zeitgeist of modernity

Venturi and Scott Brown returned to the eclecticism of the picturesque—but with a desire to undermine the traditional and stable meanings upon which Vanbrugh and Hawksmoor had relied.

1
Neil Levine, "Castle Howard and the Emergence of the Modern Architectural Subject," *Journal of the Society of Architectural Historians*, vol. 62, no. 3 (September 2003): 326–51.

2
Ibid.

3
Robert Venturi, *Complexity and Contradiction in Architecture*, 2nd ed. (New York: Museum of Modern Art; distributed by New York Graphic Society, 1977, 1966), 59.

and its place proposed a vocabulary of supposedly universal forms. In the 1960s, Venturi and Scott Brown offered an entirely different perspective: to them, Vanbrugh and Hawksmoor's picturesque offered a sensitive and generous treatment of the architectural subject in its flexibility, acceptance of complexity, and attention to perceptual experience. The drawback of this eclectic approach was not its engagement with historical styles, but rather the rigid traditionalism that tended to govern the selection and reproduction of stylistic precedents—a rigid traditionalism that persisted in modernism, namely through formal rules asserted by such early modernists as Le Corbusier. Rebelling against the reigning prescribed modernist aesthetics, Venturi and Scott Brown returned to the eclecticism of the picturesque—but with a desire to undermine the traditional and stable meanings upon which Vanbrugh and Hawksmoor had relied.

The Benjamin Franklin Memorial and Monument in Philadelphia by Venturi Scott Brown.

The results of Venturi and Scott Brown's theoretical approach are plainly legible in a trio of related monuments completed by their firm, Venturi Scott Brown, between the 1970s and the early 1990s in Philadelphia's Old City neighborhood. Each of the monuments takes historically derived forms—a Georgian house, a symmetrical plaza, and an obelisk—but the historical associations of each form are undermined in the monuments' materiality, scale, and structure. The first is a memorial and museum for Benjamin Franklin on the site of his house. The monument recreates only the skeleton of the original house through a metal frame, and serves as a sharp reminder—located near the heart of American historicist pageantry—of our inability to return to a past world. The second is a plaza that miniaturizes the Philadelphia street grid with marble pavers. At its center stands a comically undersized statue of William Penn while a tiny model of Penn's long-demolished house marks the Plaza's location. This "Welcome Park," as a large sign proclaims, raises the specter of an empty city and critiques the fetishization of Penn's historical figure. The third is an obelisk commemorating Christopher Columbus. This monument is formed of thin galvanized steel panels, each panel separated by three-inch gaps that reveal a skeletal structure within. The deconstructed, skeletal obelisk flouts the norms of monumentality; in place of solidity there is hollowness. The effect is ambiguous and contradictory—accepting of Columbus's importance as an iconic figure for Italian Americans but suggestive of the hollowness of worshipping a figure responsible for the brutal murder of Indigenous American peoples. With each of these monuments Venturi Scott Brown ask the viewer to rethink interpretations of the monuments' meanings by challenging expectations of what a monument should be and by offering a space for the viewer to draw their own conclusions.

This trio of projects by Venturi Scott Brown demonstrates not just the restoration of a lost formal technique but an ability to engage with the social meanings that underlie it. Though *Complexity and Contradiction* is focused on architectural form, rather than larger social concerns, a careful reading of the text begins to bring out passages where these concerns for the identity and structure of society, and perhaps most importantly the subjectivity of the viewer, momentarily come to the fore. Consider, for example, Venturi's comparison of the facade of Vanbrugh's now-demolished mansion Eastbury to Jasper Johns's paintings of superimposed American flags.[3] The mention in the text notes only a formal similarity, but the subtext is clear: Vanbrugh's techniques are as rich and critical an artistic expression for our own time as Jasper Johns's. Venturi Scott Brown's work, as evinced by the Philadelphia monuments, actualizes this subtext. In their work Vanbrugh and Hawksmoor's empowered subject returns, transformed and made relevant once again.

How does design create meaning, and how much is our understanding of design swayed by narrative?

Isaac H. Pollan (MArch I)
Buildings, Texts, and Contexts I
Instructors: Erika Naginski and K. Michael Hays

Dear Sir,

I am writing to you from the unfortunate vantage of someone who feels that there are certain matters of crucial importance that have been ignored. Ignored by you, I'm afraid.

I am speaking, of course, of an element of your most recent construction—your so-called Hidden Room project. The issue that I take with your project pertains to your choice of site. Before you came along, the site on which your project sits was sublime in its infinite emptiness. It was a landscape of pure white: an elegant binary one could really let their soul sink into. It was a nearly nonexistent kind of place! Now, as I look out over the landscape upon which you have built, I cannot help but see an utterly detractive blip (your project).

I understand that your building relies on infinite, uninterrupted sight lines from its interior so as to create some sort of positional confusion (who knows why you should want to confuse your guests) but I'm sure you could have found some other location to build on. Perhaps you could have chosen a site from one of your draft files. Some place you had already muddied up to some degree. There was no need for you to introduce new and innocent bytes into all of this. It's just wasteful is what it is.

Sincerely,
Dr. Laura J. Michaels
« The Techno-Naturalist »

Preface
Included in this document are a selection of original letters from a variety of interested parties addressed and delivered to Isaac H. Pollan, the architect of the "Hidden Room" project (completed in the autumn months of the year 2018). The letters take on many voices and slowly tease out a number of different themes in the building. Each contributor brings their own specific set of interests and criticisms as they describe the built environment. Through these various narratives an experience of the building begins to coalesce . . . though it would be impossible to describe with absolute certainty.

Additional letters in this document include correspondence from Hans H. Hildebrand (the Curator); Willow (the Wind); Trenton Smith III (the Developer); The Brad Nails (the Band); Roberta (your Grandmother (with the bad hip)); Detective Dejesus (the Detective); and Isaac H. Pollan (the Architect).

To The Architect,

We have just shipped your final order of marble to site. As specified, it is of the snow white variety encrusted with reflective prismatic flecks. I hope that you continue to find our product satisfactory. And I hope that this is the last order that you will need. . . .

Because we also wanted to inform you that your project has exhausted our quarry of stone and as a result we will be closing our doors after 72 years of operation. We knew that this day would come. But admittedly, we thought we still had a numbers of year's worth of stock left.

I understand that it is appealing on both intellectual and lavish grounds to construct a modern building completely of fine stone, though I wonder if it is entirely necessary that this include all of the unexposed structural elements, or the plumbing for that matter. Not that we are complaining, thank you for funding our retirement.

Nice Doing Business With You,
Meonardo Lichelangelo
« The Quarry »

How can materials actively engage with subjectivity? How can we amplify the ambiance that seems to surround a person?

Delaram Rahim (MDes ADPD)
and Maharshi Bhattacharya (MDes Tech)
Digital Media: Ambiance
Instructor: Allen Sayegh

"In Bloom" manifests the feelings that are hard to express in words and otherwise become evident in one's body language or on the skin through occurrences such as goosebumps, blushing, and pallidity. As a second skin, "In Bloom" senses the proximity to another person and reveals the bright or warm-colored inner layer that is camouflaged by the dark-colored outer shell as another person gets closer to the one wearing the skin. We see it as a tool to visualize social anxiety, or attraction and repulsion; however, we do not wish to attach a definitive meaning to the skin and leave it to the wearer to explore their own interpretation.

The circuitry is such that when the sonar sensors detect a person within a two-foot radius, an air pump (diaphragm) is activated, filling the air chambers within a silicon jacket.

The jacket is made of two layers of silicon cast into the desired shape, with air chambers in between. Both layers have differing consistencies: while the top layer is thinner, more flexible, and elastic for ease of inflation, the bottom layer is thicker and more rigid in order to prevent it from stretching during inflation.

The jacket is then covered with a bright orange elastic fabric, and finally slitted packaging paper is fixed atop the fabric. The chambers inflate to push open the slits in the paper and the orange fabric becomes visible through the dark-painted slits over time, providing visual contrast.

How do we foreground personal identity in design? What can urban planning pedagogy learn from goth ideology and Sufism?

Sidra Fatima (MUP)
Independent Study
Advisor: Abby Spinak

Introduction

Hi everyone, my name is Sidra Fatima, and I am excited to have you all here with me in what is going to mostly be an experiment. Feel free to move around, grab a snack, dance if you want to, and "disrupt" the room at any time.

Welcome to this journey, which is part-experiment, and will hopefully be a positive experience—with both reflections and invitations. It is an attempt at communication, to see if you can see the tangle of web in my mind: how I find goth ideology, Sufism, and urban planning to be counter-hegemonic movements in the face of current capitalist extractive oppression. It is both personal narrative and future fiction. It is both outrage and resolution. It is repetitive, but new. I am not here to convince you, but to tell you of the ways in which identity, ways of knowing, and embodied practices can be urban planning, without it being rationalized.

> I have spent a lot of time—waiting; And I am feeling impatient because I have sat here; And hoped for it: For a change, For a movement, For a reckoning; With a trust that someone would do it. And I admire all those before me, and with me, who do, and who have, and who are; But this vow of silence—taken from not being understood or legible—is going to end here and now.

ACT I: Ways of Seeing

Identity is a big thing to unpack. Anything is possible if you sound Caucasian on the phone.

There is an inherent violence in the action of categorization and othering. We don't choose the color of our skin, where we are born, or what we inherit, and this is where aesthetics comes in. From ways of seeing, to how I am seen. Moving beyond the inheritance of a world obsessed with beauty and equating that subjectivity into goodness; adding layers of whiteness, and European features, and the dominion of colonialism as it values certain aesthetics and leaves others out—I am tired of these ways of seeing. They create a collective imaginary that may condition and constrain the sense of justice that binds a community.

Professor Annette Koh recently said, "Decolonizing planning requires that we take a long look at planning's project of making things better, which has always been subjective and rooted in exploitation. Our concepts of the public good and collective improvement are anchored in the history of colonial dispossession. Even if the designs have changed from car-centric sprawl to walkable New Urbanism, the logic remains the same."

ACT II: Ways of Being

So how is this relevant to planning? As a planner, I see pain and suffering all around me.

Our liberation is bound up with each other.

I'd like to begin by recognizing the labor of women of color and the burden to radically bring empathy into every space you are in. It means giving energy and one-sided exchanges. The amount of labor we give without taking anything back—this is the paradox of voluntary martyrdom; no credit, glory, or payment.

In *The Undercommons* (2013), Fred Moten and Stefano Harney describe us as: "after all, the subversive intellectual came under false pretenses, with bad documents, out of love. Her labor is as necessary as it is unwelcome. The university needs what she bears but cannot bear what she brings. And on top of all that, she disappears. She disappears into the underground, the down-low low-down maroon community of the university, into the undercommons of enlightenment, where the work gets done, where the work gets subverted, where the revolution is still black, still strong."

Radicality is simply grasping at the root of things.

So I've been working with vulnerability, and what possibility there is in not knowing.

ACT III: Ways of Knowing

Transformation is about learning to be vulnerable, seeing things a different way, and being open to radical adaptation. You have to let go of maturity to be remade.

Goth, for me, is a survival infrastructure—both in music and as ideology. In music, I am free, because of the multiplicities the medium allows. Anything can be goth. Picasso is goth. Goth has its origins in subversiveness: from Mary Shelley's *Frankenstein*, to Dante's *Inferno*. Bauhaus is goth. Because these moments are those of pushing back on prescriptive ways of being and ways of knowing. In ideology, it is a counterculture that is more critical of the status quo. It is fluidity, embracing the fullness of the human experience, and letting go of a fear of the unknown.

Truly, the only thing I know is that it will be uncomfortable. Yet discourse can be a way of life—aspirational approaches through many situations; to move through something that is partial and inconsistent. I would argue that planning, if made accessible, has the potential to shift our mode of living because it explicitly counters the ideological oppression that shapes the way people think.

Identity is inherently multiple. In addition to planner, goth, and artist, I am also Muslim. Sufism, at the core of Islam, invites the abstract, the illegible, the thing that cannot be articulated. The most fundamental principle of Sufism is that of unity in multiplicity.

What does your liberation look like?

What are current student and faculty perspectives on addressing social issues in design pedagogy and curricula?

Fiona Kenney (MDes HPDM), Brian Lee (MArch I), Gio Shin (MArch I)
An Unsentimental Look at Architecture and Social Craft (Seminar) and Independent Study
Instructor and Advisor: John Peterson

Amid current divisive and fast-paced political, cultural, and ecological conditions, formal pedagogy of design school can seem to linger too far behind the pressing social issues that drive many students into the design fields. In such cases where coursework and curricula do not adequately address contemporary social issues, these issues become consigned to informal education settings such as guest lectures, electives, and student groups. The result, for some, is concern for the relevance and impact of design and design pedagogy in contemporary and future worlds.

This project seeks to understand and contextualize this perception amid others that circle around design and design pedagogy's ability or responsibility to address social issues. The project was conducted in two parts. Part one surveyed Harvard GSD students in an effort to quantify the extent to which they believe social issues have been addressed in their formal education—and whether they even ought to be. Responses were collected from over a third of the student body. They indicated the majority of students have a strong belief in the agency of design to affect social outcomes, and a wide dissatisfaction with the extent to which this agency and responsibility are currently explored in the School's core curricula.

If the issue could be improved by more clearly articulating social dimensions in core project briefs, then how can these questions be reframed?

Part two aimed to spark dialogue between students and faculty about the role of design in shaping social outcomes, and the responsibility of the School to acknowledge this role. Faculty reactions to the initial student survey were gathered through interviews in order to build a deeper understanding of discourse at the GSD, and to identify underlying issues and potential solutions. Faculty members acknowledged that more could be done to address social issues in core curricula and posed various potential solutions, but also noted deeply rooted challenges to each. While there was no consensus between faculty on specific strategies, there were overlaps between student and faculty proposals. Multiple students and faculty interviewees, for example, proposed mandatory ethics courses. Many cited a lack of suitable vocabulary or language surrounding this issue as a main obstacle to progress; this lack often hindered communication in interviews as time was spent on both sides clarifying word choice and interpretation.

The study concluded with a roundtable discussion, to which faculty interviewees and all students were invited. The intention was to bring together all players in the conversation, discuss results, and explore paths forward. This year-long project has demonstrated, most importantly, that there is much more common ground than expected within the entire Harvard GSD community. This can be leveraged to sustain this dialogue and collaborate on implementing change. It is our hope that the results of this project, and their subsequent dissemination, will encourage the GSD to institutionalize or formalize a means to address social issues in design.

Ethics
Independent Study
Pedagogy
Seminar

"Why, in the face of reality, are we continuing to study only Western architecture at Harvard? We know that many great architects, Wright, Le Corbusier, and Kahn among them, drew extensively from other architectural tradition. Is there something we do not know? [. . .] If we are not designing for a mixed culture of the 21st century, nor for the people of our present society, for whom are we to design?"

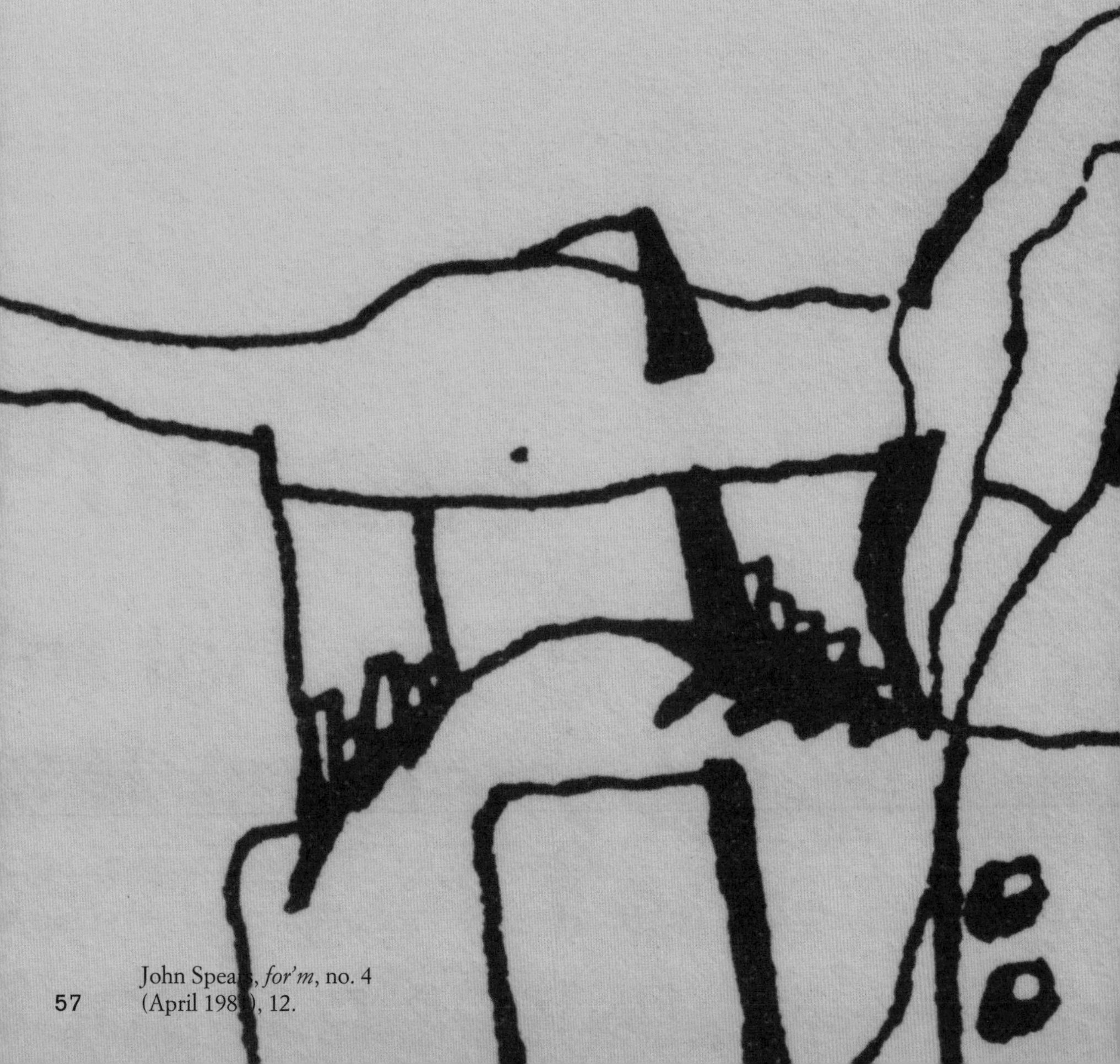

John Spears, *for'm*, no. 4 (April 198[illegible]), 12.

Who are we designing for? What if the needs of trees were valued as much as the needs of humans?

Kira Clingen (MLA I, MDes RR), Carson Fisk-Vittori (MLA I),
Shira Grosman (MLA I AP, MDes ULE)
Landscape Architecture IV: Four Semester Core Studio
Instructor: Rosalea Monacella

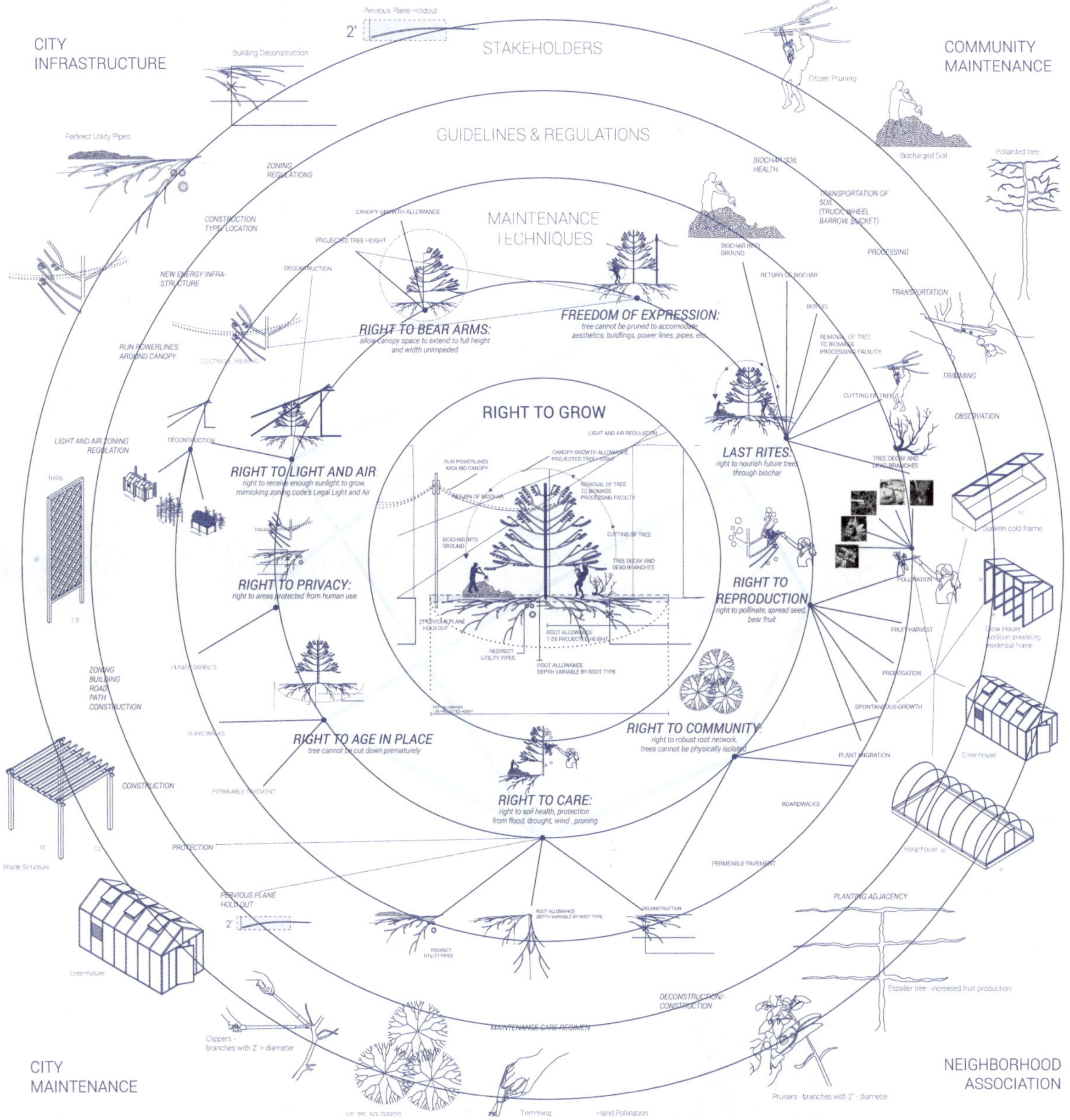

It is easy to assign monetary value to the city tree. A dollar value quantifies how much carbon they absorb, how many health benefits they are estimated to offer, how many gallons of rainwater they catch, and even their aesthetic appeal. But this form of value and evaluation limits the view of city trees to utilitarian, anthropocentric perspectives, and it limits our investment in their life—the city tree has a seven-year life expectancy. This project critiques the valuing of trees as resources for human benefit and instead proposes the revaluation of trees as intentional purposeful beings. This requires a reconfiguration of the urban assemblage.

Climate Change
Core Studio
Justice
Plants
Policy

Right to Grow Manifesto

Right to Community
Prioritize robust root networks and physical connections, plant in communities not as specimen species, allow root community to prosper through permeable surfaces.

Last Rites
Continue the life cycle of local tree communities by harvesting dead biomass and nourishing future trees through biochar.

Right to Expression
Do not cultivate or prune to accommodate aesthetics or utility infrastructure.

Right to Age in Place
Do not cut down the tree prematurely.

Right to Bear Arms
Allow canopy space to extend to full height and width unimpeded.

Right to Care
Prioritize soil health and non-aesthetic trimming; protection from wind, flood, drought; space-free utility infrastructure.

Right to Privacy
Protect areas from human use.

Right to Light and Air
Receive adequate sunlight to grow based on Zoning Code's Legal Light and Air.

Right to Reproduction
Pollinate, spread seed, and bear fruit; plant with male and female companions; stewardship through hand and artificial pollination; construct beehives and pro-insect gardens.

This project sets forth a catalyst for this shift in the form of an ordinance, "Right to Grow," inserted into zoning code and illustrated by a projective case study in South Boston. The "Right to Grow" ordinance prioritizes trees' needs in an urban environment. It reconfigures the false urban binary between people and woody plants by establishing spatial rights of tree communities. This ordinance expands space for plant communities, and therefore challenges prevailing planting conventions. This project also expands typologies to form empathetic spaces within cities in order to reframe conventions of habitation between people and woody plants.

Whose "camp" are we living in? What is queer architecture?

Bradley Silling (MArch I)
Architecture Thesis
Advisor: Jennifer Bonner

The premise of this project is to locate an architecture between two definitions of the word "camp." One definition offers a queer way of seeing and making culture, but has rarely resulted in architecture. This definition includes a love for defiance found in strong characters, a naively disengaged attitude towards content, and a suspension of the kinds of moral seriousness and diagrammatic dogmatism we find in architectural modernism. The dismissal of good-bad binaries has proved invaluable to queer culture, and while "camp" and queer are not synonyms, they are intrinsically related.[1]

The other definition of "camp" conjures the pastoral, and though it always results in architecture it has rarely been theorized. This type of camp needs no quotations around it. It connotes a peaceful innocence and a rural setting that manifests most clearly as summer camp. While summer camp was first institutionalized at the turn of the 20th century to rescue American boys from domestic life while on school break, the phenomenon eventually evolved to welcome and stimulate a myriad of identities: Girl Scouts, Black Panthers, Jews, theater kids, communists, and many more.

Summer camp might be the best tool we have for rehearsing the performance of our other selves in another kind of home. The experience of another kind of home is mirrored in spaces of queer collectivity, for example in Harlem's drag scene in the 1980s. Facing rejection from their biological families or working-class communities, members of Harlem's drag community lived together in Houses. Lead by a self-proclaimed "mother" or "father" who supported their "children," these Houses gave language and legitimacy to self-made family structures of queer collectivity,[2] and provided protection from physical and sexual violence.[3] But, unlike summer camp, they never found their own architectural form.

Houses in the Harlem drag scene were assembled from ill-fitting stock apartment buildings—someone else's definition of home. Sometimes single apartments were shared by a small group of performers; other times, entire floors of tenement buildings were turned into a sprawling assemblage of rooms. These were spaces of living, but also spaces for performers to work together on their craft. Hallways, for example, acted simultaneously as living room, runway, and circulation space.[4] Michael Cunningham describes these spaces as "baroque fantasies of glamour and stardom, all run on Singer sewing machines in tiny apartments."[5] Between performance and domesticity there are rich implications for an architecture of "camp."

"Camp" needs an architecture that can be lived in, but the practice of architecture must also be moved by "camp." Architects tempted to make spaces that "suit" a particular set of inhabitants may also try to "read" bodies according to normative (physical and familial) structures. However, "camp" and queerness defy this practice. The messy and ill-fitting domestic spaces of the House are not indicative of spatial poverty; rather, they are practices of self-design resistant to moral binaries and diagrammatic natures. Queer life is unrepentantly disordered, non-repetitive, and always contingent. We can see this in the normative space of the Harlem apartments, in their incommensurability with heterodox domestic collectivity of the House, and in the improvisation needed to live inside them anyway.

1
In "Notes on 'Camp,'" Susan Sontag tried to define "camp" and site it historically. In response to the shape-shifting character of the phenomena, she chose to write her essay as a series of 58 loosely connected "jottings," each of which lends some texture to the concept of "camp," but never sharply defines any of its boundaries. Susan Sontag, "Notes on 'Camp,'" *Partisan Review* 31, no. 4 (1964): 515–30.

2
Some of the best firsthand accounts of these Houses come from the 1990 documentary, *Paris is Burning.*

3
If a House were able to occupy an entire floor of a building, they could ensure a greater degree of safety. Trans sex workers suffered extremely high murder rates by johns. The Houses' collectivity meant that those who worked in the sex industry could avoid being fully alone with a stranger.

4
Marlon M. Bailey, "Gender/Racial Realness: Theorizing the Gender System in Ballroom Culture," in *Feminist Studies* 37, no. 2, (2011): 365–86.

5
Michael Cunningham, *Spirit of Harlem: A Portrait of America's Most Exciting Neighborhood* (New York: Doubleday, 2003).

Taking a site in Los Angeles, zoned for heavy industry use but now largely unoccupied, this project aims to make a space of camp that results in architecture while remaining staunchly committed to the oddities of queerness. (Camp loves a good cliché, so we might call this an "urban wilderness.")

The plan operates through an estrangement between the stable house-like forms of the massing and the promiscuous units that fill it. Like summer camp, its gabled roofs are a foil for the weirder dynamics they shelter.

The unstable and jittery rooms of each unit slip in and out as needed. Deep inside the house, neighbor relations become increasingly strange. It is only possible to perceive the shape of a neighbor's home through glimpses of their lives seen across courtyards. A mash-up of otherwise polite domestic forms produces internal relationships foreign to the normative image of home.

How can designing with a gendered lens create a public realm that better meets the needs of women and girls, and by extension all residents?

Carolyn Angius (MUP) and Sudeshna Sen (MAUD)
Gendering Urban Development
Instructor: Chelina Odbert

The City of Mendoza, Argentina is preparing to implement Phase 5 of a federal settlement upgrading program, PROMEBA. In Mendoza, PROMEBA Phase 5 will be focused in parts of La Favorita, an informal settlement to the west of the central city near the foothills of the Andes Mountains. This studio was tasked with redesigning the neighborhood's central plaza, Plaza Aliar, and developing a neighborhood plan focused on building a more gender-equitable public realm in La Favorita. During research on the ground, the studio facilitated participatory workshops over two days to learn more from women in La Favorita about their daily lives, what they like and don't like about La Favorita, and what they envision for the future. The studio also heard from federal and municipal staff and previous outreach efforts.

"Multiple Mobilities" interrogates the relationship between the built environment and gender equity and envisions a public realm that equally supports and reflects community members of all gender identities. While inequities between genders are often cultural and societal, the design disciplines must adopt a gendered perspective to ensure our built environments do not replicate such disparities. Through planning and designing with a gendered lens, we can realize a public realm in which all genders have access to diverse activities, feel their identities are reflected and celebrated, and can achieve their independent visions of the future.

"Multiple Mobilities" proposes a set of interventions that, while spatialized in La Favorita, can also provide a framework for planning and designing for gender equity in similar environments across Argentina.

Gender
Mobility
Option Studio
Public Space
Social Equity

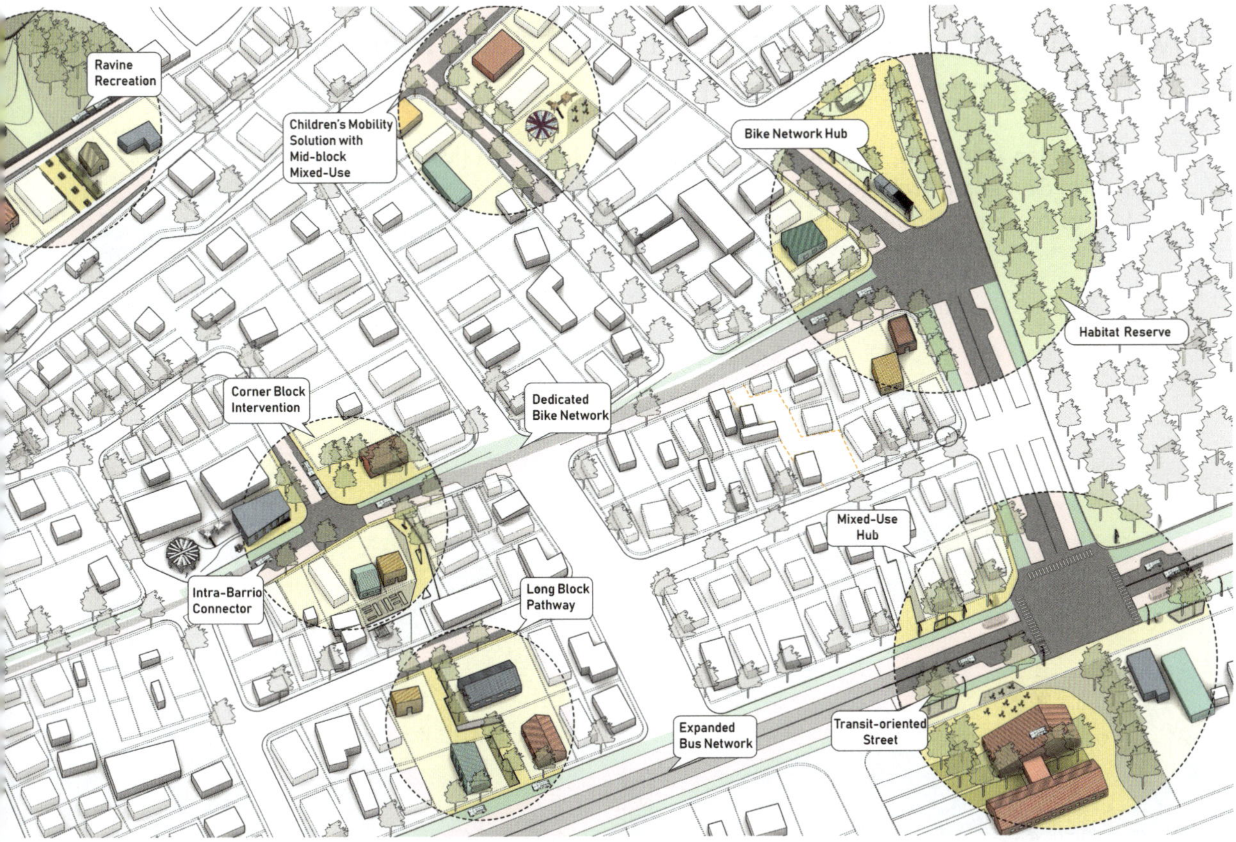

Ravine
Recreation
Children's Mobility
Solution with
Mid-block
Mixed-Use
Bike Network Hub
Habitat Reserve
Corner Block
Intervention
Dedicated
Bike Network
Mixed-Use
Hub
Intra-Barrio
Connector
Long Block
Pathway
Expanded
Bus Network
Transit-oriented
Street

Supermarket
Daycare
Cafe Seating

Commercial Use
Bike Shelter
Communication
Station
Bus Shelter
Sidewalk Seating

Playground
Promenade
Shaded Seating
Community Garden

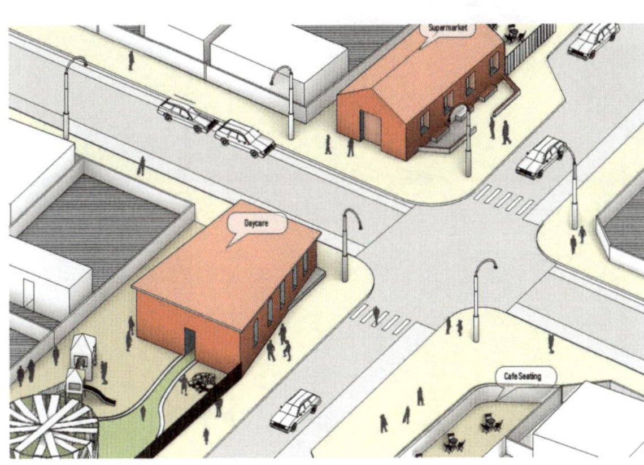

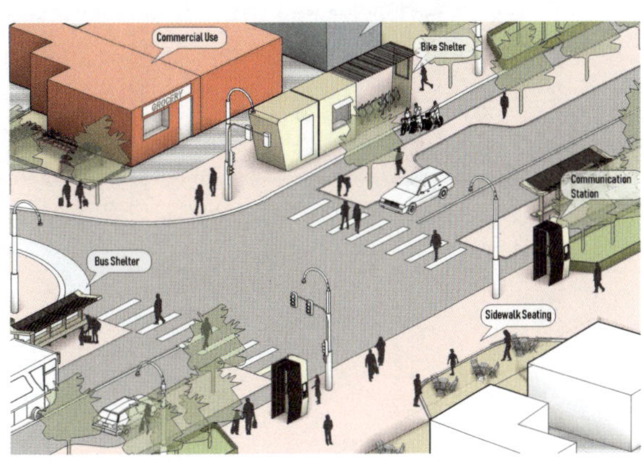

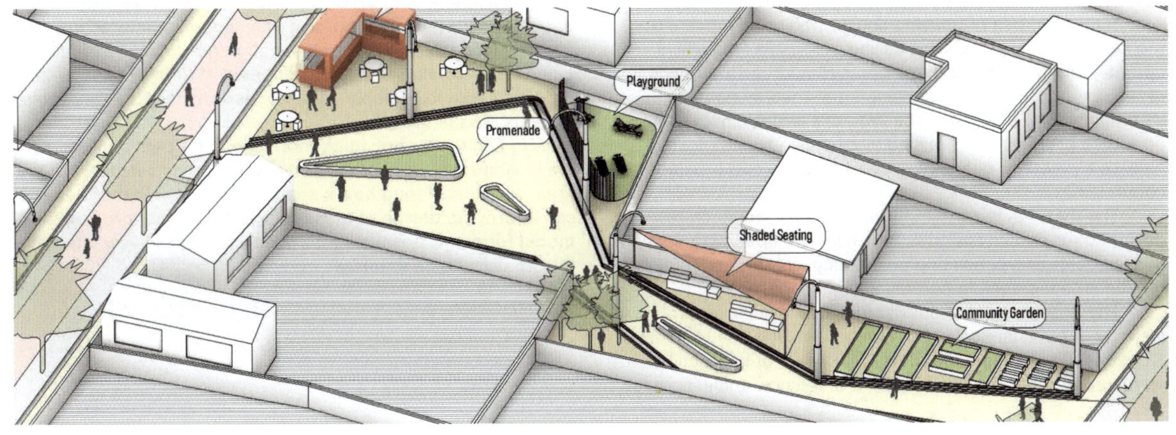

How can architecture designed for people and their pets be a means of connecting new residents with existing communities?

Jamie Han (MArch I), Yuna Kim (MArch I), Julia Schubach (MArch I)
Fourth Semester Architecture Core: Relate
Instructor: Jenny French

"Union Square Crossing" is a cohousing project that deals with multiple scales of housing design while reinterpreting the assumed scale at which housing proposals typically operate. The project's primary aim is to address the needs of the neighborhood by proposing a pet-friendly cohousing community for Somerville. The project's larger aim is to provide a prototype for housing that creates spaces for pets as a means of connecting new residents and existing communities.

The thesis of this project proposes that architecture designed for people and their pets has the capacity to connect the residents of a cohousing community and to connect those residents to the existing communities.

The project is a mat-courtyard hybrid organized around a series of medium-scale common houses that aim to foster a community of people and pets. Four types of interaction were supported in the spatial and architectural qualities of the project: human-pet interaction, human-architecture interaction, pet-architecture interaction, and human-human interaction. These relationships are expressed through similar formal languages and spatial qualities but exist at different scales in order to serve its multiple types of residents and visitors (pets, humans, and neighbors).

In addition to providing more space for pets and pet owners in Somerville, connecting new and existing residents of the area, and considering how a scale smaller than that of humans can inform the design of architecture, the project proposes a model for one way housing proposals can sensitively integrate into an existing community.

What happens when possessions or objects become the tool for designing domestic space?

David Kim (MArch II)
The House: The Waken Desire
Instructors: Tatiana Bilbao and Iwan Baan

Think about visiting an empty house. Imagine living in it. You enter through the front door and probably see a living room or a drawing room. Depending on the house, maybe a kitchen is close by, followed by a series of bedrooms and closets. In the closet, you imagine your clothes inside. In the bedroom, maybe a new bed frame, your bookshelf, and a desk. In the hallway hangs art given to you by your friend. In the kitchen, your favorite dining table, and in the living room, maybe a new TV and grandma's hand-me-down L-shaped sofa. If you're a filmmaker, where does your film equipment go? If you're a musician, what about your guitar and drums? You can see it all, there in the empty house. Your objects and belongings are what make this your home. The architecture is set, and in your mind, you imagine yourself and your things in it.

But what happens if you flip this mentality around? What if your possessions and objects and belongings lay in front of you, and the architecture didn't exist? No empty house, no walls or defined spaces like kitchens or bedrooms. After all, aren't these constructs created by someone else? What if you instead imagined the architecture? What spaces emerge from this thought? Now, maybe, clothes don't necessarily need to go into the closet, and the bed doesn't need to be in the bedroom alongside a nightstand and a lamp. By inverting the object-and-architecture relationship, not only is the idea of traditional domesticity liberated, but you also rethink the definition of any given space.

Domestic space can now be defined by the objects, not by the architecture.

How can form and program reclaim spaces made inaccessible due to exclusionary practices?

Aria Griffin (MArch I)
Third Semester Architecture Core: Integrate
Instructor: John May

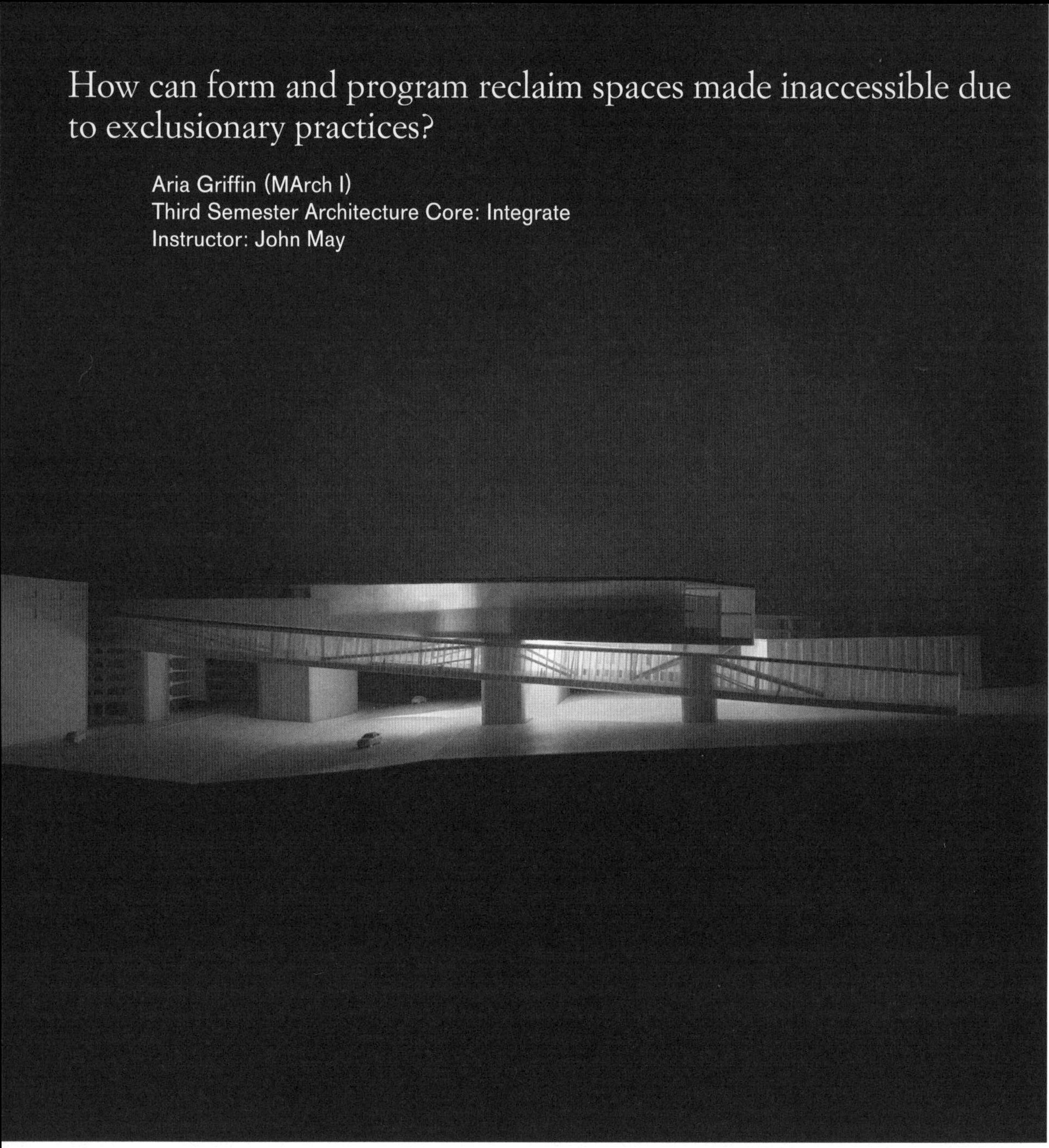

This project inserts a Yale-owned night school attached to the Paul Rudolph garage, which will serve the New Haven communities that have been severed by the construction of Interstate 95. The highway, built originally in the 1950s to connect suburbanites to shopping centers in the downtown area, cut off the Hill neighborhood (located south of the site) from the heart of the downtown and hastened the Hill's decline.

Such a provocation contemplates the exclusionary practices of Yale University in New Haven, and those practiced historically within the hotel typology. This project references the work of photographer Carrie Mae Weems. Her haunting portraits shift the antiquated power dynamic to one which includes the black body—standing in for the "lost" (under-represented, or buried) figure throughout history. The viewer is reminded of the hidden contributions written out of our collective history. In this way, this can be read as redemptive work—a reclaiming of the spaces and narratives that were previously inaccessible to us.

A growing demand for more affordable higher education asks us to critically examine the elite pedagogical models and reinvent them to become more attainable and equitable. In New Haven, this disparity is heightened by the built environment and made obvious by stark neighborhood divisions.

The night school in this proposal includes a hotel for commuting students and visitors that will help revitalize both the downtown and the Hill in the evening hours. Large community event spaces and a ghostly monumental pedestrian bridge align with the major street axes across the highway. Therefore, the building's volumes act as stitches to suture the city back together.

Core Studio
Program
Race
Social Equity

What can architecture help us feel into?

Morgan Starkey (MArch I)
Architecture Thesis
Advisor: Andrew Holder
Recipient of the James Templeton Kelley Thesis Prize

"The joint, that is, the detail, is the place of the meeting of the mental construing and of the actual construction"
—Marco Frascari, "The Tell-the-Tale Detail" (1983)

Gravity connects us to inanimate matter—literally. This attraction is the reality of our physics. Perhaps more importantly though, gravity links us figuratively and emotionally as we empathize with the load-bearing members in an assembly because we too are burdened by the same force. Empathy is the connective tissue between the construing of our mind and the construction of matter and it permits us to "feel into" the objects in our environment; our bodies themselves becoming parts in these assemblies. Furthermore, the creative resistance of force in architecture produces machines that are abundant in potential energy, rendering a perceived instability that is decidedly human. It is the tectonic expression of joints holding together these codependent parts in precarious equilibrium that allows for an assembly to be coherently understood as representative of a larger order, idea, or system.

If the joint is the nexus between the mental and the physical aspects of architecture, where tectonic metaphors tell stories about the society that constructed it, these details then become synecdoche for architecture itself—that is, a mode of human creativity that imbricates the metaphorical, the allegorical, and the imaginary with the physics of reality. This thesis contends that at its best, a building can be read as a single detail, a simple machine of expressive elaboration of the work done to resist the gravity that wants to destroy it. It makes legible the flow of forces at play in coordination with and choreographed to its program and the ideas it is tasked to represent as a unified whole.

Detail
Form
Materials
Thesis

. . . A conversation about the Just City . . .

Identity
Justice
Social Equity
Urbanism

"The Just City Assembly," Discussion and Workshop, April 12, 2019

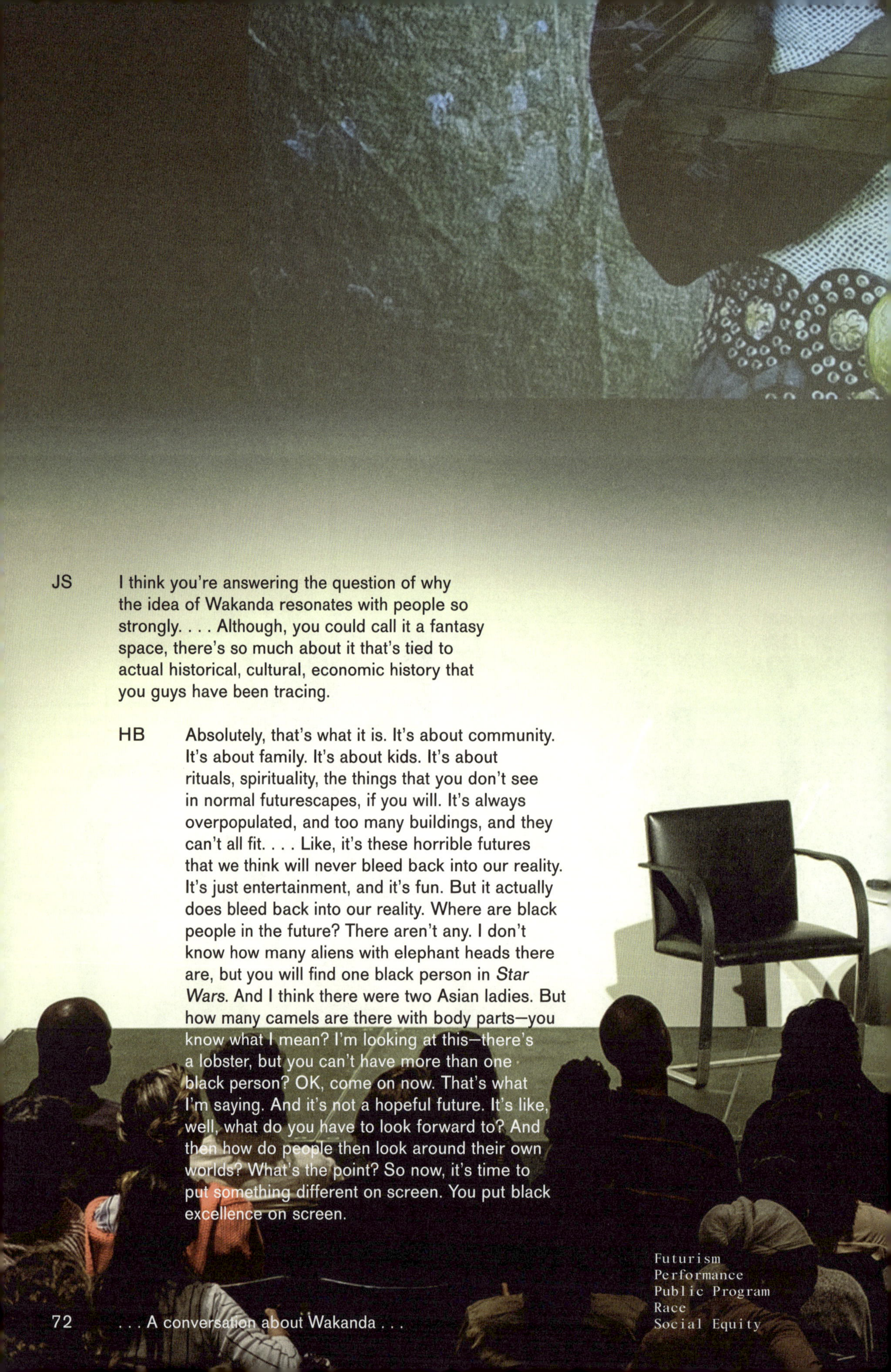

JS I think you're answering the question of why the idea of Wakanda resonates with people so strongly. . . . Although, you could call it a fantasy space, there's so much about it that's tied to actual historical, cultural, economic history that you guys have been tracing.

HB Absolutely, that's what it is. It's about community. It's about family. It's about kids. It's about rituals, spirituality, the things that you don't see in normal futurescapes, if you will. It's always overpopulated, and too many buildings, and they can't all fit. . . . Like, it's these horrible futures that we think will never bleed back into our reality. It's just entertainment, and it's fun. But it actually does bleed back into our reality. Where are black people in the future? There aren't any. I don't know how many aliens with elephant heads there are, but you will find one black person in *Star Wars*. And I think there were two Asian ladies. But how many camels are there with body parts—you know what I mean? I'm looking at this—there's a lobster, but you can't have more than one black person? OK, come on now. That's what I'm saying. And it's not a hopeful future. It's like, well, what do you have to look forward to? And then how do people then look around their own worlds? What's the point? So now, it's time to put something different on screen. You put black excellence on screen.

Futurism
Performance
Public Program
Race
Social Equity

Hannah Beachler with Jacqueline Stewart,
Rouse Visiting Artist Lecture, Lecture and Discussion, October 4, 2018

What would your city be like if you felt that your city as a space, as a community, included and centered black women?

Chandra Rouse (MUP)
Urban Planning Thesis
Advisor: Lily Song

Rae Chardonnay, Tracie Hall, Isis Ferguson, Maya Bird-Murphy, Jacqueline Stewart, Tonika Lewis Johnson, Amanda Williams. The story of these seven black women space-makers in Chicago is one of resistance, adaptation, innovation, and agency.

As a strategy, space-making is an old tradition in black communities, which have scarcely been able to rely on urban planning institutions to protect their interests.[1] The necessity to turn inward for leadership development, mutual reliability, and community care produced a legacy of space-making that these women were borne from and build upon. In this way, black women space-makers comprise an institutional practice that is not new—but seen in the context of urban planning, their work offers a valuable and value-laden perspective on alternative spatial practices and the various spatial knowledge that can produce them.

Analyzing the particular histories of black women creative practitioners in Chicago, and their positioning within persistent but unfixed social hierarchies, is an important research practice. While such a focus narrows research findings to a particular regional demographic, nuanced analysis of how those who go beyond expressing survivalist agency and express creative agency can create a more solid foundation for deeper comparative analysis of black women space-makers and other spatial imaginaries across various cities. In accordance with extant literature on critical geography and black feminism, these particular women create new geographies that reflect themselves, and in doing so create new possibilities for many to engage. They imagine new spatial possibilities for their lives and communities—despite structural violence rather in direct response to it.

The work of these women transforms space often abandoned by urban planning entities, and focuses on celebrating black women and similarly situated communities in Chicago. While their work is interested in creating human experiences rather than meeting objective and quantifiable goals typical of modern planning strategies, their practice is also rigorous, responsive, and intentional in how they accommodate and manage conflict between multiple audiences and multiple truths. As they often discussed, the audience must see differently in order to see their work, and consequently see these women as legitimate space-makers.

Like these black feminist space-makers, planners must dare to assert visions of a world that we all deserve, and the hope that will get us there.

1
See Clyde Woods, *Development Arrested: The Blues and Plantation Power in the Mississippi Delta* (New York: Verso Books, 2017).

A

B

A
Tonika Lewis Johnson and Folded Map: Johnson's Folded Map™ Project visually connects residents who live at corresponding addresses on the North and South Sides of Chicago through interviews, interactive mapping, a companion website, and a Chicago West Side study. She investigates what urban segregation looks like and how it impacts Chicago residents.

B
Tracie Hall and Rootwork Gallery: Founded in 2016, Hall's gallery, Rootwork, showcases artistic expression that has healing, reconciliation, or the investigation of folk, street, and indigenous cultures at its core.

Race, Space, and the Poetics of Planning: Toward a Black Feminist Space-Making Practice

C

D

E

G

F

C
Rae Chardonnay and Nick Alder and Party Noire: The #PartyNoire community is an inclusive cultural hub celebrating black femmes, QWOC, and black womynhood along the gender spectrum and holds space especially for queer, trans, and genderqueer and gender non-conforming black people. Cofounders Chardonnay and Alder are divinely connected in their mission to affirm, uplift, and celebrate black womanhood along the gender spectrum.

D
Maya Bird-Murphy and Chicago Mobile Makers: Chicago Mobile Makers creates programming that encourages Chicago youth to become change makers in their own communities through design-focused skill-building workshops. Their objectives are to engage and empower youth through making and skill building; to train and support future public-interest architects, designers, and makers; and to advocate for social, economic, gender, and racial diversity in the architecture and broader design fields.

E
Jacqueline Stewart and the South Side Home Movie Project: The SSHMP seeks to increase understanding of the many histories and cultures composing Chicago's South Side, and of amateur filmmaking practices, by asking owners of home movies (shot on 8mm, Super 8mm, 16mm film) to share their footage and describe it from their personal perspectives.

F
Amanda Williams and Colo(red) Theory: Williams's series, "Color(ed) Theory," painted the exterior of soon-to-be-demolished houses on Chicago's South Side to mark the pervasiveness of vacancy and blight in black urban communities.

G
Isis Ferguson and Arts Block at Arts and Public Life: Ferguson currently develops process, narrative, and projects for the Arts Block, a geographic site and ideological approach that exist at the unique nexus of community development, urban planning, and art.

What is structural racism, where does it occur, and how can we counter it?

Loyiso Qaqane (MAUD), Laier-Rayshon Smith (MUP), Isaac Stein (MLA II, MDes RR)
Urban Design and the Color-Line
Instructor: Stephen Gray

In 1911, Baltimore became the first city to pass a zoning ordinance separating space through the classification of skin color. This blatantly racist act lead to the establishment of similar ordinances across United States municipalities, until it was deemed unconstitutional in 1917 by the Supreme Court.[1] But the reality is the separation for the built environment existed before Ordinance 692 and continues today through mandates that are supported either overtly or covertly by municipal legislation and practices. Often these measures are reinforced by private sector development with the coordination and approval of local officials. In Baltimore today black and white populations are still divided. Lines dividing people by skin color take the form of topography (a ravine between hills), infrastructure (Greenmount Avenue and Interstate 83, which limit access between parts of the city), and economic incentives (for companies such as Amazon) that bring investment and further gentrification to white enclaves.

Across the United States, color-lines manifest as roads, highways, buildings, and other physical interventions. Sometimes, these lines develop because of policies, strategies, and plans made by planners and policymakers. These manifestations of color-lines implicate all professionals involved in the urban decision-making process. If design has created physical manifestations of color-lines, how can design address the same inequities and injustices?

To say that racism in South Africa was structural and overt is an extreme understatement. The philosophy behind the creation of the country was to create a European nation on a continent that is almost completely black. This sounds like an absurd idea, but there are so many countries that have implemented this idea—countries such as Australia, New Zealand, Canada, and of course the United States. Though they manifest through different demographic dynamics, the structures of white supremacy that guide the racist philosophies behind these countries are widely similar."

—Loyiso Qaqane, personal essay

The color-line, as a tool of racial segregation, has been instituted on many levels throughout society. It is imperative to acknowledge the arsenal of exclusion that has been utilized by planners and designers to weaponize the built environment as harmful and not as innocuous design features or planning strategies. Dismantling these systems will require significant change within the processes and systems that have instituted racism in our society.

—Laier-Rayshon Smith, personal essay

It is our task as designers to help guide our clients (city officials, developers, community members, homeowners, etc.) to actively promote anti-racist agendas and design decisions. Furthermore, as designers we have the skills and duty to reveal and represent disparities and opportunities that lie within the work we do with these power brokers in order for them to have perspective on the impact and lineage of the work proposed."

—Isaac Stein, personal essay

"An ordinance for . . . promoting the general welfare of the city by providing, so far as practicable, for the use of separate blocks by white and colored people for residences, churches and schools."[2]

1
Garrett Power, *Apartheid Baltimore Style: the Residential Segregation Ordinances of 1910–1913*, *Maryland Law Review* 42, no. 2 (1983): 289.

2
Baltimore Mayor J. Barry Mahool. May 15, 1911. Ordinance 692.

Identity
Infrastructure
Race
Seminar
Social Equity

What is infrastructural racism? How are the ways we draw connected to the ways we plan?

Andres Quinche (MLA I, MUP)
Urban Design and the Color-Line
Instructor: Stephen Gray

The collages created during this course served as a type of archaeological excavation. Archival research sought to unearth the histories of Mexican American and African American communities in Los Angeles. By digging, cutting, and piecing back together we are able to better understand the past and plan for the future. As designers we have a duty to reckon with the histories of the communities that we engage with, both written and unwritten. These collages explored both the damages inflected upon Latinx and black communities (redlining, predatory lending, highway construction, illegal deportations), as well as the communities' desires, aspirations, and livelihoods (community organizing and protesting for education, healthcare, and housing). Collectively, these collages represent a layering of stories, a palimpsest of past and present, and a new way to represent history.

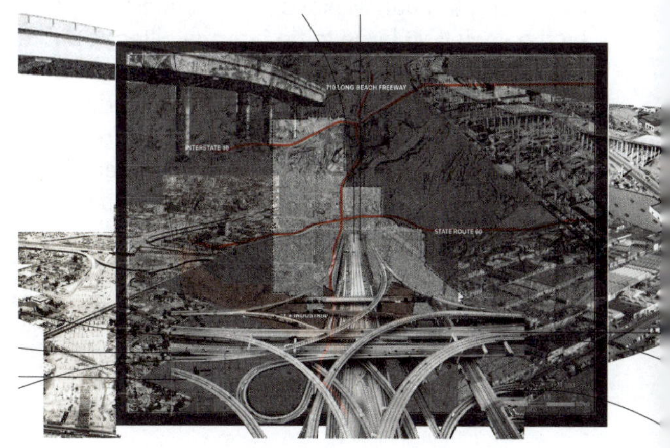

Infrastructure
Race
Seminar
Social Equity

How can a purposeful redefinition of terminology promote the agency of low-income residents in Nigerian urban environments?

Esesua Ikpefan (DDes)
Experimental Infrastructures
Instructor: Abby Spinak

Nigeria is a country where dominant social groups, from British colonial masters to ethnic and religious majorities, have used narrative to shape the built environment. These stories persist from one generation to the next and, according to Toyin Falola, resulted in "the manipulation of historical memory for politics and for resistance to people of African descent who attempt to reinvent that false memory; the transition from the control of people to the conquest of land; and the response by dominated people to reclaim their own past and their struggle for inclusion."[1] In order to understand Nigeria's deeply rooted ethnoreligious contestation over political agency and physical space, the creation of purposeful tension between Nigerian ethnic and religious groups by European colonizers must be acknowledged.

Due to this constant search for approval by the Nigerian government and urban society at large, value is placed on homogeneity and sameness. This is overtly expressed in Lagos, Nigeria's largest urban and economic hub, where the elitism of the Yoruba ethnic majority has its foundations in Western education. Certain architectural typologies and infrastructural systems are praised for their Western advancement, while others are seen as disturbances to the social and spatial construct hoped to be achieved by the societal elite; "planned" is better than hybrid, which is better than "unplanned." Thus, Ikoyi, the former European quarters, is better than Popo Aguda, a Brazilian returnee settlement with Afro-Portuguese architectural typology, which is better than Makoko, a waterside community of the urban poor. Lagos is better than Lagos, which is better than Lagos. Just as the construct of Yorubaness and its elitism in Lagos has no room for ethnic minorities and urban poor, infrastructure, as defined by the dominant sociopolitical ethnic majority, does not include the systems and networks created by those outside of its contrived identity.

This project, the construction of a "Subjective Dictionary of Nigerian Urban Infrastructure," embraces the multiple meanings of land, architectural typology, and relationships to built environments as a means of confronting hegemonic social, political, and economic control over space through dominant narratives in Lagos, Nigeria. Specifically, it focuses on narratives circulating through Makoko Iwaya Waterfront, a part of the city deemed by the society at large to be informal, illegal, and dirty. The "Subjective Dictionary" presents Makoko as possessing valuable and legitimate systems integral to understanding indigenous Nigerian forms of urbanity. It tells a different story of Makoko in hopes of confronting urban planning processes in Lagos and the histories on which they rely. Each concept or term is chosen to provide an expanded understanding of Lagos as a city, both referencing its colonial heritage and, at the same time, claiming its freedom and independence. By using poetry and song, image and text, the dictionary hopes to present not only multiple definitions of space, but also multiple means used to derive these definitions.

HOME
The place where one lives permanently, especially as a member of a family or household.[2]

SLUM
A place of love; of value; of culture; of urbanity; of infrastructure; of rethinking futures.

ROAD
A wide way leading from one place to another, especially one with a specially prepared surface which vehicles can use.[2] Makoko possesses an intricate road network in the form of waterways.

1
Toyin Falola, "The Slave Mutiny of 1839: The Colonization of Memory and Spaces," in *The African Diaspora: Slavery, Modernity, and Globalization* (Rochester, NY: University of Rochester Press, 2013), 53–72.

2
Oxford English Dictionaries, 2nd ed., s.v. "home" and "road."

How can landscape processes be leveraged in post-Confederate monument sites to unearth the physical environment of racism?

Ann Lynch (MLA I)
Landscape Architecture Thesis
Advisors: Danielle Choi and Emily Wettstein

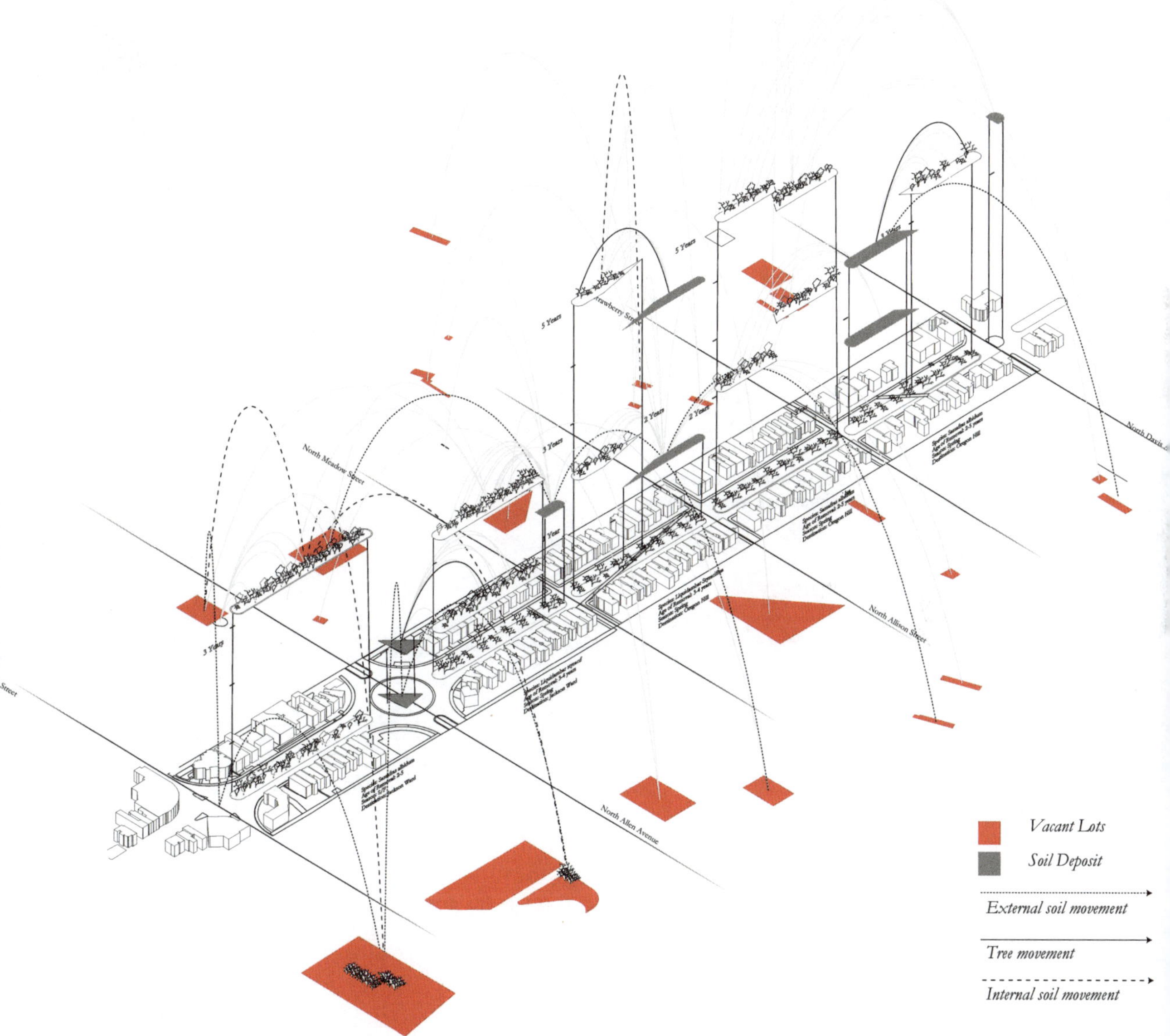

The removal of Confederate monuments from public spaces throughout the New South has created a spatial typology: the post-monument site. These places contain a trace of the original monument, most often the pedestal, a vestige that calls into question the structure's actual and perceived spatial extents. "Inveterate Scars" takes up the productive instability of the post-monument site, ultimately determining that Confederate monuments remain fixed in an idea of the past through their consecration in the present.

"Inveterate Scars" begins on Monument Avenue in Richmond, Virginia. The avenue established a memorial archetype in the postbellum South, merging monumental forms with city infrastructure. Five Confederate monuments are situated on the avenue, each at traffic circles.

History
Identity
Monument
Race
Thesis

Inveterate Scars: Confederate Monument Removal in the New South

Small or irregularly shaped pieces are crushed and used as aggregate. This improves soil drainage and monument cladding becomes new pathways.

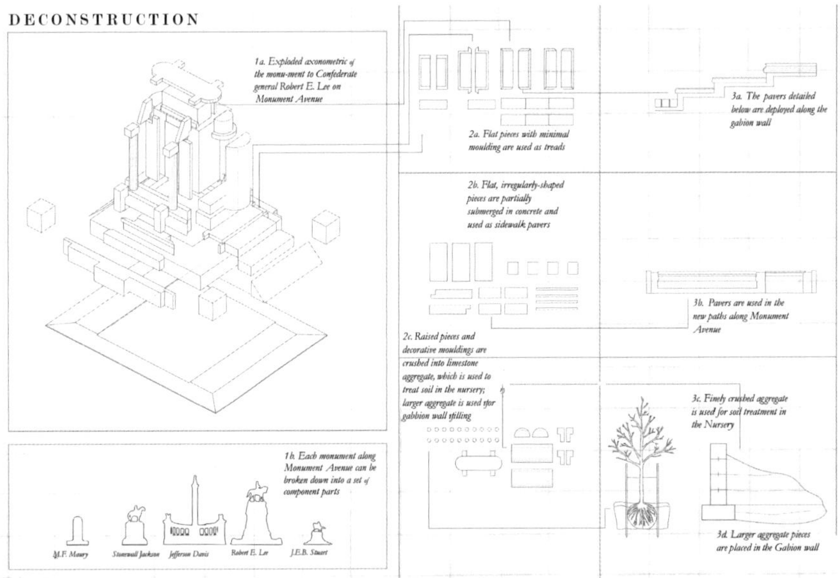

This project chronicles the process by which new historical sites are identified and made visible through the processes of archaeological survey and excavation. This thesis proposes excavation as both an impetus toward and a generator of design. In removing excavated ground from these new sites to Monument Avenue, a silenced history reveals a new reality. By removing the figurative element of these monuments, we see the pedestal is composed of the urban surface. As such, a deconstruction of the pedestal requires the deconstruction of the city itself. This thesis confronts landscape architecture's complicity in constructing the physical environment of racism, and proposes a new future for the discipline—one in which the processes of landscape are leveraged to unearth silenced truths.

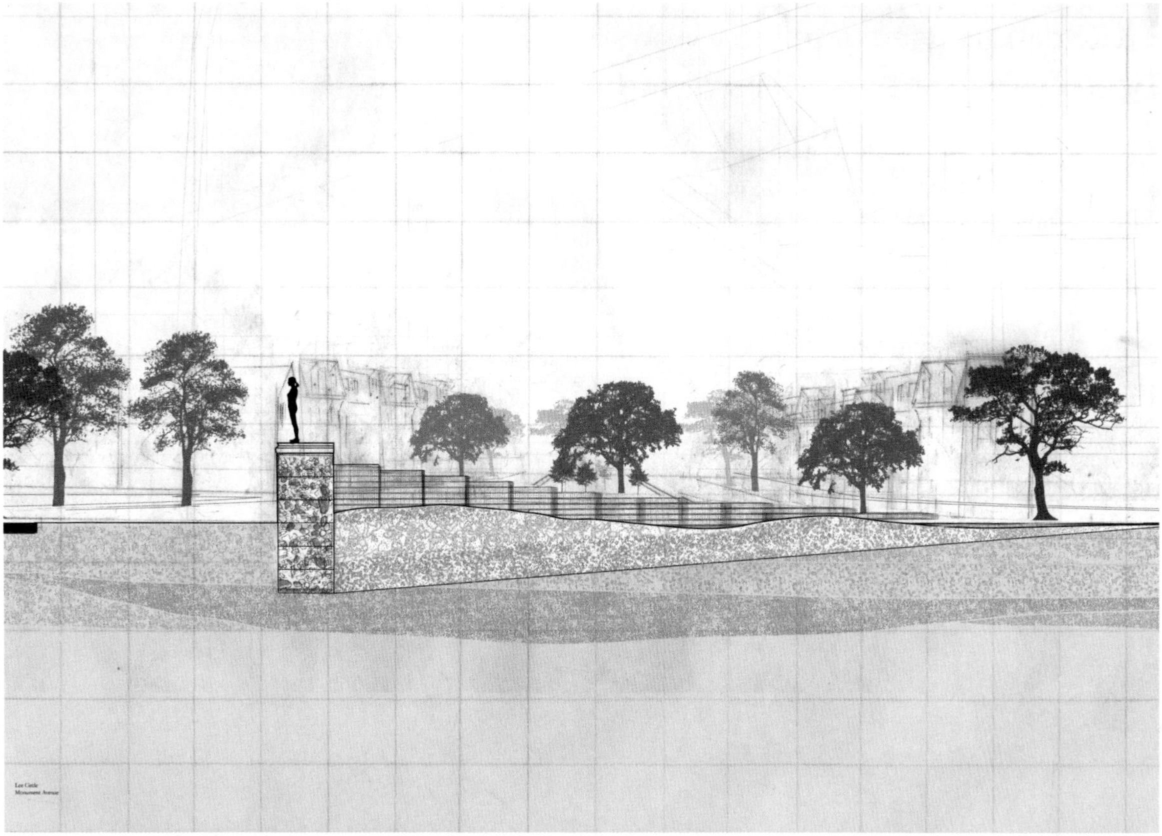

A scalable gabion wall serves as a vantage point as well as a retaining mechanism for soil deposits; monument claddings become stair treads.

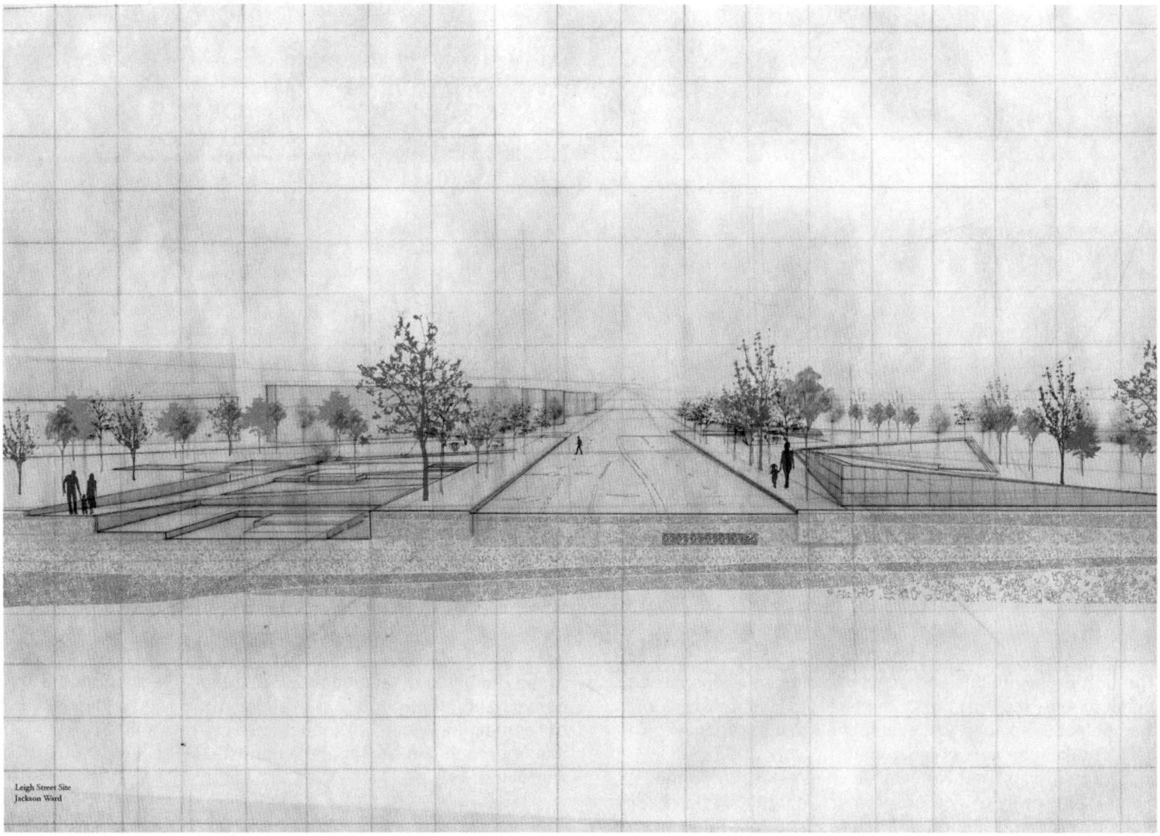

Before the construction of I-95, Leigh Street was narrower and lined with houses; these sunken plazas are derived from excavated housing foundations.

How can we view a territory or space, specifically the Greater Boston area, with the lens of indigeneity?

Andrea Reimer (Loeb Fellow '19)
Constructing Visual Narratives of Place
Instructor: Francesca Benedetto

The first project in this course was to choose a lens through which to view the territory of the Greater Boston Area, and then select 10 places that exemplified that perspective. This project takes the lens of indigeneity.

"The Things That Remain" is an atlas exploring the history and reality of a territory where indigeneity has been violently erased. This project requires a deeper interrogation of the definition of "indigenous," and thinks less about the context and more about the qualities of objects, a kind of remnant indigeneity. While necessary given the facts, this approach is fundamentally opposed to an indigenous worldview.

History
Indigeneity
Memory
Seminar
Territory

How do we perceive the social reality of the Midwest?

Adam Sherman (MArch I)
American Gothic: Monuments for Small-Town Life
Instructors: Pier Paolo Tamburelli

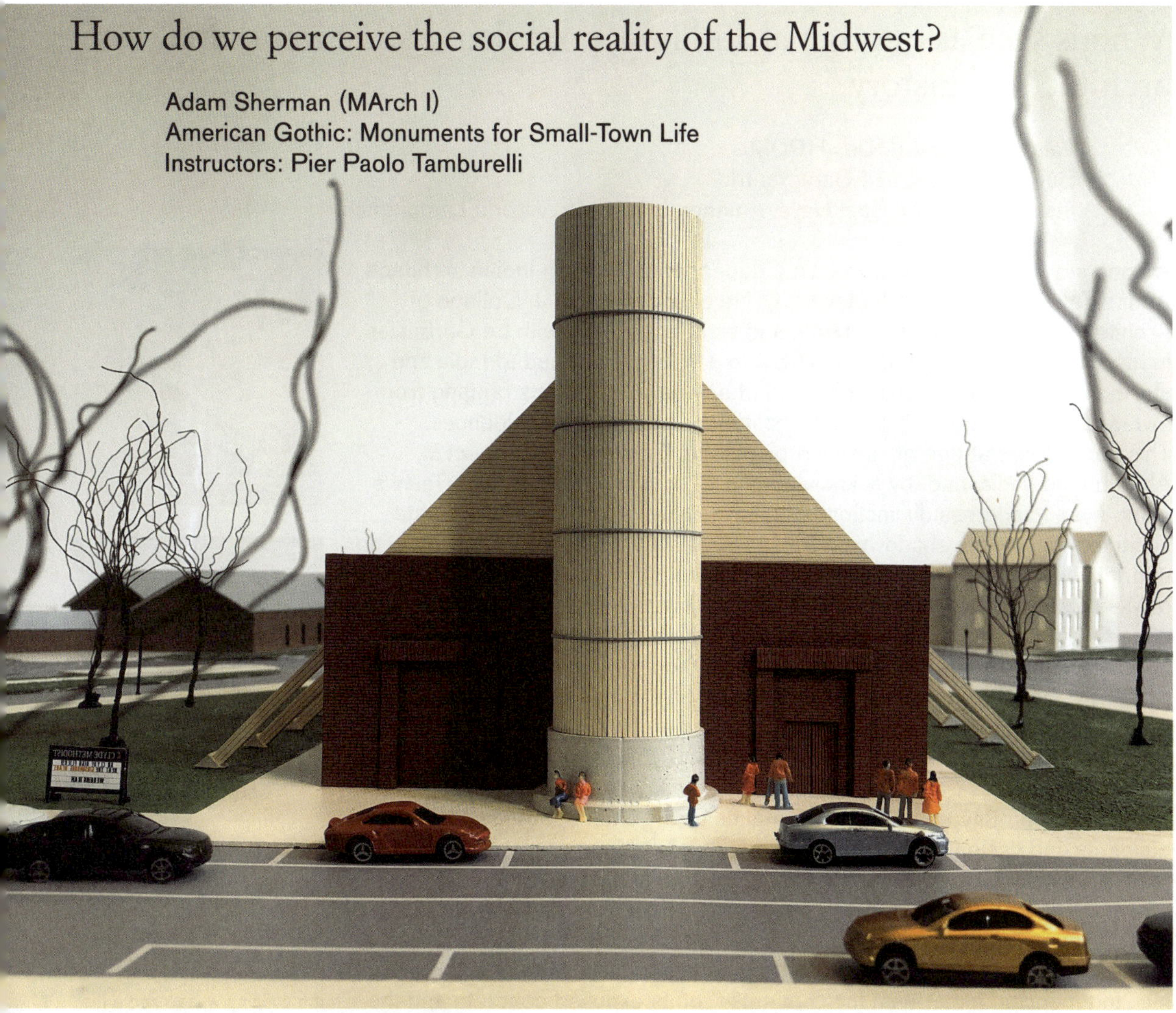

In the era of "Make America Great Again," factory towns in the American Midwest are witnessing confrontations between small-town traditions and new modes of contemporary life. The design of this Methodist church in Clyde, Ohio, explores how architecture can react to this tension.

The building evokes imagery of both religious and industrial vernacular architecture in service of multiple symbolic roles as a church in a factory town. Acknowledging both the possibilities and the limitations for architecture to respond to political changes, the church offers itself as a monument for contemporary small-town life.

Who is seen as unoriginal and how does that distinction shape architectural history?

Vaissnavi Shukl (MDes HPDM)
Buildings, Texts, and Contexts III
Instructors: K. Michael Hays, Amanda Lawrence, Vittorio Lampugnani

Among stories of lesser-known post-independence modern Indian architects, Arvind Talati's is especially noteworthy. He attended the J. J. College of Architecture in Bombay from 1947, and went on to work with Le Corbusier in his Paris studio from 1954 to 1957. In 1958 he returned to India and started his own practice that consisted of a variety of projects ranging from low- and middle-income housing to institutions and private residences. This paper looks at one of Talati's projects, the Bank of India project in Ahmedabad, India, and, by acknowledging Corbusier's influence on Talati's work, aims to address distinctions of unoriginality which perhaps relegate Talati too far into the shadows of architectural history. Questions surrounding unoriginality include: How can originality be reconciled with the transposition of Western architectural ideas into a country that has just gained independence from yet another Western idea of colonialism? For gaining a deeper understanding of what came to be known as modern Indian architecture, in what ways can the works of Indian architects be situated beyond studying them as derivatives or compilations of modern architectural projects from the West? Lastly, how did the interpretation and cultural appropriation of Western influences translate into the emergence of new, original "Indian" architectural prototypes? This paper makes an argument about how such buildings and design processes are products of a complex nexus that transcends ideas of derivatives, generics, and compilations.

Completed in 1965 (demolished a couple of decades later), the Bank of India was located within the dense urban fabric of the eastern part of Ahmedabad. The program is rather simple: the building was to serve the function of a bank and support daily banking activities which included spaces for cashiers, accountants and managers, a strong room and safe deposit vault, working space for bank employees, a canteen and a small living quarters for visiting officers.

The Bank of India was completed in 1965, around eight years after Talati's return from Paris.[1] To an untrained eye, the building is the epitome of modern Indian architecture, representing an avant-garde idea of a postcolonial, independent India. With the "grayness" of its exposed concrete and the "whiteness" of its walls, the building embodies an uncommon aesthetic that emerges from new ideas, new materials, and the need for new institutions to build a new nation.[2] Though Corbusier designed a variety of public buildings and public housing during his career, he never directly encountered a program which focused exclusively on functions of banking. How then can the Corbusian influence on Talati be situated? In lack of a parallel building type as an origin to draw inspiration from, the main concern in this case is not Talati's imitations of Corbusier, but rather, of cultural and contextual appropriation within the west–east schism. Thus to study the influence of Corbusier on Talati, this venture into distinctions of originality avoids a direct comparison between how Talati's buildings look with respect to Corbusier's, and instead focuses on examining individual elements that embody modern qualities.

To begin, the Bank of India building does not demonstrate all five features of Corbusier's modernist manifesto: it is not raised on *piloti*, does not have a free ground floor plan, nor does it display an entirely detached facade. On the contrary, the building is deeply rooted in the ground it sits on, through the creation of a basement. The structural layout of the columns does allow for a free plan, but Talati opts for a more disciplined interior arrangement, which adheres to the existing grid lines. Partly responsible for this arrangement is the program, which demands a layout that maximizes the use of available space by steering away from the use of curvilinear partition walls. Similarly, the structural grid allows for the creation of a free facade, but Talati restricts himself to modifications within the existing grid-and-fin structure—modulating the widths of the openings with a fixed height, creating a series of ribbon windows to make up the facade.

The ribbon windows are the first indicator of Corbusian influence. They are not located on the same plane as the wall infill; rather, the windows are offset from the columnar plane and form an added layer of skin on the exterior. The horizontal openings along with the fins were conceptualized as sun breakers to control the harsh tropical sunlight. The evolution of these elements as a mechanism to address the local climate can be directly attributed to Talati's time at Corbusier's office, and especially to his studies for the Tower of Shadows in Chandigarh. The development of the brise-soleil can be traced back to Talati's initial projects after his move from Paris; it becomes a continuing element in his future projects and also becomes a general marker of critical regionalism in subsequent modern architecture projects in India.

Among Corbusier's "Five Points of Architecture" in *Towards a New Architecture*, one feature most recognizable in the Bank of India is the terrace garden. While there was no garden on the terrace in Bank of India, the articulation of the terrace itself bears immense direct resemblance to most of Corbusier's roof gardens. Talati's roof is enclosed on the sides with an extension of the facade and left open to the sky, thereby framing views of the city from the terrace. The design of the terrace in itself is a very conscious choice of imbibing the Corbusian character; in one of his axonometric sketches, Talati makes a note of how he wants his terrace to be and where he draws its reference from. He notes, "TERRACE FUTURE EXPN (expansion)," under which he writes "(VILLA SAVOYE)." So strong was the influence of Villa Savoye's terrace on Talati that he chose to replicate and adapt it not only in a completely different geographical context but also in a building whose function is far from that of a private residence.

The representation of Bank of India as a white cube with structural elements is a modernist image of the project. As the prevailing image of the Bank of India, it is an example of the widespread influence of Corbusier, direct in cases like Talati and indirect in others. While the Bank of India was one-of-its-kind around the time it was built, we know by now that it was not a tabula rasa. Talati's architecture was a product of active engagement with his past experiences. It was a transposition of Western ideas, modified and applied to fit the cultural and geographical Indian context he was practicing in. This could be seen as an unoriginal compilation of Western ideas. But, in the process of transferring design principles from one context to another, one building type to another, there is immense potential in creating new architectural prototypes. The Bank of India, then, should be considered in this more fluid and complex understanding of originality. Repetition of such building styles—the modern Indian banks—subsequently gave rise to a new archetype. In that sense, Talati is a successful, yet unrecognized, critical regionalist architect.

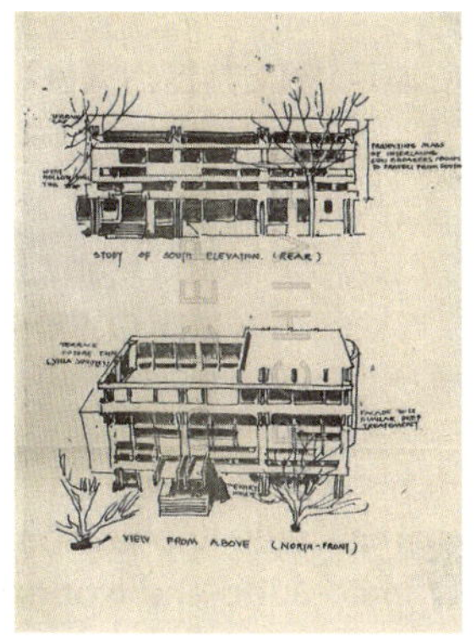

1
In the years preceding Bank of India, Talati had successfully worked on commissions of private houses; Nutan Gujarat Industrial Estate (1961); Baroda Stadium and Sports Centre (1961); a hostel and dining hall for the Mahavir Jain Vidhyalaya (1965); and his most recognized work at the time, Jeevan Sadhana School (1963). Though the Bank of India has gestures that indicate Western influence (crispness of building surfaces, composition of the facade, and presence of a flat roof), read within the context of his previous works the Bank of India reveals Talati's development of his own style. It demonstrates rigor in contextualizing his learnings from the west and finding optimal ways of application to make them relevant in the geographic location he was practicing in.

2
The unprecedented form reinforced expectations that this bank would redefine traditional banking functions.

Image credits: Arvind Talati.

Can architecture overcome its normative terms and open itself to ad hoc associations and the projections of new meanings?

Phillip Denny (PhD)
Factory of the Sensible and the Political* (Equipping Experience)
Advisor: Catherine Ingraham

In his 1967 essay "Art and Objecthood," the art critic Michael Fried dismissively applied the term *literalist* to sculptural work by minimalists like Donald Judd and Robert Morris.[1] Fried condemned these artists for making a virtue of sculpture's objecthood as opposed to striving for objecthood's transcendence. In his estimation, the sum of their efforts amounted to nothing more than theatricality; that is, "the experience . . . of an object *in a situation*—one that, virtually by definition, *includes the beholder*."[1] According to Fried's logic, literalist art thus produced at least two fundamental displacements to the precepts of modern sculpture: first, the singular art object was replaced by an unbounded, indefinite situation; second, detached perception was overtaken by embodied experiences that unfold in time.

For Fried, the theatricality of literalist art meant the negation of modern ("true") art's precept that a discrete object could be understood instantaneously, "not because one *in fact* experiences a picture by Noland or Olitski or a sculpture by David Smith or Caro in no time at all, but because *at every moment the work itself is wholly manifest.*"[1] By contrast, sculptures such as Morris's *Untitled (L-Beams)* of 1965 (to which Fried was, in part, responding), frustrate total apprehension. In these works, viewers are part of the situation and can attain only partial representations of the whole—a view from this side, another from the opposite angle. The mobile beholder's changing position, close then far, constitutes new relations among presences, bodies, and sculptures alike. On that basis, Fried declares literalist sculpture to be "paradigmatically theatrical."

Although Fried posed literalism as an object to be overcome and a provocation to artists to "defeat theater," the literal reappears now as a rich theoretical reserve. Arguably, a "literalist sensibility" in architecture has developed from these same precepts to produce new forms of experience, ways of being in the moment, of presentness. By Fried's description, architecture is fundamentally theatrical: the built environment is experienced durationally by embodied subjects which are indissociable from their situation. This literalist sensibility is exemplified by an elaborate scrapheap in the side yard of the Los Angeles art and architecture gallery Materials and Applications. This is "The Kid Gets out of the Picture," an installation by The Los Angeles Design Group (The LADG), led by principals Andrew Holder and Claus Benjamin Freyinger, in 2016.

Almost all architecture begins and ends with images, but in "The Kid," the picture in the title is never there; it can only be imagined, alluded to, or suggested. And even if it, the proverbial Kid getting out of the picture, were "there," what would it be a picture of? The work seems designed to defy description by any but the most straightforward means, say an inventory of its diverse parts: corrugated aluminum culvert pipe, 8˝ x 8˝ nominal pinewood posts, concrete masonry units, milled plywood, plaster. These materials are piled up, stacked, or bolted together, but their coherence as a whole is not beholden to any unifying grid or familiar form. Even seeing the entire work in an orthographic plan or elevation would communicate little about the situation. Looking for a clue to "The Kid"'s logic in the appearance of a junk pile is

The object stands in relation to the subject who beholds it in the present, itself becoming a kind of presence in space that, like "the silent presence of another person" in a room, "distance[s], or crowd[s]" the subject."[2] Image by The LADG.

1
Michael Fried, "Art and Objecthood," in *Art in Theory, 1900–1990: An Anthology of Changing Ideas*, eds. Charles Harrison and Paul J. Wood (Oxford: Blackwell, 1992), 822–34.

2
"The Kid Gets Out of the Picture," The LADG, www.theladg.com/The-Kid-gets-out-of-the-Picture.

3
See also Jennifer Bonner's "Another Axon"; Jonathan Rieke's "Teh Developed Surface" [sic]; Ellie Abrons and Adam Fure's (of T+E+A+M) "Rock Hut"; David Eskenazi's (D.ESK) "Column & Copy"; McLain Clutter and Cyrus Peñarroyo's (of EXTENTS) "SRFC_PLAY."

like trying to gather pieces of an unsolvable puzzle. The emphatic draping of a thick, pink surface over a muscular, gridded shell destabilizes its reading as a pliant surface that has been haphazardly laid over the structure. The sturdy posts, bolted to beams, do not in fact consistently lift anything at all. In some places, they have no contact with the pink surface, which warps away from the beams as if repelled by a force field. Nearby, modest ziggurats of dry-stacked concrete masonry units simply occupy space, fully indifferent to the assemblies around them. Without the binding logic of a consistent tectonic rationale, these elements cannot be understood as harmonic in either composition or structure, but only as collected parts. Yet, the appearance of this assembly, in the gallery setting of Materials and Applications, leads visitors to search for the intentionality and logic that holds it all together.

"The Kid" frustrates the spectator's presumption of a synthetic unity of parts to a whole: whether received as an image or experienced in situ, the work apparently resists any overarching organizational schema. The logical correspondence between representations and their realized counterparts was a key premise of the picturesque. In "The Kid," this relationship between representation and realization remains fundamental but is reconfigured. According to The LADG, The Kid engages the aesthetic principles of picturesque landscape architecture to "ask how these [picturesque] tactics can be deployed in reverse, extracting the qualities of images and literalizing them in the real world."[2] As invoked by the architects, the picturesque is uniquely invested in the translation of images from two dimensions to three, from the privileged picture into space and back again. But rather than privileging a coherent picture, the Kid is received by its beholders as a convergence of fragments, a provisional figure. This aesthetic tendency, "the experience . . . of an object *in a situation*—one that, virtually by definition, *includes the beholder*," persistently evades apprehension of the whole as anything more than the sum of its parts. In denying the revelation of any coherent organizational logic, this architecture elicits the perceptual absorption of spectators in their efforts to reconnect the fragments and reconstruct a sort of whole.

By recovering the anthropomorphic terms of Fried's critique of literalism, I am suggesting that current work, such as LADG's "The Kid," reinvests architectural objects with this paradigmatically theatrical mode of relating to subjects and experience. This theatricality has its fundamental basis in presentness, in the unfolding *here and now*. This work favors the tangible and the material, the haptic and the close at hand, the embodied and the felt. This sensibility is not a rejection of architecture's medium-specificity (its particular objecthood) in deference to either sculpture or theater. Rather, it suggests a recovery of the inherent theatricality of all architecture: the durational quality of its experience is the basis of architecture's situatedness in the world.

The literalism of this work is part and parcel of this renewed focus on the experience of unknown subjects—each particular, partial, differently embodied—for whom this work waits. It does not claim proper subjects of architecture as such; rather, this work produces situations open to other bodies and relations not bracketed by the normative terms of architectural experience. These works not only criticize architecture's obsession with producing icons—buildings as enduring images—but also suggest a politics of infinite openness to *ad hoc* associations and the projection of new meanings onto the work. This architecture's rejection of given systems of tectonic organization, such as the trabeated frame or the column grid, gives the work of schematization to the viewer. The situation of these works form a sort of whole only for as long as the encountering subject can hold the pieces together in the present.[3]

This sensibility is not a rejection of architecture's medium-specificity (its particular objecthood) . . . Rather, it suggests a recovery of the inherent theatricality of all architecture: the durational quality of its experience is the basis of architecture's situatedness in the world.

How can the hubris of a modernist parking garage be dissolved and reoriented to address its community?

Don O'Keefe (MArch I)
Third Semester Architecture Core: Integrate
Instructor: John May

New Haven, like so many American cities, undertook a series of disastrous urban planning experiments in the mid-20th century. The Temple Street Garage, a two-block-long parking deck designed by Paul Rudolph, is one of the more contradictory artifacts of this era. A landmark structure that expresses the ambitions of the modernism, the garage is also a symbol of the hubris of the design professions.

This intervention preserves much of the structure while reimaging the ground floor and top surface of the deck as microcosms of the city. The architectural language of the constituent parts of this scheme read as background elements in the larger cityscape. The building is intended to be slowly accepted into the community, relying on soundly considered details and a sensitive treatment of landscape and paving to create a textured addition to the urban fabric.

In solidarity with the critiques of modernist planning, this project attempts to restore scale, rhythm, and programmatic variety while retaining a sense of optimism about the ability to the urban environment to improve, not simply be repaired. The scheme accounts for flexibility across time scales: seasonal variation, temporary events, long-term spatial reconfigurations and phased construction.

This project aims to arrive at a positive architectural outcome by connecting a social ethic directly to tectonics and skipping over the intermediate stage of a concept: a potentially narcissistic construct that should be suppressed. Keeping in mind our most sincere aspirations for a future urbanism, this project suggests that we move by way of incremental steps, designing through a series of small decisions. Thus, this project argues that in architecture, an aggregation of tactics constitutes a strategy.

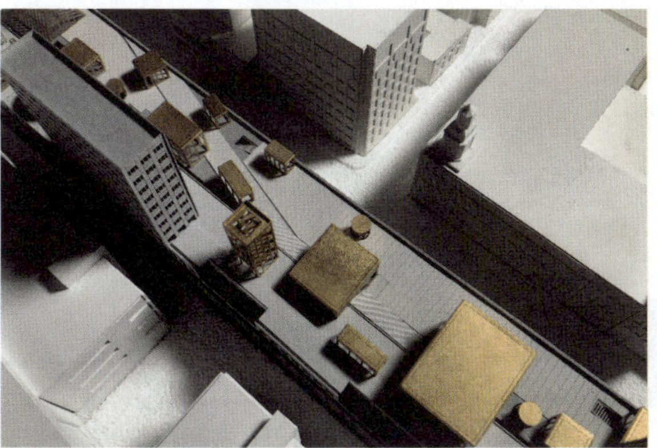

Parking Garage Renovation, Buildings
Added to Top

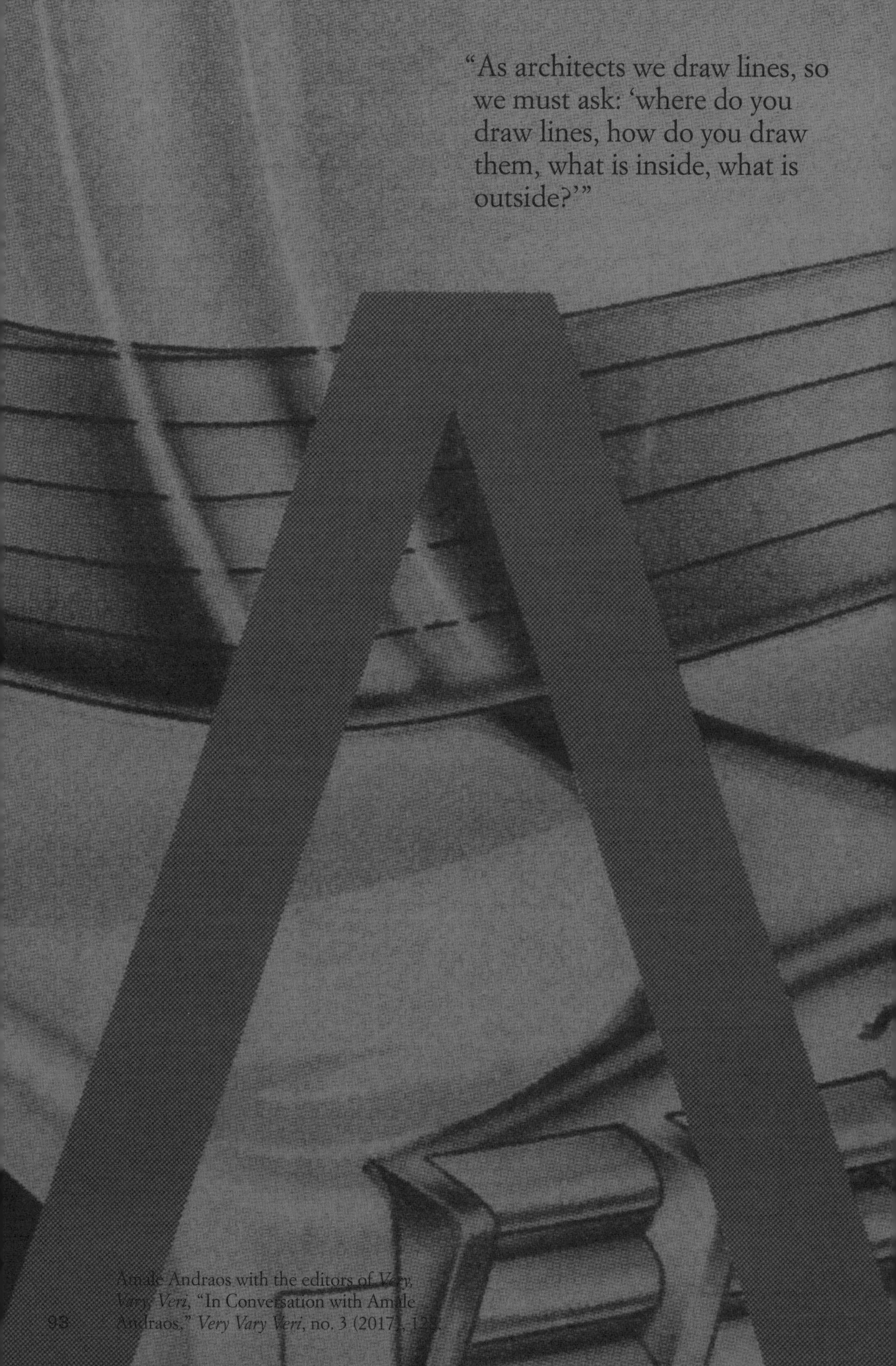

"As architects we draw lines, so we must ask: 'where do you draw lines, how do you draw them, what is inside, what is outside?'"

Amale Andraos with the editors of *Very, Vary, Veri*, "In Conversation with Amale Andraos," *Very Vary Veri*, no. 3 (2017), 12[illegible].

How can architecture make the border between the United States and Mexico visible?

Marianna González-Cervantes (MArch I)
Architecture Thesis
Advisor: Mack Scogin

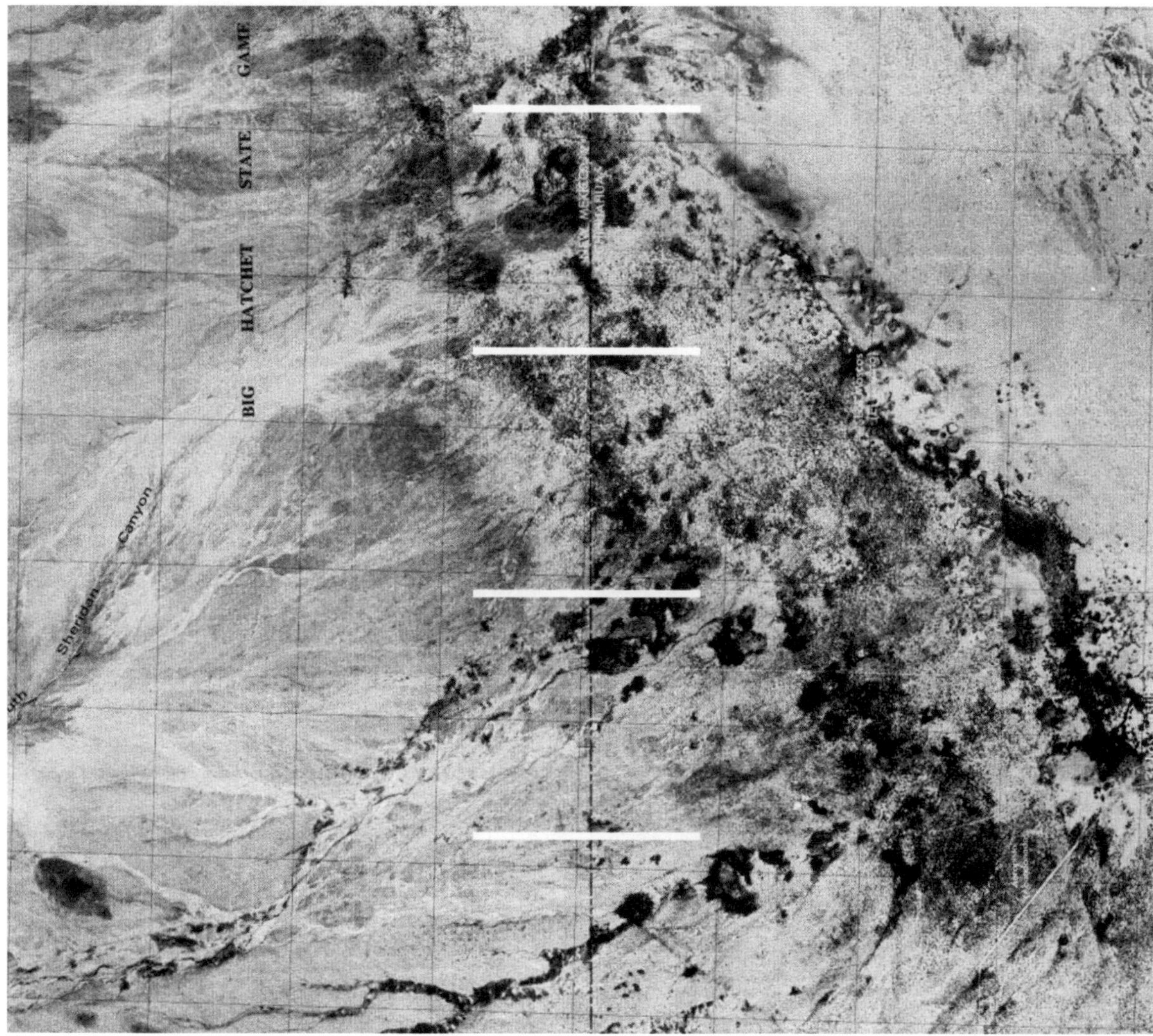

"Architecture Beginning to End: A Building to Build a Building" focuses on an architecture at the edge of becoming, and the thesis focuses on how it came to be rather than what it is.

Buildings have conventionally been understood to be the defining factor of architecture, but architecture's definition as being preoccupied with the production of buildings inevitably creates a condition in which things are and are not considered to be architecture. In an unproductive binary of *is* and *is not*, the edge between the two presents a possibility that points to a shared thickness in which one thing becomes another. In saying something is or is not, we make clear our own assumptions of where this defining edge lies, at least for ourselves.

The border between the United States and Mexico is not so different. In 1849, the Joint United States–Mexican Boundary Commission mapped and marked the boundary line. The 258 obelisk-shaped markers placed on the very line itself are a physical thickening of a border that was previously an imaginary line. These monuments stand unchanged through time as precedents for sacred ground agreed upon and shared by both countries: a condition possible due to an edge existence.

This thesis proposes 30 one-mile-long monuments along a 31-mile-long site that are meant to mark a thickness between two countries. In considering of the construction of these lines, six steps were investigated: measure, plot, dig, level, place. A series of tools were devised for each of these steps to understand what would be needed to construct these new markers. These steps question whether the specificity of the reinvented monuments could begin to generate new kinds of architecture or a new way of thinking about architecture, beginning to end.

Borders
Migration
Monument
Territory
Thesis

Step 1—Measure: This structure draws parallel lines along the site that extend half a mile into each country.

Step 2—Plot: This structure transitions measurements via large-scale tools to plot and prepare the ground.

Step 3—Dig: This structure marks points where digging would need to occur.

Step 4—Level: This structure is a liquid leveler made into a family of pools that can be carried independent of one another.

The relationship between new monument markers and the old obelisk monuments reconstructs the line they serve to mark.

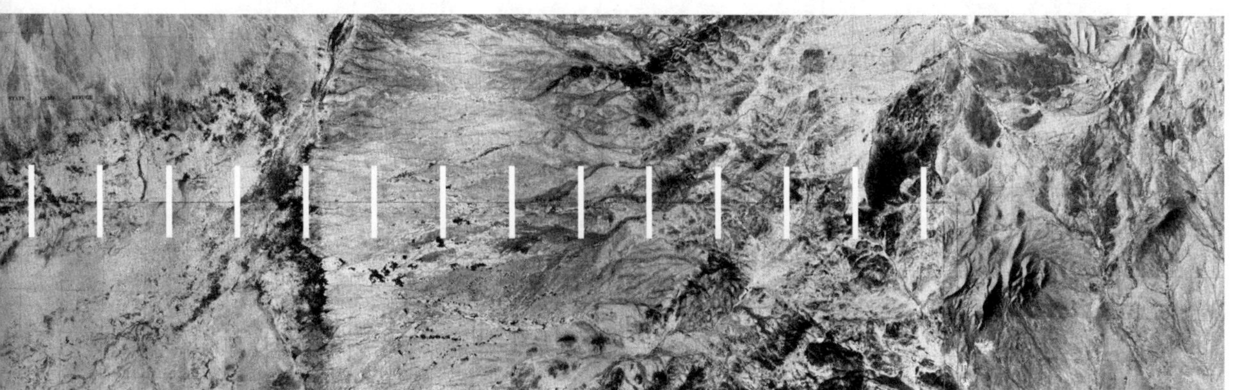

Proposed monument markers along the United States–Mexico border.

Where is the center of the United States? What is its significance? How does it shape conceptions of the heartland?

Grace McEniry (MArch I)
Architecture Thesis
Advisor: Megan Panzano

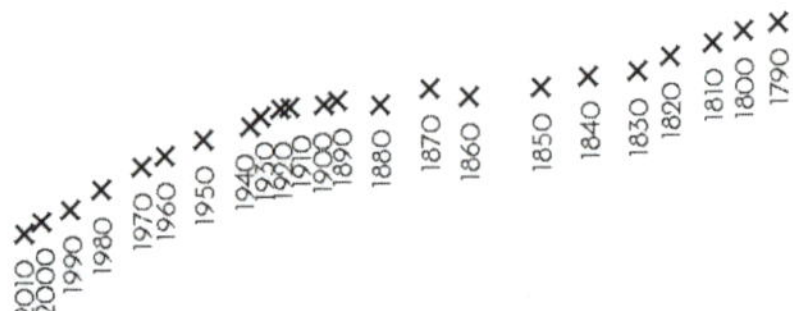

Center implies two things: both a point and its surroundings—an area whose middle can be identified. The center has always been important to understanding our place in the world. With infinite ways to describe the us-and-world relationship, it is necessary to invoke and be critical of assumptions made in the identification of geographic center points.

This thesis studies the Mean Center of Population of the United States, which the Census Bureau describes as a fulcrum around which the country would balance if it were flat and weightless and an equal weight replaced each person. The mean center has been pulled across the country, from Maryland in 1790 to Missouri in 2010, by forces of history, capitalism, and culture. Looking where these centers land

American City
Monument
Population
Thesis
Typology

Site of proposed monument for the 1820 Mean Center of Population in Hardy County, West Virginia.

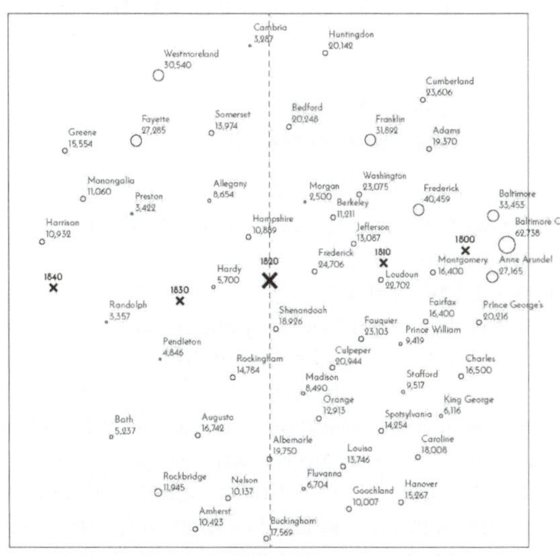

Roof apertures and respective 1820 population by county.

exposes a delta between the ground truth of these points—in cornfields and parking lots—and the measured one.

This project inhabits the space between the limits of Census data, Google imagery, and firsthand exploration at 23 mean centers of population. There, Google imagery provides both planimetric satellite images and perspectival views of varying resolution, synthesizing the seeming objectivity of seamless surveys with the egoism of firsthand perspective.

These centers quantify cultural and economic forces and invite a design project allegiant to a different set of ideals—those typified by curiosity and a desire to explore and expose the richness of the ordinary American heartland, simultaneously the middle of nowhere and the center of everywhere.

How are conceptions of state defined through water?

Naomi Woods (MDes RR)
Design Studies Thesis
Advisor: Diane E. Davis

By asserting that the collapse of the Somali state in 1991 was an end to the centralized state apparatus but far from the vacuum purported by dominant international relations (IR) theories, this thesis seeks to elevate the example of the water system of Mogadishu as an instance of ongoing state regeneration, adaptation, and reformulation in a unique but instructive setting that can inform how state formation is understood by the wider community of practice. Indeed, practice is the key—by observing the practice of state and statehood, at the scale relevant for governance, which is much smaller than that of the central state—the concept of collapse ceases to have salience, or is restricted to the level of central government. In other words, this thesis seeks to propose other ways of understanding state formation through the lens of the water system in Mogadishu from the late 1950s to the present.

The characteristics illuminated by this water lens begin to compose the "other ways" of state formation being sought. Constraints impacting the water system are mainly the following: a lack of definition of what constitutes the state within the wider framework of institutions, capacities, and responsibilities; problems with trust and legitimacy on the part of citizens and levels of government; established market failures; and undercapitalization. When juxtaposed against the opportunities also presented, they form a basis for the opportunities available to the water system.

It is not the function of this thesis to propose solutions for governance and statehood in Mogadishu or Somalia. Rather, the methodology of using a smaller lens like the water system of Mogadishu proposes that by shifting perspective from macro issues, such as the stabilization of Somalia, alternatives for action or coalition-building might become more apparent or take on a fresh perspective. The endurance of the water system in Mogadishu at the very localized level is indicative of such a shift in perspective. Where there has been collapse, in fact, there was a sustained effort to continue adapting, reinventing, and reimagining the idea of statehood throughout the time of the war from the private sector, alternative governance modalities and scales, and the citizens who were left without the state apparatus per se. This thesis does not attempt to be comprehensive in its assessment of Somali history or geopolitics and the iterations of statehood or governance that occurred in and around Mogadishu after 1991, nor does it seek to underplay the tremendous suffering experienced by the Somali people in the lead-up to the 1991 war, and the violence and displacement that ensued. This thesis does not ignore the persistent, complex insecurity experienced by residents of Mogadishu to present day, and the horror of the bombings that occur there on a regular basis.

This thesis does, however, aim to introduce a new focus—that of the resilience and adaptation of the systems and the people behind and within these systems who have created innovations and possibilities for reimagining the state that otherwise might not have been conceived. The experimental laboratory of the site of Mogadishu today presents enormous possibilities for innovating a responsive idea and iteration of the new state of Somalia, learning from the past and reimagining the future on that basis. The lens of water indicates the level of granularity and inter-sectorality possible in

By observing the practice of state and statehood at the scale relevant for governance—much smaller than that of the central state—the concept of collapse ceases to have salience.

improving understandings of state formation, using the same framework of analysis applied to Sana'a, Yemen, or Damascus, Syria, to illuminate and collect wisdom from these systems and how they have interfaced with state formation in the past and could do so in the future. This thesis also tests the ground for integrating spatial and urban-design-oriented thinking with IR and policy analysis, demonstrating how a reframing of scale and perspective can inform a different set of policy outcomes. For instance, take the idea of the modular state—what are the implications of modularity for systems that are resilient to climate change? What are the efficiencies that can be gained through entrepreneurship and modularity versus monopolistic, hegemonic, and universalist systems of the modernist past? Is there another role for the public-private partnership, whereby the public is the junior partner—and is there an equitable way not yet widely practiced for the private sector to perform those functions considered public? Could such a new approach be an avenue for citizen engagement where one has not previously existed?

In addition, this thesis tests the possibility of evaluating a specific sector of the capital city of a "collapsed state" in order to show the granularity of understanding statehood and state formation, and explore the possibilities of state formation reframed at this alternative scale. At a time when climate is playing an increasingly significant role in the flows of populations and constraints faced by the state, as it forms, this scalar alternative offers the possibility of new scenarios for envisioning a future Mogadishu and, by implication, Somalia. What are the interventions that can take place to form an idea of the state from the household level? That of the neighborhood or district? Can the water system be used to facilitate these interventions?

The grand solutions of the late 21st century are no longer the only option for providing essential services and the role of the state moving forward: the state is a sum of its parts, and those parts may well be at the level of the city, neighborhood, and household. Micro-solutions are part of this equation, and may provide more cumulative impact at the local- and state-formation levels than they have previously been given credit for. By demonstrating one such instance of this potential, scalar ideas for making the future of Mogadishu will become a reality in the innovative laboratory of Somalia.

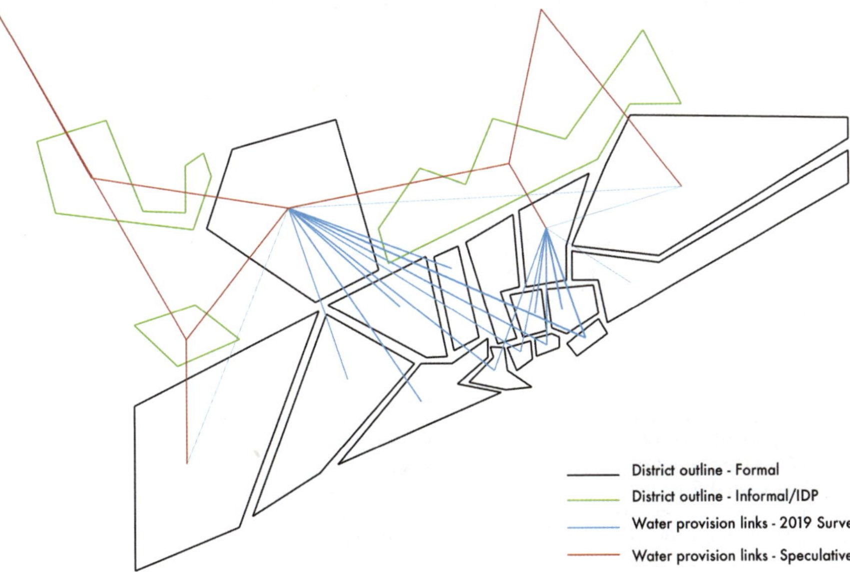

Abstraction of the water system of systems in Mogadishu. Supply chains traverse district divisions in varying proportions, denoted by the line weight of the blue lines linking the districts, representative of 2019 surveyed supply connections in formal settlements. Red lines denote potential existing or future connections from the Afgooye and Stage 2B well fields, imagining the linkages between geographically demarcated systems and supply systems traversing the space.

How can landscape practices reclaim indigenous territory?

Emily Hicks (MLA I) and Melody Stein (MLA I)
Landscape Architecture Thesis
Advisors: Rosetta S. Elkin, John Koepke (University of Minnesota)
Recipient of the Landscape Architecture Thesis Prize

The homeland of the Fond du Lac band of the Ojibwe people in the St. Louis River Estuary was once blanketed with wild rice. Wild rice (*Zizania palustris*) is a culturally and spiritually important wild grain that has been hand-harvested from the lakes and rivers of the Great Lakes Region for thousands of years. Today, wild rice harvest remains a treaty-protected right for all Ojibwe people in Minnesota. As the estuary lost its wild rice to land dispossession, resource extraction, and industrialization, the people of Duluth have also lost their estuary. This thesis proposes recovering the St. Louis River Estuary through the practice of wild rice harvest. This project takes the necessity of access to the lands and waters where wild rice grows as a framework for design and the first step toward recalibrating shattered relationships between people and land.

Colonialism
Ecology
Food
Ownership
Thesis

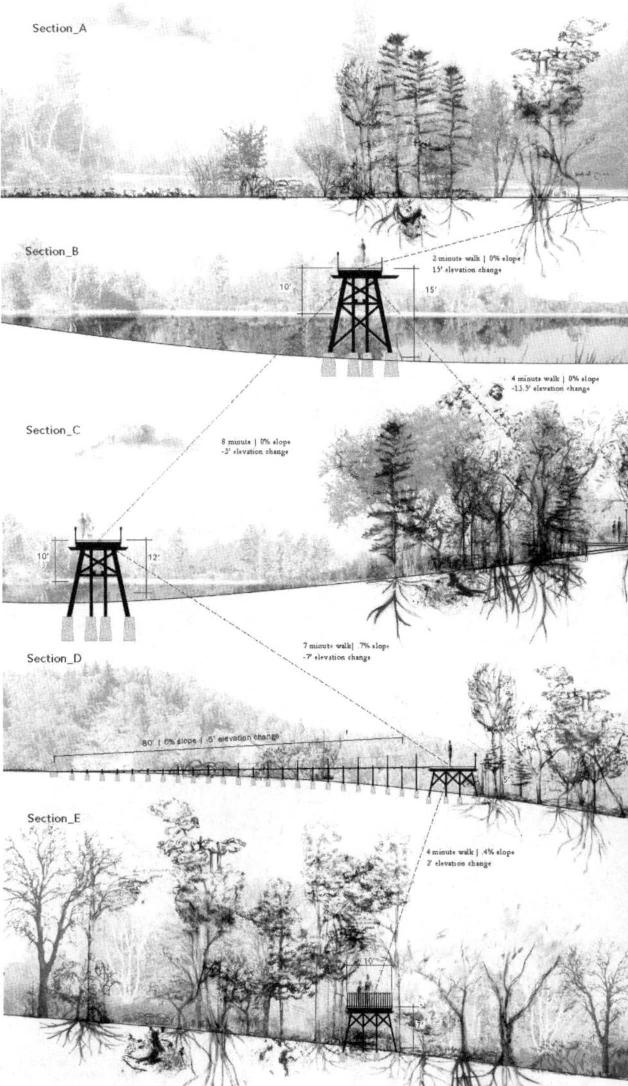

Above: A proposed walkway between the estuary and Spirit Island provides access, both physical and visual, to important cultural spaces.

Left: The Grand Portage was once measured by its stops, or pauses, and though their location has been lost to time the entrance to the portage remains near the present-day dam. This project proposes 12 portage pauses at the newly public entrance to the Grand Portage.

CONSTRUCTION DETAIL
THRU STATION "O"
~ SCALE 3/8" = 1" ~

What is statelessness? What is nationality? What is the role of art and design within a bureaucratic deadlock?

Hanna Kim (MDes ADPD)
Design Studies Thesis
Advisors: Krzysztof Wodiczko and Malkit Shoshan

Statelessness—a condition of not being "considered a national by any State under the operation of its law"—is a global human rights crisis absent from the public dialogue. Stateless people are unable to seek legal protection from any nation-state and are often barred from movement. They cannot legally travel across borders and are often at risk of detention and discrimination. Although the United States acknowledges the phenomenon, its government does not recognize the full tragedy of the problem and has not designated an office for addressing the issue of statelessness within its borders. Without a legal apparatus for dealing with statelessness, the U.S. state perpetuates a lack of awareness of the issue and paralyzes any political will for change.

The U.S. Citizenship Initiative for the Stateless (USCIS) is a visionary agency that aims to break fear, apathy, and the bureaucratic deadlock that perpetuates the invisibility of stateless people.

The exhibition of USCIS resembles a bureaucratic immigration office. Here, the public can be educated and mobilized to act on these issues. Waiting in a winding queue with little instruction, visitors begin to understand the frustrations and challenges of being stuck in legal limbo. They then engage their immigration officer, actually a stateless person swapping roles. This radical reversal of authority gives agency to someone who, outside the exhibition, faces consistent intimidation and humiliation by the state. Taking part in nonviolent activism, the public then fills out a petition to be mailed to (the real) USCIS field offices, government officials, and politicians as a provocation. USCIS thus renders the solution tangible, even if it remains unreal. It envisions an alternative future where justice is restored to stateless people in the United States. And it creates room for critical dialogue and action on nationhood, citizenship, rights, and the definition of humanity itself.

Borders
Democracy
Justice
Policy
Thesis

SOLIDARITY

U.S. Citizenship
Initiative for the
Stateless
Take a
Number.
Please wait until your
number is called.

U.S.
LIDARITY

How can architecture offer a new paradigm for community-oriented development in refugee camps?

Nadyeli Quiroz (MLA I AP, MDes ULE)
Architecture as a Tool to Improve Lives: Development of a Day Care Center for Rohingya Children
Instructor: Anna Heringer

"Walls of Time," a day care center for the Rohingya children in the Kutupalong Refugee Camp in Bangladesh, is composed of three elements: a mud-wall prototype, the day care center building, and a playground. When fully realized, the project creates an enclosed and protected public space for children shaded in the perimeter, with a central patio and an almond tree. This design prototype can be replicated in other tents in Kutupalong, and the design's material choices consider the future abandonment of the camp, with the anticipated return of the site to the forest.

Community
Justice
Materials
Option Studio
Structure

Daycare for Children

House A

House B

House C

A NEW POSSIBLE FUTURE

20 30 40 50 60 70

Who is a global citizen and what is the impact of global citizenry on shared environments?

Sofia Xanthakou (MDes ULE)
Design Studies Thesis
Advisor: Antoine Picon

Today, the rise of the notion of the "global citizen" (i.e., that one's identity transcends geography or political borders), along with the current form of international tourism it has spawned, has created many anxieties surrounding the traditional linkage between cultural identities and their geo-specific rootedness. This thesis asks: Are we witnessing today the demise of transnational tourism at the hands of global citizenry? This project's basic contention questions whether, if taken to its extreme, global citizenry would spell the end of transnational tourism. That is, if in its most extreme form, being a global citizen entails (A) belonging to the community of the world, and (B) the absolute freedom to access any and all parts of the planet, then binaries such

as local vs. tourist, insider vs. outsider, or citizen vs. (im/) migrant shall cease to exist.

This project provides a historical and conceptual analysis of international tourism, since this form of tourism most typically entails the presence of cultural insiders ("locals") and outsiders ("tourists") within a common place. This project concludes with the development of a series of visual provocations that articulate the two main responses to the death of transnational tourism: (A) preserving transnational tourism, which is largely predicated on ethno-nationalism and, as such, results in such problems as today's immigration crises; or, (B) accepting the decoupling of cultures from landscapes in order to decrease our footprint on the wider natural environment, thereby better preserving it.

Who is the public for world heritage? Who is the "we" to which the aesthetics of world heritage apply?

Andrew Scheinman (MDes ADPD)
Design Studies Thesis
Advisors: Susan Snyder and George Thomas

Decapitated of its iconic ancient buildings by Islamic State destruction in 2015, the city of Tadmur, Syria, known internationally as Palmyra, was nonetheless at its acme in global presence that year. Thanks to a deluge of obituaries, archival photographs, and memorial reproductions that saturated Western media, this singular "obliteration" of our ancient past in Palmyra made headlines even as scenes of actual, ongoing death in situ were overlooked. Tributes like the one-third-scale model of the Triumphal Arch of Palmyra, fabricated in 2016 by the Institute for Digital Archaeology (IDA), used media to weaponize architectural likeness on behalf of the cosmopolitan world and its received aesthetics against "unique barbarism" in the Middle East. Touring moneyed and powerful capitals like London, New York, Washington, and Dubai, the replica Arch was staged for photographs against buildings of recognizable political and cultural might, implying global ownership through juxtaposition while eclipsing the greater humanitarian crisis in Syria. These images were, in turn, disseminated at the behest of wide-reaching media outlets, recalling and reiterating a historical, orientalist "ruin lust" that imagined the heroic architecture as abandoned, as if an image of antiquity made three-dimensional. Considering these events and drawing on a rich literature from heritage and memory studies to postcolonial and media theories, this thesis challenges the premise of architectural heritage like that of Palmyra belonging truly and absolutely to the world at large. It posits that the Arch replica and similar memorials engage only a world heritage public—a splintered nation at the receiving end of media outlets, bound together by a discourse of apolitical aesthetics—perpetuating a cultural and actual war very much contradictory to the idea of a singular, universal world.

Unlike human blood, spilled upon the very materialization of cultural heritage, the logic goes, ancient structures like those in Palmyra "'belong' to us, Europeans and Arabs alike," as one Middle East correspondent puts it. For those readers who find this language appalling, the same crop of writers provides reassurance, as in a 2015 *Guardian* article by Julian Baggini titled "Why it's all right to be more horrified by the razing of Palmyra than mass murder." The author writes:

> "Caring about how people live also means caring about those aspects of human culture that speak to more than our needs for food, shelter, and good health. It involves recognizing that there are human achievements that transcend our own lives and our own generations. We come and go, but we are survived by the fruits of our peers and those who came before us. There is a humility in seeing, as Rick did in *Casablanca*, that the problems of a few 'little people don't amount to a hill of beans in this crazy world.'"[1]

To whom the plural "our" refers is a lingering, unanswered question in this and arguments like it, but the presumed, idealistic answer vis-à-vis world heritage is the total population of the planet. That is, world heritage belongs to all people in all the world for all time. It is, in material form, the essence of humanity at large, a cosmopolitan metonym for everyone

Today, when we lament the loss of the Greco-Roman ruins at Palmyra—and build traveling monuments to that loss, as did the IDA—we are, by way of our aesthetic judgment, channeling centuries of romantic, orientalist ruin-gazing centered on the "cradle of civilization" that is, we assume, the modern-day Middle East.

everywhere. Human bodies—that is, only some people, somewhere—are barely a hill of beans in comparison.

Most striking about this "our" is the assumption of an audience in common—that we, readers of the *Guardian*, are the dispensable who come and go; that we are survived by the fruits of our peers; that our lives are transcended by human achievements, broadly defined. No matter the brand of alarmist rhetoric, the one consistency in all this discourse is an assumption of a worldwide audience on the basis of global history, understood as world heritage common to all cultures, everywhere.

But heritage and history are not the same. "Heritage is not a testable or even plausible version of our past; it is a declaration of faith in that past," David Lowenthal reminds us.[2] Where history, in its pure, analytic, and critical form, is a reconstruction of the past as detached from the present, always already over and done with, heritage is an active social marker, an ongoing relationship to the past used to justify well-delineated cultural identities. "Prejudiced pride is not the sorry upshot of heritage but its essential aim. Heritage attests our identity and affirms our worth." As such, heritage requires recognition of something else, a thing apart that is plainly, obviously not our heritage. On a global stage, therefore, the bombastic positioning of cultural heritage as the material history of everyone—an endless identity group—is inherently paradoxical. Heritage by its very definition exists to be the material of a select few, never universal. Could heritage truly, absolutely apply to the world at large, it would cease to be heritage at all.

Consider once more that *Guardian* article, specifically its first-person plural "our." That "our," we can safely assume, is the same "our" to which the mantra from the IDA, "our past is their past," applies.[3] Following the social theorist Michael Warner, who defines a public—not *the* public, but one of many—as a collectivity "that comes into being only in relation to texts and their circulation," that is, "by virtue of being addressed,"[4] we might define the audience of the *Guardian* piece and the Arch as well as the parishioners of world heritage more generally—the "we" here—as a world heritage public. This is a public that accepts the tenets and aesthetics of world heritage as indisputable, a public that participates in a discourse of material valorization based on mutually understood definitions, value systems, and language about the past, and a public that, despite its claims of universality, shores up the exclusive boundaries to the "civilized" world by way of that very discourse.

1
Julian Baggini, "Why it's all right to be more horrified by the razing of Palmyra than mass murder," the *Guardian*, August 24, 2015.

2
David Lowenthal, *The Heritage Crusade and the Spoils of History* (Cambridge and New York: Cambridge University Press, 1998).

3
The Institute for Digital Archaeology, or IDA, is a collaboration between Harvard and Oxford Universities, the British Council, the Dubai Future Foundation, and UNESCO among others.

4
Michael Warner, "Publics and Counterpublics," *Public Culture* 14, no. 1 (Winter 2002): 50.

"Landscape of Trans-Nationality: Trans Siberian Railway (TSR) and Alternative Nature," Studio Trip, Spring 2019

This lecture by Demita Frazier, a life-long black feminist, social justice activist, thought leader, writer, and teacher, presented a personal exploration of the impact that the city landscape of Chicago had on this precocious and observant African American mid-century woman's aesthetic evolution.

. . . A conversation about aesthetic Apartheid . . .

History
Identity
Public Program
Race
Social Equity

Demita Frazier, "Aesthetic Apartheid: Gender, Race, and Socio-economic Class, and the Impact on Perception, Engagement, and Experience," International Womxn's Day Lecture, March 7, 2019

Where do we draw the lines that define a woman?

Mindy Seu (MDes ADPD)
Design Studies Thesis
Advisors: Jeffrey Schnapp and Malkit Shoshan
Recipient of the Design Studies Thesis Prize

1. "A CYBORG MANIFESTO: SCIENCE, TECHNOLOGY, AND SOCIALIST-FEMINISM IN THE LATE 20TH CENTURY"

15. BLACK TO THE FUTURE

17. L0VE0NE

19. WILL THE REAL BODY PLEASE STAND UP?: BOUNDARY STORIES ABOUT VIRTUAL CULTURES

55. MY BODY, A WONDERKAMMER

56. OLD BOYS NETWORK

104. CYBORG MEMOIRS

117. "FROM CYBORGS TO HACKTIVISTS: POSTFEMINIST DISOBEDIENCE AND VIRTUAL COMMUNITIES"

218. *DIGITAL*MEDIA* JUNK*WARE*LORE*

256. "A (DIGITAL) GIANT AWAKENS – INVIGORATING MEDIA STUDIES WITH ASIAN PERSPECTIVES"

Trombone, stop the artifact thieves, help Bessie Coleman at her airshow!"

59 "TRAPPED BY THE BODY? TELEPRESENCE TECHNOLOGIES AND TRANSGENDERED PERFORMANCE IN FEMINIST AND LESBIAN REWRITINGS OF CYBERPUNK FICTION," Thomas Foster, 1997

"This essay uses Allucquère Rosanne Stone's 19 recent work on the status of embodiment in virtual systems to account for the existence of a significant number of popular narratives by women writers about virtual reality, despite Ross's characterization of cyberpunk fiction 104 as inherently masculinist. In particular, Stone's work helps explain the predominance of themes of gender and sexual performativity or cross-identification in these narratives about cyberspace. I have written elsewhere about the relevance of theories of performativity to narratives of cyborg 117 embodiment, but this considers the relevance of those theories to virtual reality computer interfaces and computer simulations, which tend to be represented popularly as technologies of disembodiment. To what extent do theories and practices of subversive mimicry and performativity function as a cultural framework for constructing the meaning of virtual reality and telepresence?"

60 "YOU ARE CYBORG" (Interview) Donna Haraway, Hari Kunzru, published in *Wired*, 1997

"But she is not talking about some putative future or a technologically advanced corner of the present. The cyborg age is here and now, everywhere there's a car or a phone or a VCR. Being a cyborg isn't about how many bits of silicon you have under your skin or how many prosthetics your body contains. It's about Donna Haraway 1 going to the gym, looking at a shelf of carbo-loaded bodybuilding foods, checking out the Nautilus machines, and realizing that she's in a place that wouldn't exist without the idea of the body as high-performance machine."

61 *ZEROS AND ONES*, Sadie Plant, 1997

This is not a book about women and technology. Nor was this book created for women. Throughout these pages, scholars, hackers, artists, and activists of all regions, races, sexual orientations, and genetic makeups consider how humans might reconstruct themselves by way of technology. What is a woman anyway?

The creation and use of this catalog is a social and political act. The aggregated texts, organizations, events, and other media push against the dominant understanding of internet history. We are taught to focus on engineering, the military-industrial complex, and the grandfathers who created the architecture and protocol. But the internet is not only a network of cables, servers, and computers. It is an environment that shapes and is shaped by its inhabitants.

Together, these works map the radical techno-critical activism that shapes a cyberfeminist counterpublic. The publication takes the name "cyberfeminism" as an umbrella, complicates it, and pushes it into plain sight for others to respond to and build upon.

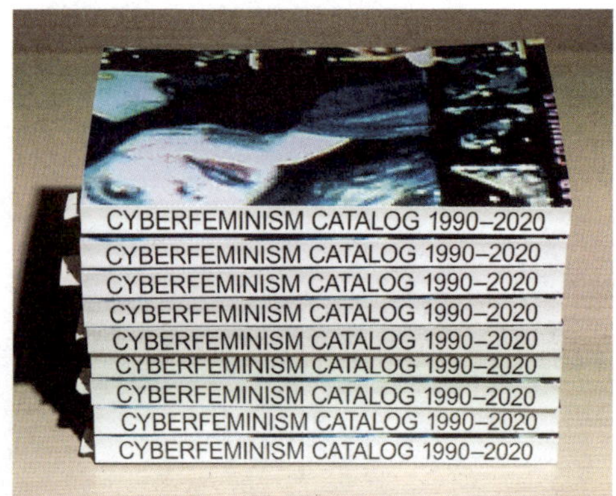

How can the lines of the body become less exact?

Daniel Shieh (MDes ADPD)
Design Studies Thesis
Advisors: Dan Borelli and Rebecca Uchill

"The Display of the Self" explores ways to talk about body shame publicly and how to retain the fluidity and multiplicity of one's identity under the categorizing gaze of the other. How can changing the visibility of one's body in physical space affect body shame and resist categorization? How can a body be vulnerable yet protected in public space? Or hidden yet visible?

Consisting of a wearable structure that veils the wearer completely and displays the wearer's body as fragmented shadows on its surface, this project allows a wearer to conceal and reveal simultaneously; the shadows at once intimately emphasize the presence of the wearer's body yet prevent onlookers from knowing exactly what the wearer looks like. Because the appearance of the body cannot be known and can only be imagined through the shadows, which are changing with every movement of the body, the identity of the wearer cannot be clearly categorized.

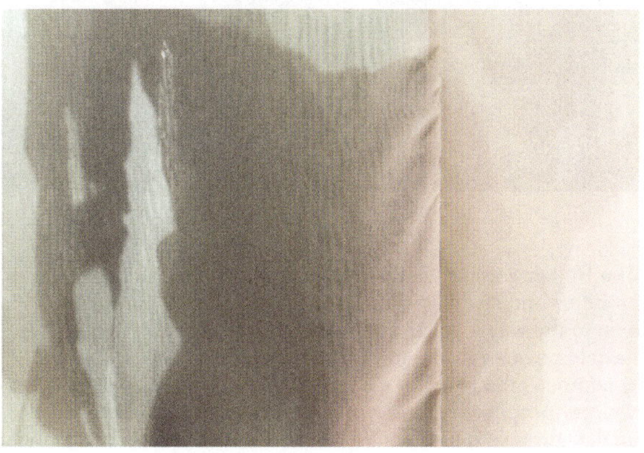

How can the lines of maps be reimagined to be less exact?

Nicolas Oueijan (MDes Tech)
Mapping: Geographic Representation and Speculation
Instructor: Robert Pietrusko

"The Pedalographer" is an analytic mapping instrument that modifies and layers information over visual mapping data akin to the way a guitar pedal does for audio data. It is a flexible device for free-form visual discovery." Developed to accompany the film *The Egg's Beirut* in 2018, it is a part of a larger proposal for more responsive and improvisational analytic mapping techniques that are looser in their interactivity than the GIS workflows institutionalized today. Combining the affordances of VHS cassette tapes, VCRs, CRT monitors, and historical maps with the programmability of microcontrollers, "The Pedalographer" reintroduces time, tactility, and spontaneity into mapping activities.

Lecture
Mapping
Play
Technology

How can designers help communities to better understand the power and implications of the lines drawn by zoning commissions?

José Carlos Fernández Salas (MUP) and Keting Zhou (MAUD)
Designing Atmospheres and Technologies for Social Interaction
Instructor: Jose Luis Vallejo

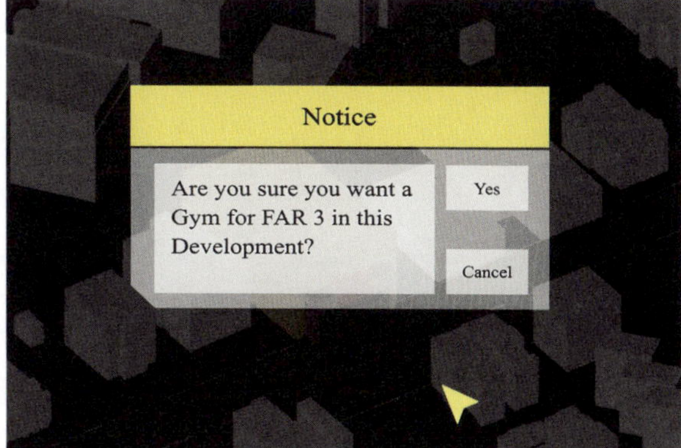

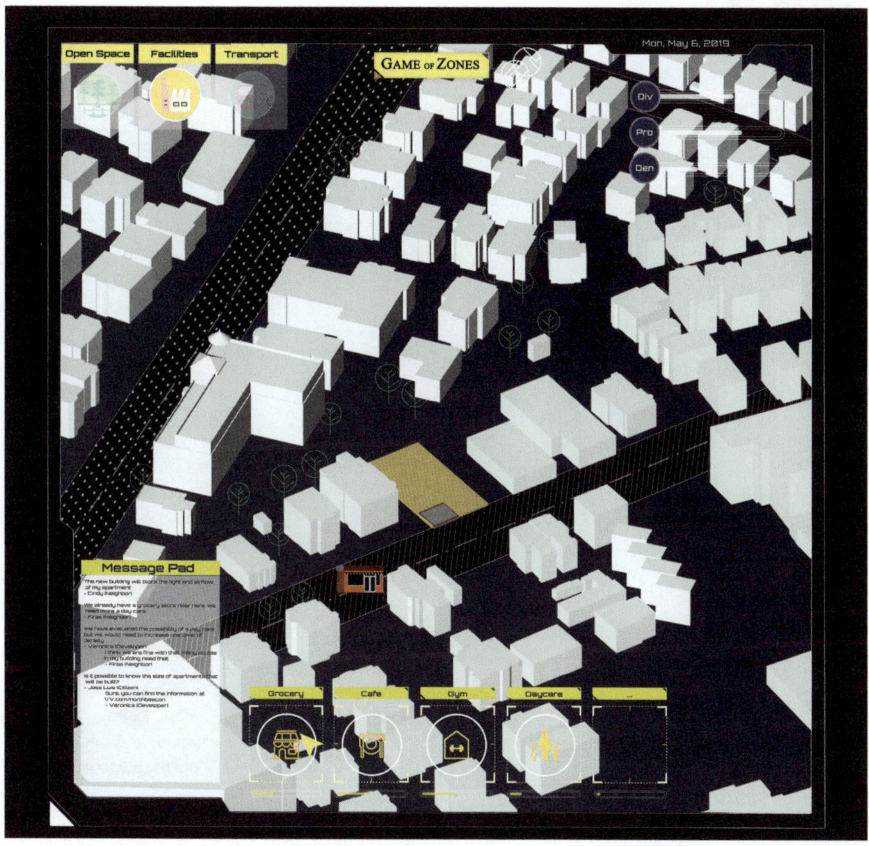

The affordable housing crisis in Boston seems like an unsolvable problem: cost-burdened residents need lower prices and neighbors want to keep or increase the value of their properties. This project explores the value of 3-D visualization tools for generating more fruitful conversations between urban stakeholders. "Game of Zones" is a digital platform for open interaction between urban stakeholders with opposing interests. It replaces traditional City Hall hearings on zoning with visualization software showing the options for building envelopes. The platform determines the amenities required of developers by residents in exchange for additional zoning incentives (e.g., density). These negotiations play out through the interactions of different users in a game-like software available on desktops and mobile phones.

Instead of using lines to mark a fixed border, how can they be used to show a changing condition such as a shifting coastline?

Isabel Brostella (MLA I AP)
Landscape Architecture Thesis
Advisor: Montserrat Bonvehi Rosich

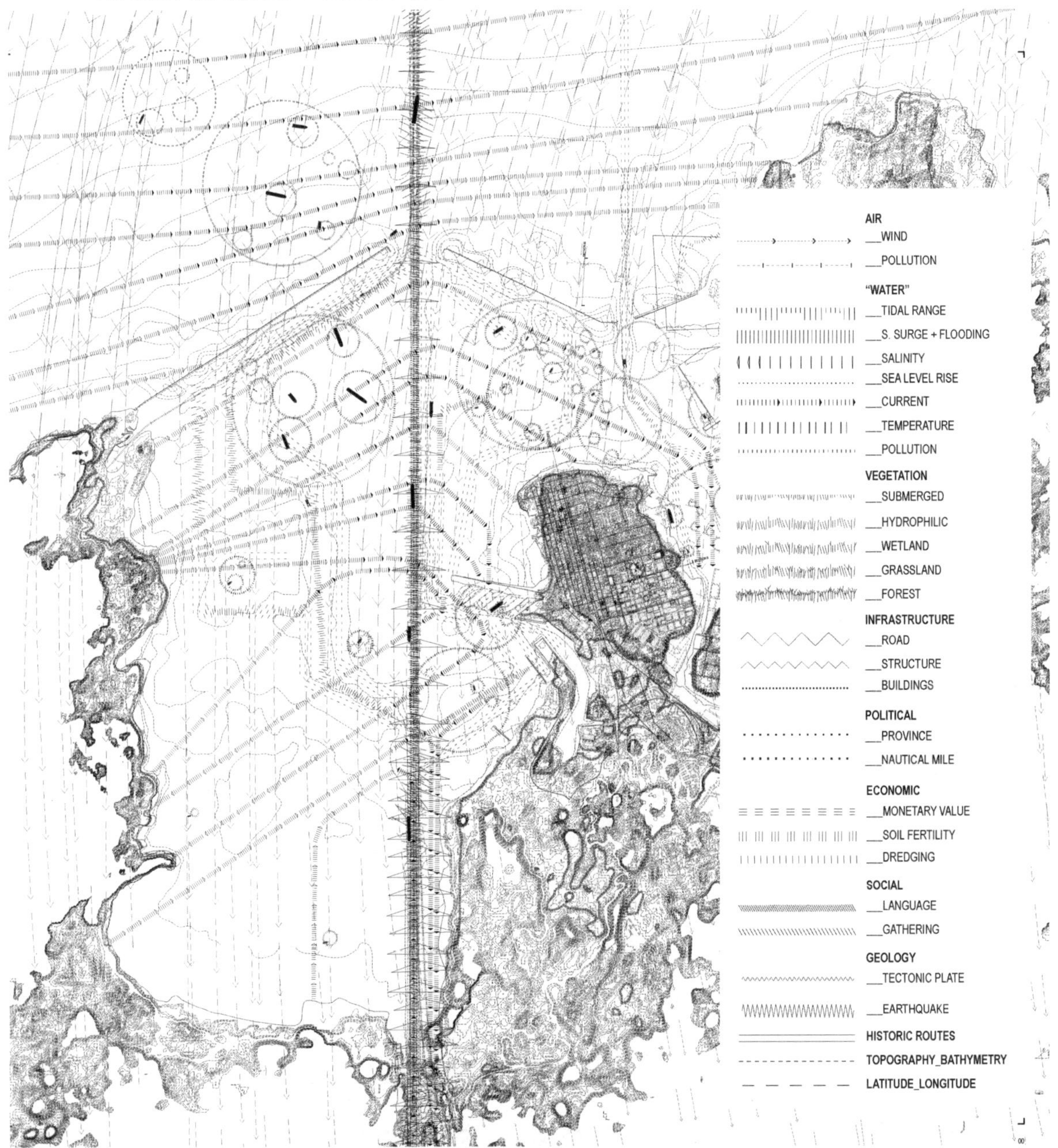

As designers, we are translators. We read the complexity in a terrain, distill it, and compose a drawing. This thesis attempts to start a conversation and push further the main and arguably only way landscape architects can work: through drawing.
It creates a methodology that explores ways of drawing the dynamism and continuous change there is in a terrain in order to prove the importance of expanding on this tool and thus on the way we read the ground.

Coastlines are complex systems that experience constant change, mainly by acting as transitional zones between two different ground conditions. "The Multiplicity of a Line" proposes coastal resilience strategies that respond to the specificity of a site read through a new method of representation. It takes

Ecology
Line
Thesis
Typology
Water

place in Panama, a narrow isthmus connecting North America to South America, and dividing the Pacific Ocean from the Atlantic, that is exposed to two differing systems. After applying this new methodology to a site on each coast, it is proven that this method can be applied to any condition and enable a different way of intervention; the ground is filled with information, expresses the movement and forces that exist there, and highlights certain patterns that allow for responsive operations to take place. This exploration demonstrates the agency a line can have while drawn with its multiplicity and allows for a different reading, understanding, and alteration of a site.

Lines are human constructions that have been used as a tool of control; their simplification has been normalized and adopted by designers ever since. Although this act is aesthetically pleasing, it almost entirely erases the complexity of a site. A drawn line dividing land and water, for instance, is a simplification responding to a single projection of a moment in time: there should not be one line, but a multiplicity of them in order to fully understand the complexity embedded in the terrain. If our way of analyzing a terrain shifts through the implementation of this representational method, the result of "controlling" the ground may be different.

How do designers respond when nature ignores the lines we draw?

Joan Chen (MLA I) and Estello Raganit (MLA I)
Field Work: Brexit, Borders, and Imagining a New City–Region for the Irish Northwest
Instructors: Gareth Doherty and Niall Kirkwood

Experimental Forest.

This project imagines a landscape of slowness for the Irish Northwest, with a focus on the territory between the Foyle and Swilly catchments. A rewilded territory arises from the significant reduction of grazing and the future flooding of low-lying lands between Lough Foyle and Lough Swilly.

The project is narrated from the year 2219, with a series of collaged vignettes that reflect actions taken in the two centuries prior. This narrative structure highlights the years surrounding Brexit as a turning point in the border landscape, and traces land-use history through a longer period of time, demonstrating the cyclical nature of this landscape. The goal of this speculation is to highlight how the region might plan not only for the immediate future, but also for the long-term.

We begin with the 2016 United Kingdom referendum to leave the European Union. This extended process unearthed both fear of a return to the border conflicts of the 20th century as well as a stronger desire to maintain historical cross-border collaboration.

Not long after, a particularly lethal strain of bovine tuberculosis appeared in Northwest Ireland. The devastation was catastrophic. Within days, complete herds of cattle and sheep were decimated. Within a year, these grazing animals were completely absent from the landscape, necessitating a new use for the pasturelands. Without the grazing animals, woody vegetation emerged, sparking discussions for deliberate vegetal rewilding through tree-planting. This landscape rewilding is facilitated by a systematic strategy for tree-planting upon previous pasture plots.

This allowed for the conception of the Inter-Loughs Mover, a water-based transportation system moving trees, people, and other goods. The system consisted of nine hubs that became a regional consolidation of forestry knowledge, whose programming included a forestry university, tree nursery, forager forest, forest playground, seed bank, arboretum, "littoretum," plant propagation facility, and experimental forest. By 2160, the "Inter-Loughs Wilds" was officially designated a shared, regional territory, functioning as a system of forest commons.

Inter-Loughs Mover.

Forestry University.

Forest Playground.

"With a predicted world population of 7 billion by the year 2000, what architectural firm is geared to handle the real problems of our times? [. . .] Retooling is an extravagance to be reserved for an occasion that absolutely demands it. The significance of crisis is that it indicates that the time for retooling has arrived. Assuming that crisis is a necessary precondition for the emergence of new theories, how do the affected parties respond?"

Allen Bernholtz, "Some Thoughts on Computers, Role-Playing, and Design," *Connection* (Winter/Spring 1968), 91.

How might future food options and dining experiences adapt to deteriorating environments?

Sinan Goral (MDE), Audrey Haque (MDE), Oliver Luo (MDE), Jake Schonberger (MDes Tech)
Digital Media: Ambiance
Instructor: Allen Sayegh

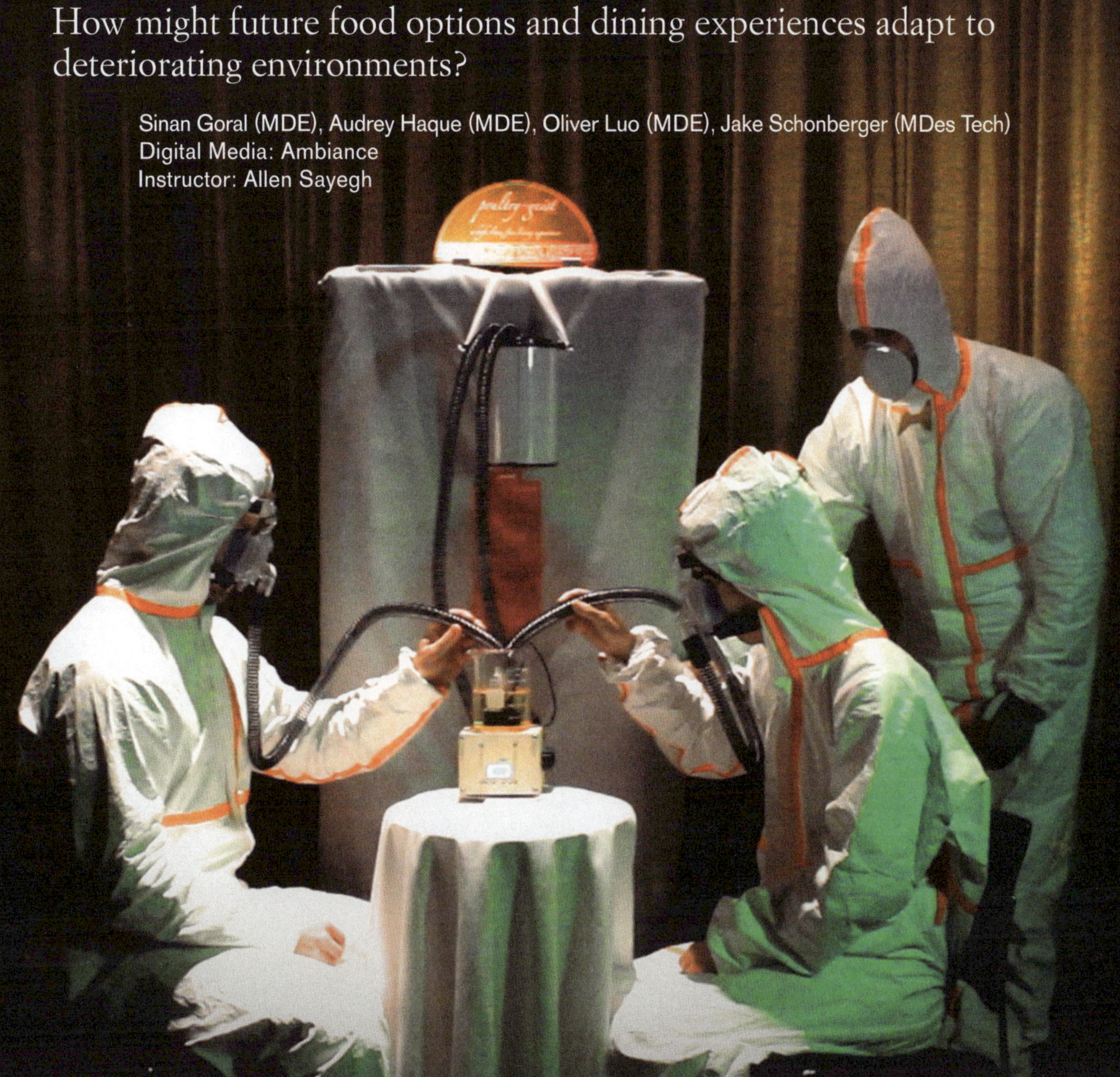

In a time when deteriorating air quality had led to the near-extinction of most forms of life, humans lost access to natural flavors that were crucial in what was once known as "cuisine." Dining ceased to be about taste and community, and food was regarded as mere sustenance. Artificial flavors engineered in labs became some of the most exquisite memories only the wealthiest could afford to enjoy.

"Poultry-Geist" explores the ways in which our dining rituals of the future may adapt to a changing environment. Set in a dystopian future many centuries from now, the story begins with a team of archaeologists recovering an archival video dating from the year 2389 that depicts fine diners enjoying food. The video depicts how humans in 2389 had cleverly adapted to the changing climate and diminishing air quality by implanting air filters onto their faces. Cleanliness and sterility were luxurious, as most of the earth was covered with dirt.

In the installation that follows the recovery of this video, participants are invited to equip themselves in sterile suits and face masks to experience 24th-century dining, where bland gruel slurped through tubes is augmented with poultry scents pumped into the nosepiece.

How might future food options and dining experiences adapt to an environment that is deteriorating? What might be the implications for our values of dining rituals in a world facing pollution and air quality challenges? Centuries from now when we look back at today's cuisines, how might flavors of the past be reexperienced and appreciated anew? These are some of the questions that have driven this project's design process and that "Poultry-Geist" participants are encouraged to consider.

Climate Change
Death
Food
Futurism
Lecture

In a post-work society, what is the role of craft and deconstruction?

Nicolás Delgado Álcega (MArch II)
Utopia/Dystopia: Living Post-Work
Instructor: Annabelle Selldorf

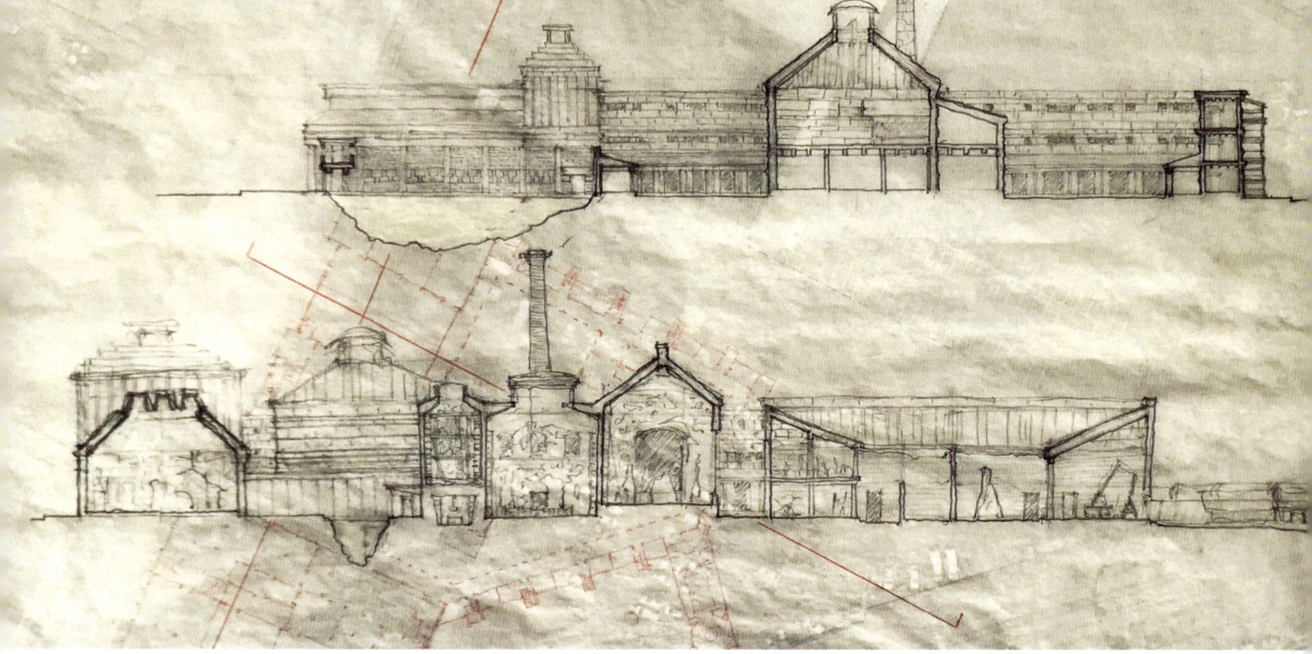

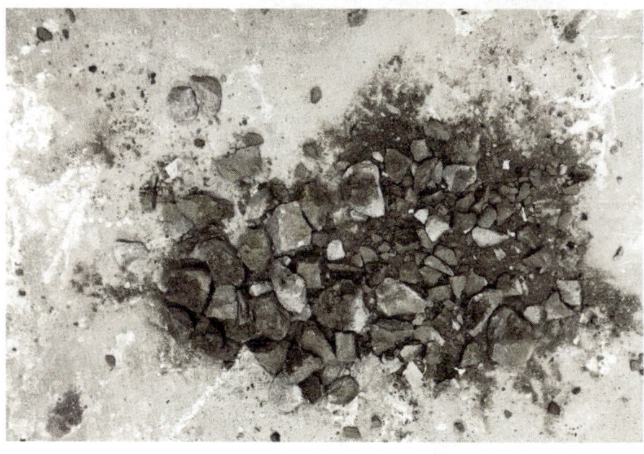

Set in 2048, the monastery is a home base for the pursuit of meaning. It is one more world amidst a context, not a model. It is a proud position, not a retreat.

The monastery is built by quarrying material within the city, the physical remains of yet another world. It produces a new future for the existing urban objects on the Framingham, Massachusetts, site in an anciently fresh way. The monastery is built from the material remains of a highway intersection being demolished nearby—principally, concrete rubble and granite curbs.

There is more thinking and less toiling. Little is wasted. A new kind of craft emerges. The common bath is a fundamental component of life in the monastery. It is communal, and yet deeply about the self and body. The spaces in the bath are sequential but open, available for a couple of minutes with one's mind elsewhere, or for much longer than that, immersed in sense perception and feeling.

The bath is not hermetic. It lets light travel into the spaces; it accepts the entry of unexpected sounds; it reverberates certain movements from the exterior, sometimes. It is a deeply internal space that nonetheless makes one aware of the forces of that which we call the "exterior," what we only understand as shadows in the walls of the cave because they exist outside of the world we have built.

How can a pavilion challenge the production, collection, and processing of waste?

Aime Vailes-Macarie (MArch II)
reCYCLO: Architectures of Waste
Instructor: Caroline O'Donnell

Climate Change
Economy
Option Studio
Reuse
Waste

How can an alternate future for decommissioned industrial sites challenge prevailing instincts of urban development?

Jonathan Kuhr (MLA I), Koby Moreno (MLA I AP), Haoyu Xhao (MLA I), Sijia Zhong (MLA I)
Landscape Architecture III: Third Semester Core Studio
Instructor: Rosalea Monacella

"Airport Archipelago" presents an alternate future for decommissioned industrial sites, one that challenges the prevailing instincts of urban development to offer integrated and innovative economic, infrastructural, ecological, and recreational systems that respond to the uncertainties of environmental change and provide greater direct benefits to surrounding communities.

The project's case study is Boston's Logan International Airport. Positioned between Boston Harbor and the neighborhood of East Boston, the airport's development over the past century has depended upon landfill operations that have allowed it to extend into the harbor. Although much of the site was built to withstand tidal flooding, and thus projected sea level rise for the next 100 years, climate change will bring major storm events that will regularly cease operations and more extreme temperatures that will make spatial demands on the airport it cannot accommodate.

This project begins with the decommissioning of the airport, developing an agenda for the site's reuse. This proposal encourages flooding through a series of canals that define new islands of operation and material flows in order to help mitigate damage to nearby residential communities. These operations (cargo, compost, co-op, agriculture, aquaculture, forestry, excavation, storage, research, and ultimately island-building through sediment deposition and material reuse) were designed with the goal of supporting a closed, sustainable economic and ecological loop, considering brownfield conditions and existing economic structures while also allowing and expecting adaptation over time.

By using earth, water, and plant material as the primary mediums for these operations, the project presents a new urban-industrial-pastoral aesthetic that might be appreciated not only for its contribution to the local economy and ecology but also for its sublime qualities in a recreational setting.

Climate Change
Core Studio
Infrastructure
Landform
Public Space

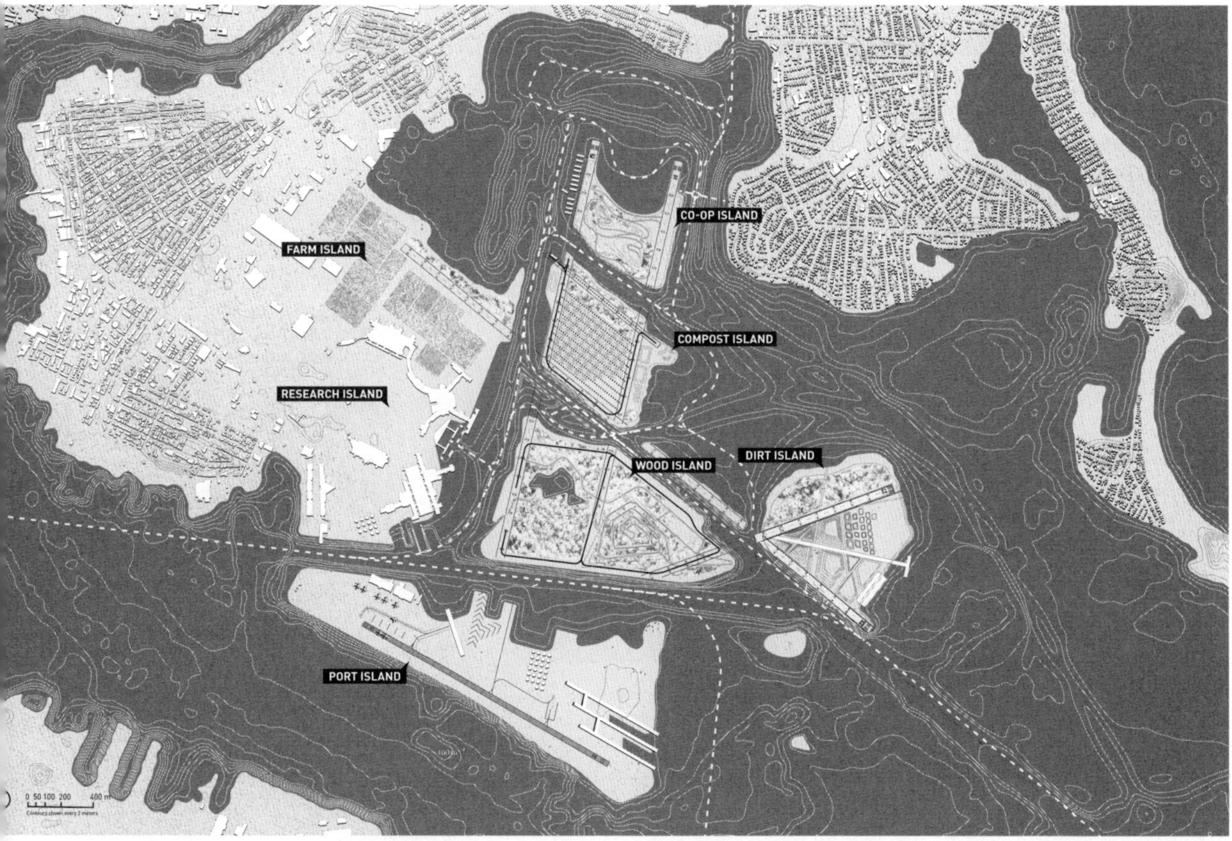

CO-OP ISLAND
FARM ISLAND
COMPOST ISLAND
RESEARCH ISLAND
WOOD ISLAND
DIRT ISLAND
PORT ISLAND
0 50 100 200 400 m
Contours shown every 2 meters

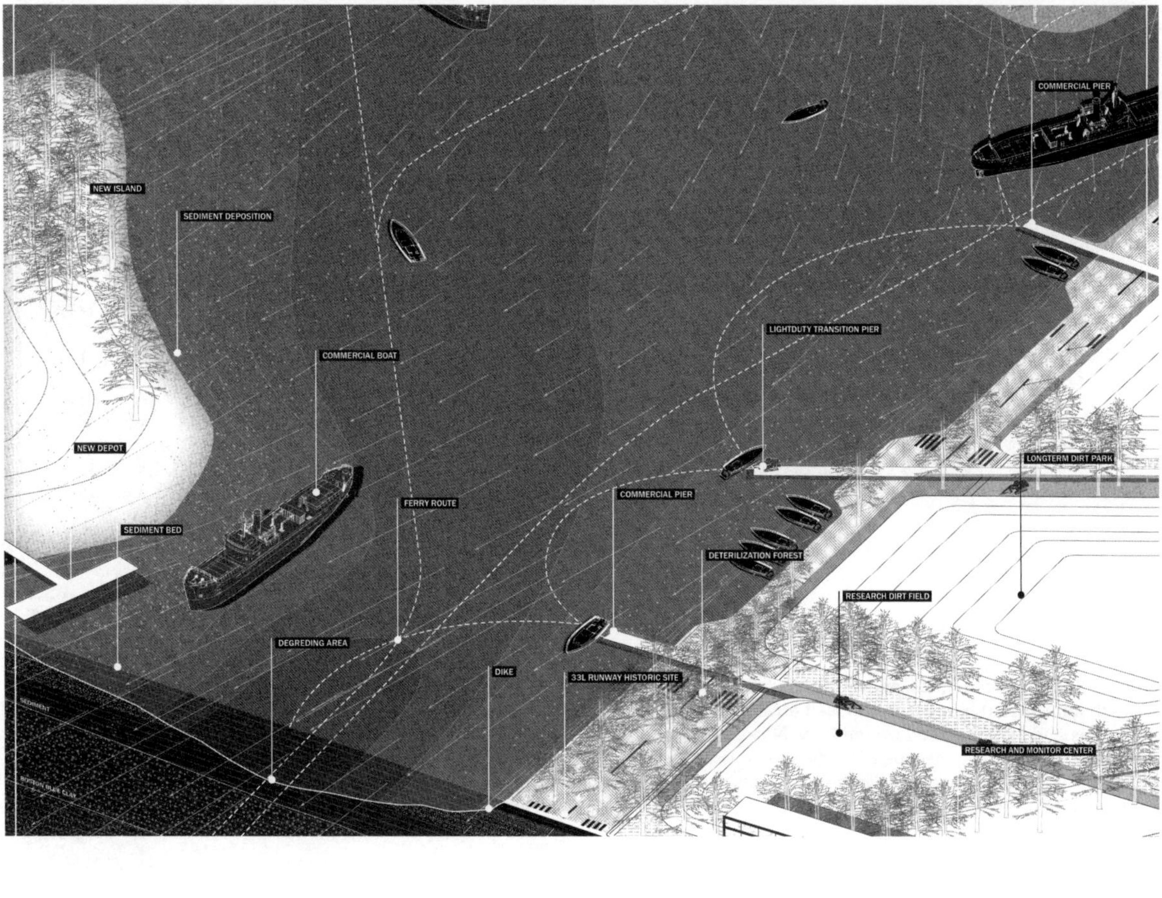

COMMERCIAL PIER
NEW ISLAND
SEDIMENT DEPOSITION
LIGHTDUTY TRANSITION PIER
COMMERCIAL BOAT
NEW DEPOT
LONGTERM DIRT PARK
FERRY ROUTE
COMMERCIAL PIER
SEDIMENT BED
DETERILIZATION FOREST
RESEARCH DIRT FIELD
DEGREDING AREA
DIKE
33L RUNWAY HISTORIC SITE
RESEARCH AND MONITOR CENTER

Can farming positively contribute to ecological and social resiliency?

Malone Matson (MLA I)
Landscape Architecture Thesis
Advisor: Danielle Choi

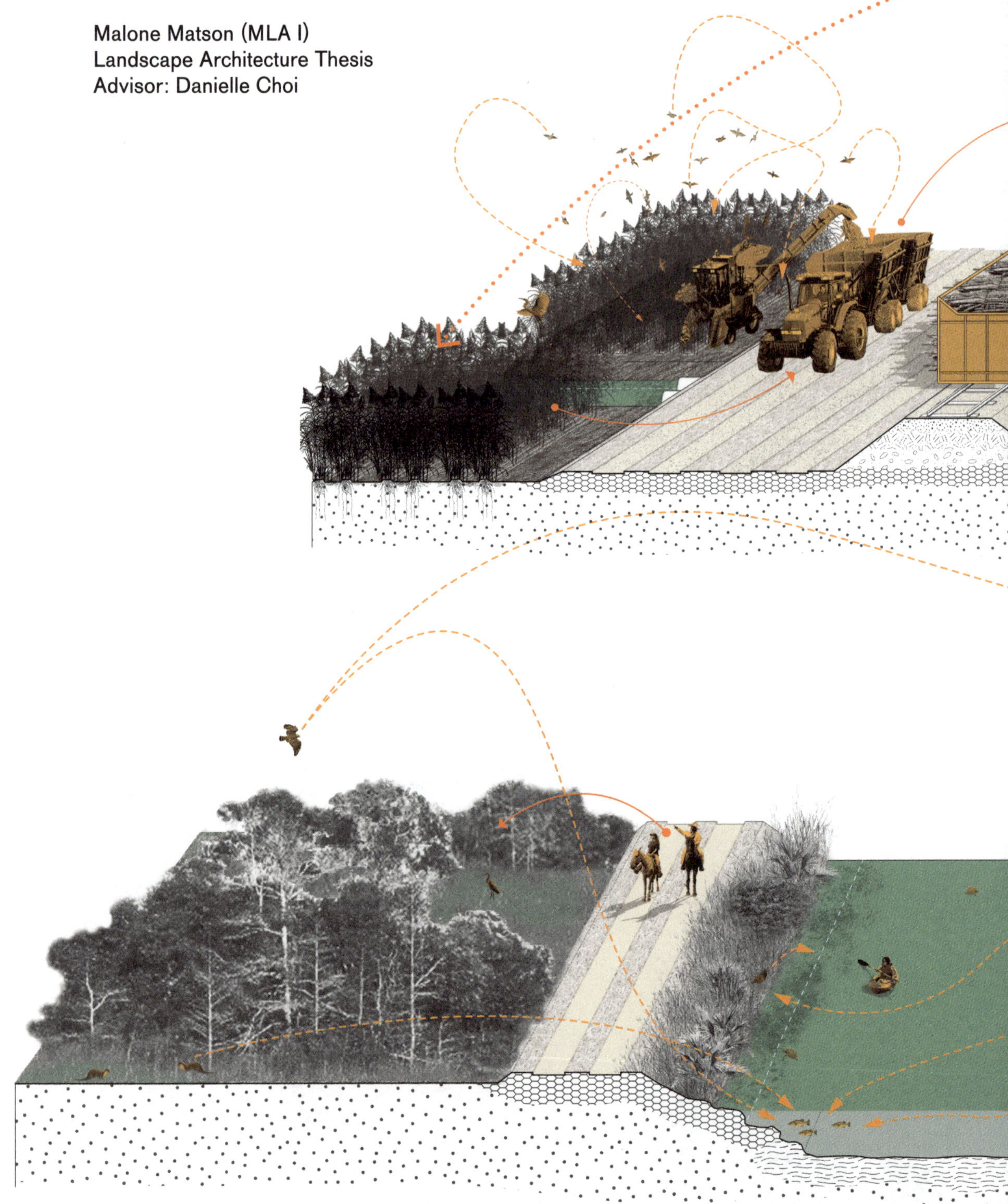

Much of the American landscape today has been produced through constructed binaries like those between humans and nature, us and the other, and wet and dry. Nowhere is this more evident than in landscapes of industrial agriculture. An ecofeminist critique of these landscapes reveals the drastic limitations of binary thinking.

This thesis examines the Everglades Agricultural Area, a 700,000-acre site at the center of Florida's critical freshwater system dedicated to industrial sugarcane farming. The state's ongoing Comprehensive Everglades Restoration Plan continues to operate with a dualistic logic, providing the singular solution of a monolithic water storage infrastructure that fails to upset the status quo or greater ecological implications. The proposed design

Agriculture
Ecology
Economy
Social Equity
Thesis

Above: Proposed drainage swale doubles the quantity of water storage initially proposed by the CERP plan.

Below: Regenerative design requires that all components of a site have multiple uses.

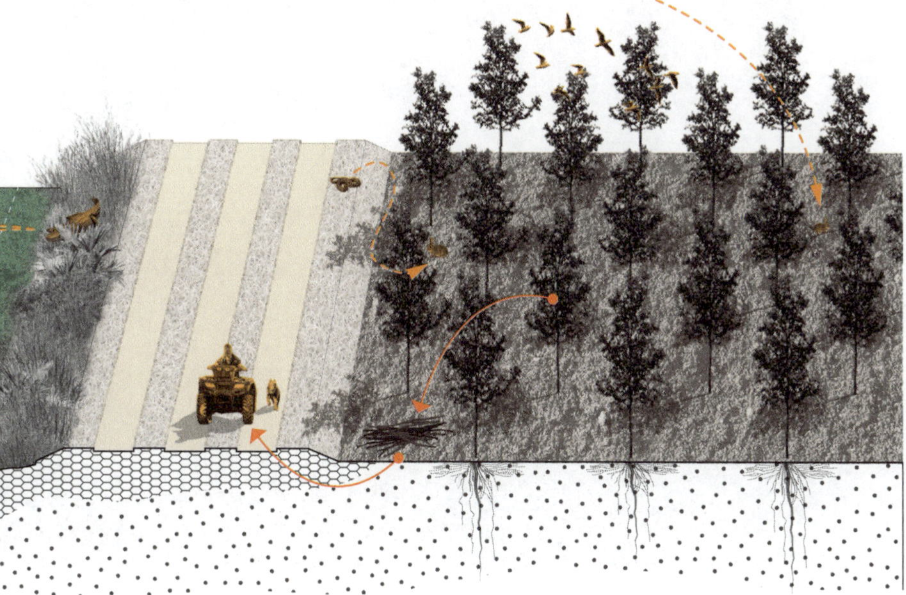

reinterprets the CERP by distributing this water storage across the EAA, disrupting the efficiency of the industrial agricultural complex and creating an opportunity for the implementation of a new regenerative farming practice, "rotational flooding," to rebuild the highly valuable but quickly subsiding muck soils.

Once a refuge for runaway slaves and Native Americans, where wetness was a foil to the white supremacist vision of nature suppressed into agriculture, the dramatic flatness of the site presents an opportunity for covert occupation. A proposed labyrinthine trail system hacks into existing infrastructures and connects the new community of farmers. Micro-topographical disturbances of the trail play with revealing and concealing amidst the vast flatness, illuminating the possibility of a landscape that celebrates life.

How can human environments adjust to nonhuman needs?

Peeraya Suphasidh (MArch II)
Recasting the Outcasts
Instructors: Jeanne Gang and Claire Cahan

This project negotiates between the structure of the existing brutalist building of Swope Marine Research Center in Woods Hole, Massachusetts, and the environment that envelopes it. It synthesizes a position toward restoration as an act done for not only the building alone, but also the ecosystem that encompasses it.

The concrete structure of the crumbling seawall in front of Swope Center will be totally removed, along with the ground level of the building. The remediation of the ground allows different species of native flora and fauna to flourish underneath the proposed visitor center as a way to foster direct engagement with those species. A gradient of wetland and dryland species run across the ground level. The

Climate Change
Conservation
Ecology
Housing
Option Studio

open courtyard on the level above captures a moment in the ecosystem and landscape, providing a window of coexistence between the occupants of Swope and the inhabitants of the environment beyond.

Instead of constructing large living units to fit to the space we demand, perhaps it is the need of the human that has to adjust in order to comply with the constraints provided by our environment. The proposed composition of the building is a direct response to the ways that humans live today. It imagines a possible future by publicly exhibiting a prototype of a visitor center as well as compacted living units, advancing the ways we imagine inhabiting this world.

How can architecture address lost residential and commercial space due to rising sea levels in Provincetown?

Ian Miley (MArch I AP)
The Future of Provincetown
Instructor: Preston Scott Cohen

This studio projects into a real future scenario in which rising sea levels present a dramatic condition of morphological reconfiguration in Provincetown. The linear, arcing form of the city, itself a product of the termination of Cape Cod's spiraling landform, provides a baseline condition from which intruding tides force a reconsideration of the town's shape. Due to the topography, the coastline transgresses deep into certain areas of the town while remaining static in others, instigating the exploration of how to reconstitute the lost residential and commercial space.

This scenario imagines 16 residential towers, referencing the vernacular Cape-style house, each demarcating a breach of the town's public thoroughfare. Connecting each set of towers is a pedestrian bridge, reestablishing the linear continuity of the city while allowing the tide to pass below, allowing new

Climate Change
Form
Option Studio
Typology
Urbanism

intra-urban beaches to shape a new coastline. While these beaches intrude into the city, an articulated bulkhead protects the areas of the city that are less vulnerable to surging seas due to their higher elevation. This new edge condition memorializes the historical patterns of habitation while reacting to the changes in elevation along the coastline.

The new residential towers perform in four essential ways: (1) Indexing the breaks in the linear continuity of Commercial Street; (2) Reconstituting the residential and commercial building stock lost to the intruding tide; (3) Referencing and naturalizing the existing Pilgrim Monument tower; and finally, (4) Providing abutment infrastructure by way of foundations for public bridges to stitch the broken city back together.

"That deafening silence coming from the White House after the new report from the IPCC two weeks ago—as Mohsen just mentioned—urging the United Nations to try, no matter how hard it appears to be, to keep the global temperature below the Paris Agreement target of 1.5 degrees can be interpreted as another proof of anti-science attitude. But for the last three years, I've been more and more convinced that the continuous, coherent, and deeply entrenched climate skepticism of the Republican Party should be seen as a mark of a great design in geopolitics, namely to redesign the United States as situated outside of Earth, and moving toward another attractor altogether."

Bruno Latour, "A Tale of Seven Planets—An Exercise in Gaiapolitics," Senior Loeb Scholar Lecture, October 16, 2018

. . . A conversation around unstable and migrating ground . . .

"The Monochrome No-Image,"
Final Review, Spring 2019

Why has the environment emerged as a category of risk that is being used to justify state-led displacement?

Davi Parente Schoen (MUP, MLA I)
Urban Planning Thesis
Advisors: Sai Balakrishnan and Abby Spinak

ISTANBUL
Turkey
Earthquake

Bogota
Colombia
Landslide Earthquake Flooding

RIO DE JANEIRO
Brasil
Landslide Flooding

In recent decades, environmental risk has emerged as justification for the planned demolition and displacement of targeted urban areas in cities across the Global South. This thesis aims to build theory on this trans-local, state-led risk mitigation strategy, its discursive justifications, and the technical determinations and tools they mobilize.

In response to both the research questions articulated and the methodological approaches that predominate existing subject-area literature, this thesis also develops an experimental, mixed-method, multiple-case-study research design. This approach attempts to understand how this strategy "travels" by comparing across the particularities of the cases in which this strategy and discursive language is being used. This research follows a set of cases, in heterogeneous contexts, in which the World Bank or Japan International Cooperation Agency has provided financial and technical support for mitigative removals.

Governing risk is not purely a technical challenge. Rather, the technical determination of risk itself, as well its use as justification, is political. As such, both the language and the tools through which risk is justified and made visible play an important part in obfuscating the contested and negotiated relationship between human inhabitation and variegated environment(s). These, in turn, frame the role governmental actors (across scales and institutions) can and should play, or not, in risk mitigation. Couching decisions about how the state should respond to risk in technical processes and representations favors certain governmental actions (e.g., removal) and precludes other ways of living with changing environmental conditions and risk.

1980

1990

Climate Change
Policy
State
Thesis

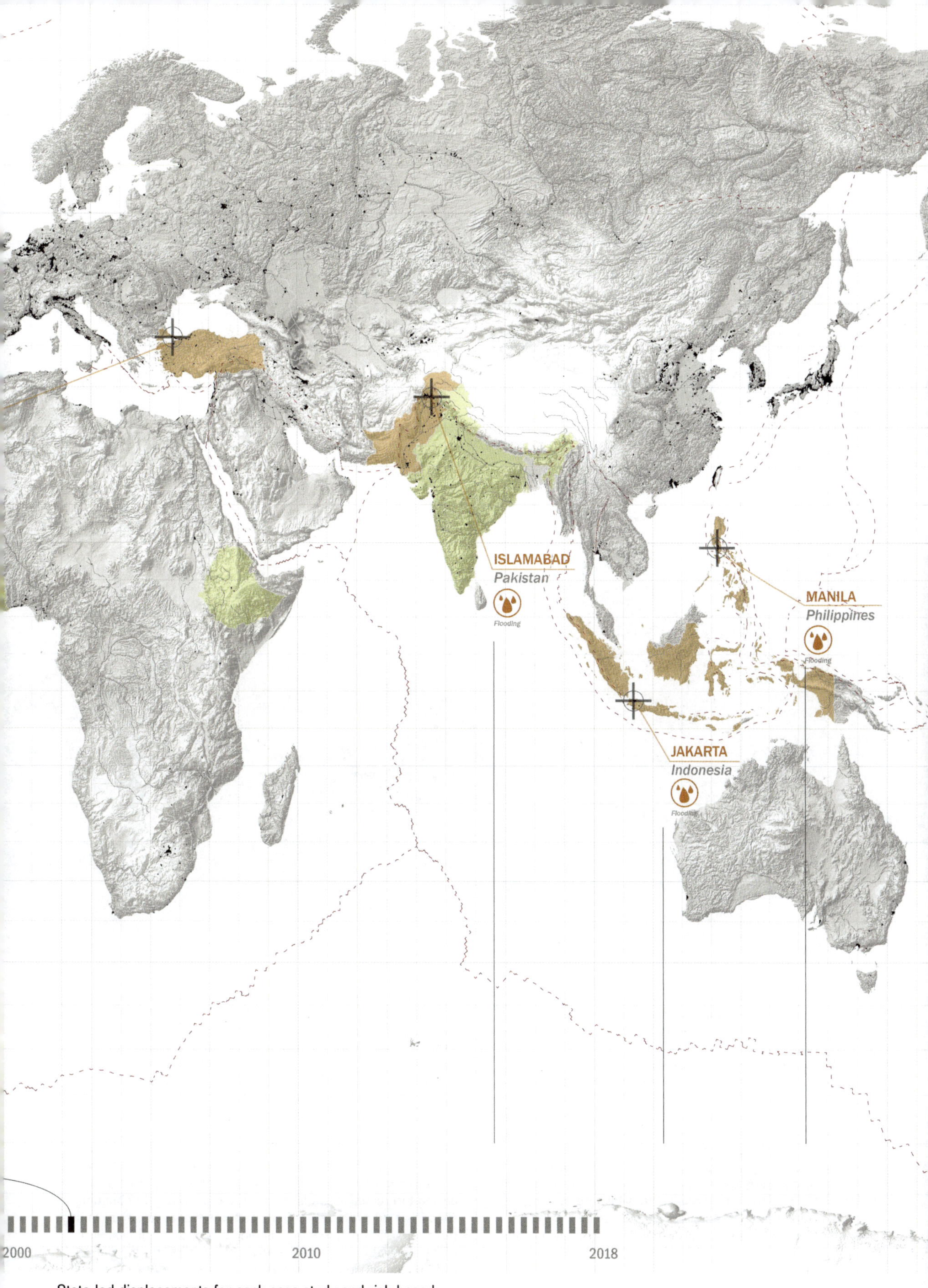

State-led displacements for each case study and risk-based justification for mitigative removals by year.

In the face of rising sea levels, how can private property on barrier islands be leveraged for public benefit?

Maggie Tsang (MDes ULE) and Isaac Stein (MLA II, MDes RR)
Design Studies Thesis
Advisor: Rosetta S. Elkin
Recipient of the Design Studies Thesis Prize

This thesis examines the role of private property in transforming the landscape of barrier islands, and proposes an alternative land trust as a redistributive approach to preemptive retreat.

On barrier islands of the Eastern Seaboard, vacation homes occupy a majority of land use, with properties held as financial assets rather than primary residences. With each successive storm, as well as with the slow onset of sea level rise and accelerated sediment erosion, taxpayer dollars are disproportionately allocated toward the restabilization and reconstruction of damaged homes and infrastructure.

This project argues that the resilience of barrier islands points not to an ecological capacity to withstand system shocks, but rather to the persistence and preservation of capital in the form of private property in predictably volatile environments.

The primary case study of this thesis takes place on Hatteras Island, North Carolina, commonly known as the Outer Banks. This project tests how to incentivize second-homeowners on Hatteras Island to gradually yield ownership along the shoreline. Ultimately, this thesis proposes a vision for a nonprofit organization whose mission is to phase out development on barrier islands.

Drawing from the economic model of a land trust, this project offers a platform that informs decision-making around real estate donations based on erosion rates and climate risk. In addition, this project rehearses and speculates on the spatial and environmental effects of the alternative land trust by visualizing the resulting landscape and the process of unbuilding. By designing protocols and procedures that reverse prevailing development logic, this trust seeks to reduce public expenditure on privatized shorelines and ultimately return the barrier island to its ecological function as a coastal defense line.

Climate Change
Ownership
Thesis
Water

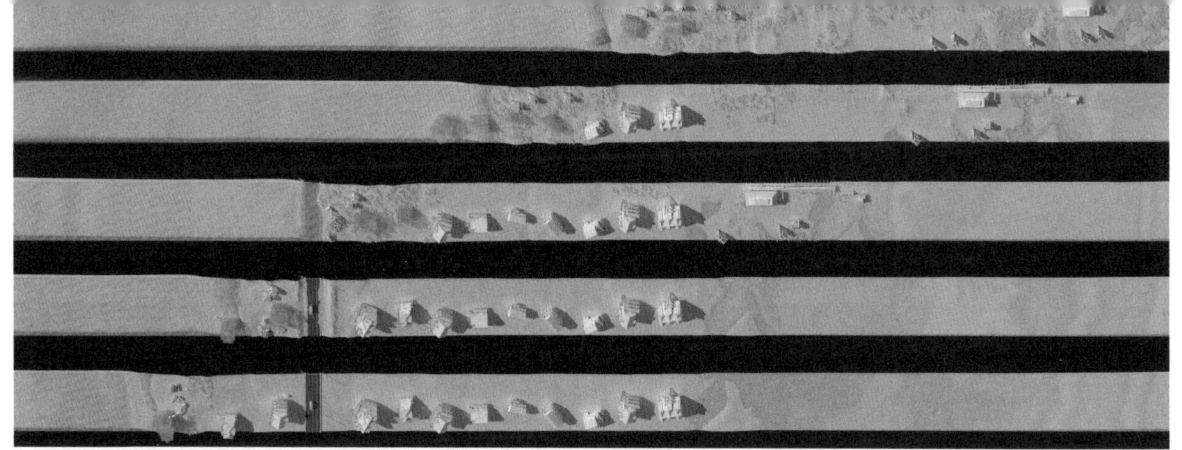

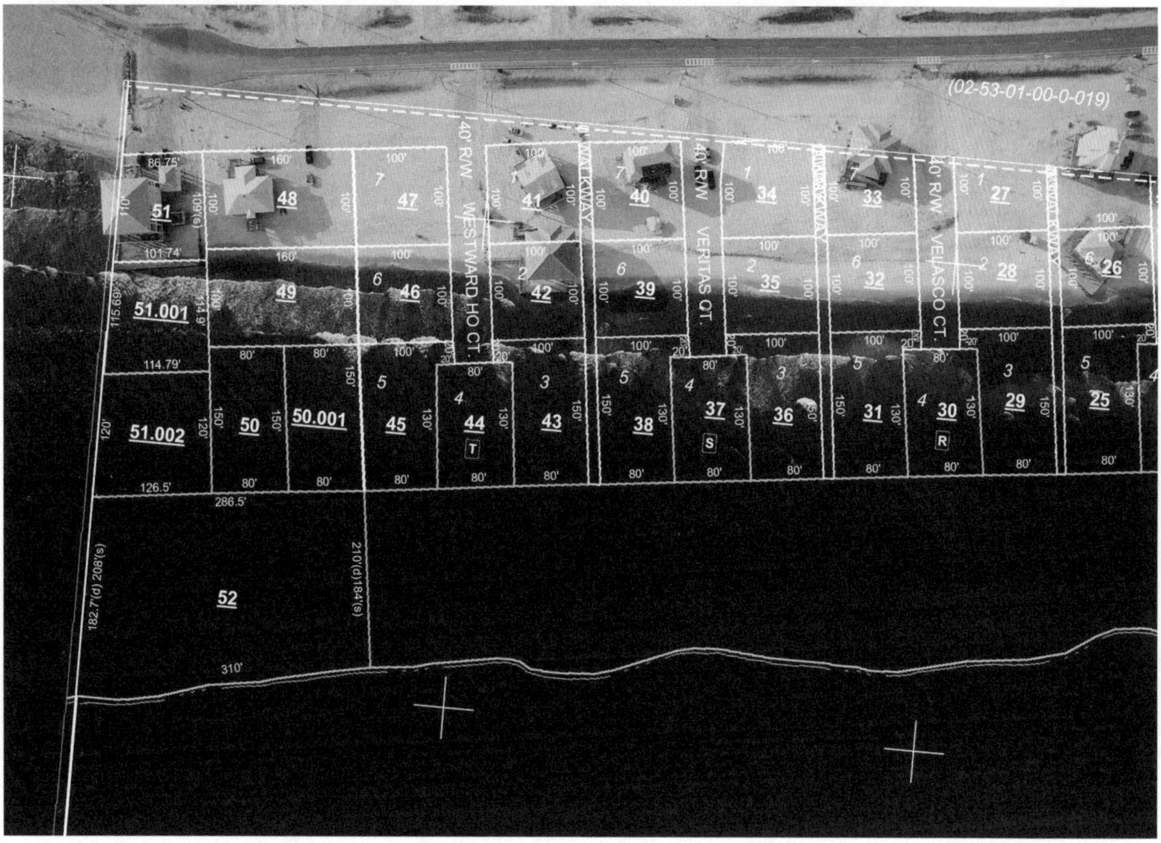

(02-53-01-00-0-019)
40' R/W WESTWARD HO CT.
40' R/W VERITAS CT.
40' R/W VELASCO CT.
WALKWAY
51
48
47
41
40
34
33
27
51.001
49
46
42
39
35
32
28
26
51.002
50
50.001
45
44
43
38
37
36
31
30
29
25
52

SORT, DISPOSE, RECYCLE BUILDING MATERIALS

SALVAGE AND COMPOST STRUCTURAL LUMBER

REPURPOSE PILINGS FOR DUNE NOURISHMENT

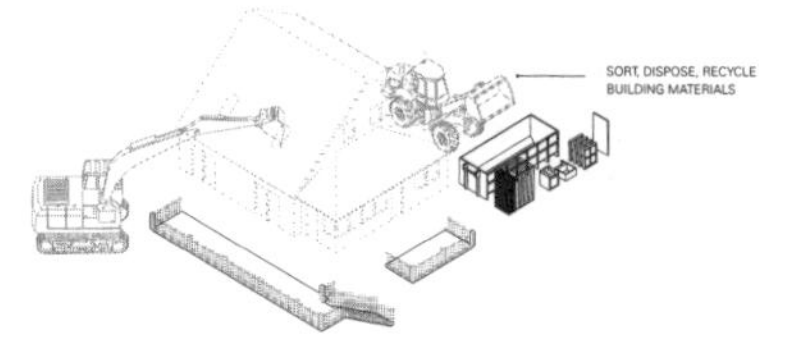

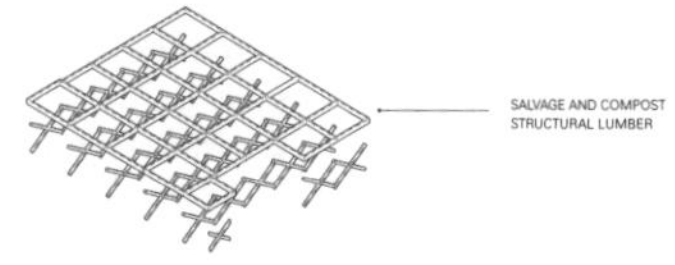

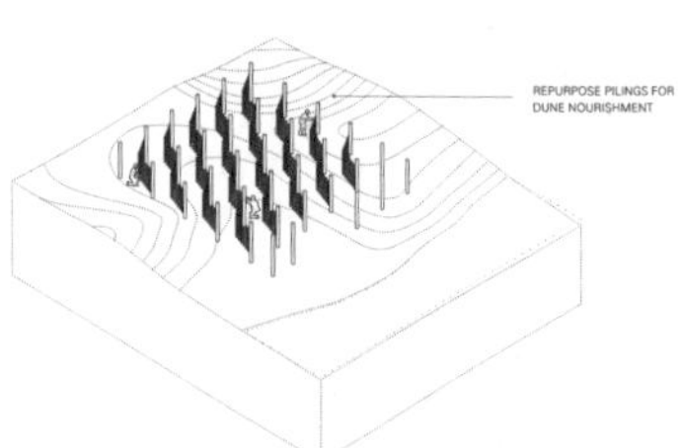

What kind of housing model can operate outside the cyclical forces of the neoliberal market?

Eduardo Mediero (MArch II)
The House: The Waken Desire
Instructors: Tatiana Bilbao and Iwan Baan

In opposition to processes of production, finance capitalism focuses on investment as the means for profit. With this, the house has become a key element for the exchange of value, simplifying its components to financial assets that allow bigger fiscal efficiency. This radical understanding of architecture as an accumulation of capital value and short-term profit has had a pronounced effect on our built environment.

One of the main problems in discerning the reasons and motives for the crisis of housing markets during the modern era is the inability to signify what housing really is. On the one hand, a house is seen as a safe haven sealed off from the banal urbanity. However, the house is at the same time a tool of real estate profit through the fixation of its functions by global market forces. This latter understanding of housing is intrinsically tied to the understanding of private property. However, private property is not only a legal designation for ownership.

Karl Marx noted that the origin of private property is the origin of owning the means of work and production. Owning something, from a mere tool to a house, was a way of owning someone's labor; claiming property over something specifically implies that it has economic value and therefore a profit. By transforming the household into private property, one inevitably exercises power over others who do not have it.

Therefore, it is imperative to create, now more than ever, a housing model that operates outside the cyclical forces of the neoliberal market. Housing that does not have economic value and therefore does not belong to anyone. Housing that cannot be exploited. A house without ownership.

How can planners and designers advance land use and ownership practices for just, equitable environments and communities?

Carolyn Angius (MUP) and Eleni Macrakis (MUP)
The Spatial Politics of Land: A Comparative Perspective
Instructor: Sai Balakrishnan

Community land trusts (CLTs) are popularly heralded as an affordable housing solution to address growing inequalities in cities where housing costs increasingly exclude low- and middle-income residents. But CLTs are not a monolith: they have diverse missions, funding structures, and scopes, and they emerge from different political and social histories, market conditions, and conceptions of shared identity in the communities they serve.

This paper presents four case studies; two in the United States and two in the United Kingdom. These studies vary in market context and represent "hot" and "cool" real estate market conditions—in other words, the degree to which real estate speculation and market demand have created exclusive and expensive private land and housing markets—in each country. The two hot-market case studies, the Atlanta Land Trust Collaborative in Atlanta, Georgia, and the London CLT in East London, United Kingdom, are in cities with competitive, expensive real estate markets, but within neighborhoods that have been the target of decades of public divestment. The cool-market case studies, the Rondo CLT in St. Paul, Minnesota, and the Granby Four Streets CLT in Liverpool, UK, are in cities with comparatively less competitive land markets and therefore less expensive private property. Across each case study, we analyzed the role of conceptions of identity and community in the origins and mission of the CLT; the CLT's organizational origins and structure; the historic relationship between the community serviced by CLT and public (dis)investment; and the financing mechanisms utilized by the CLT to purchase property and operate.

The four case studies in Atlanta, London, St. Paul, and Liverpool, underscore the critical importance of timing in establishing CLTs.

The four case studies underscore the critical importance of timing in establishing CLTs. The more limited scope of hot-market CLTs reveals the difficulty of removing property from the private market once speculation has begun: communities in Atlanta were initially skeptical of CLTs as barring their potential to accumulate wealth afforded by private land ownership, especially for households historically excluded from homeownership like those in traditionally African-American neighborhoods. The London CLT faced similar barriers to land acquisition. In hot markets, public sector construction and regulation of affordable housing may be a more effective mechanism for large-scale creation and preservation of affordable housing than establishing private CLTs at small scales.

However, CLTs may have potential to make a greater impact on perpetually affordable housing supply in cool markets. Cool-market CLTs require less funding to purchase land, and the land they acquire is less contested: both Rondo CLT and Granby Four Streets CLT encountered few barriers to land acquisition. Less competitive real estate markets also afford CLTs more flexibility: both CLTs have missions and scopes far broader than just housing stewardship. For them, affordable housing is a means to overall community development, not the end goal itself. Cool-market conditions may be more important than existing organizational infrastructure. Despite the common characterization of CLTs as affordable housing tools in cities with exclusive real estate markets, they should also be considered a protection against economic downturns in cool markets and ways to institutionalize existing affordability before it is threatened by new development in relatively affordable communities.

How can new mobility options address transportation injustice in Los Angeles?

Sunmee Lee (MLA I AP) and Yuebin Dong (MAUD)
Future of Streets in Los Angeles
Instructor: Andres Sevtsuk

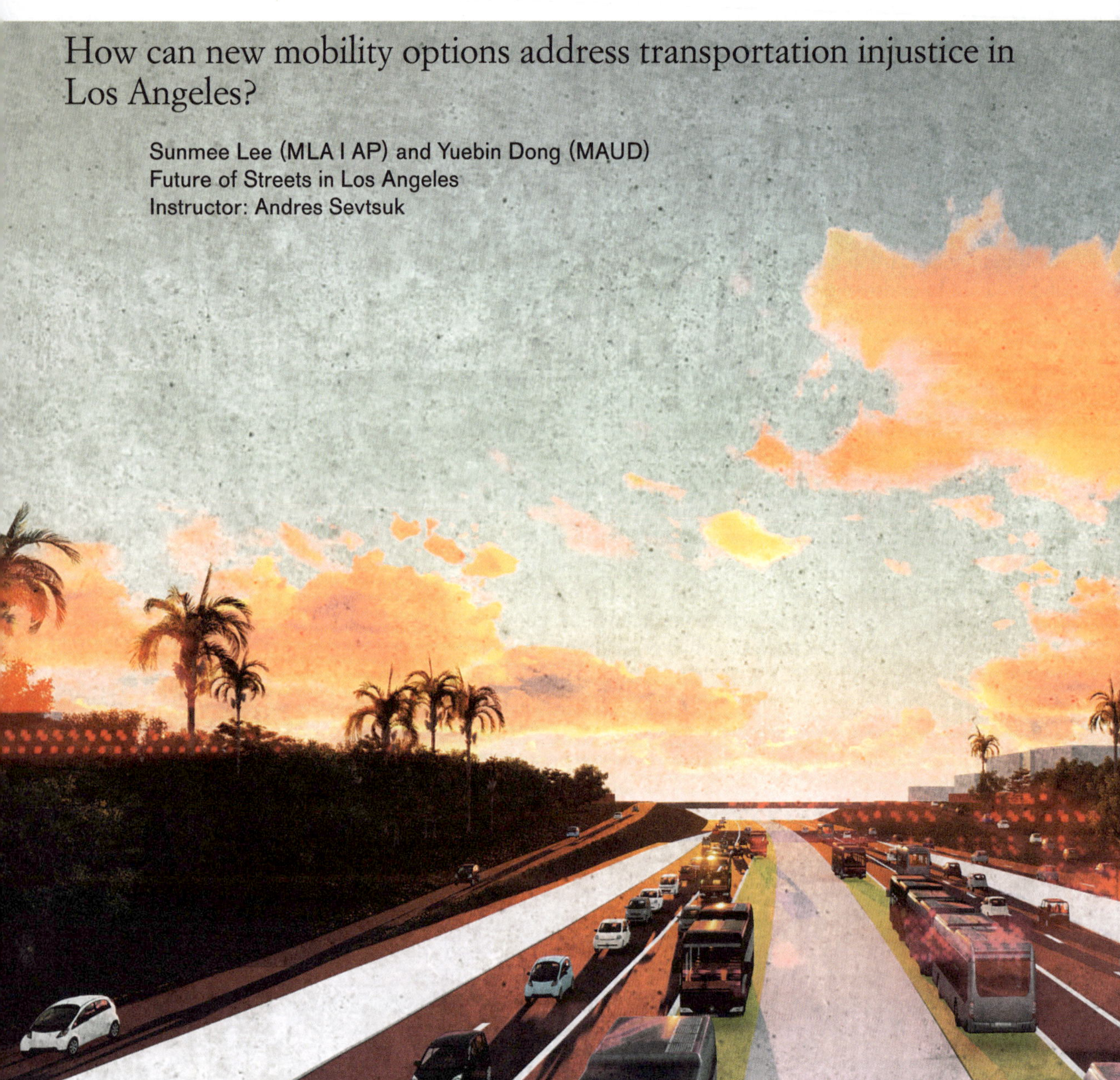

"Highways as Public Transit Infrastructure" explores an alternative to the rail expansion planned in Los Angeles Measure M. For the same budget, a public transit network on existing highways could be 5.4 times longer than newly planned rail lines, and it could serve 3.5 times more low-income households highly dependent on public transit.

Since the automobile era began, transportation injustice in Los Angeles has been reinforced. Highway construction repeatedly causes displacement of marginalized communities. Lower-income households and communities of color spend more time to travel and have limited accessibility, as they cannot afford a car. Often even Metro Rail projects associated with transit-oriented development trigger rapid gentrification, resulting in low transit ridership and displacement of existing communities. This project suggests bringing public transit to the places in most need while respecting local communities in order to offer more equitable and efficient mobility in the future of Los Angeles.

Infrastructure
Justice
Mobility
Option Studio
Social Equity

BICYCLE

What is the role of public markets in urban food supply distribution throughout Cameroon?

Amirah S. Ndam Njoya (MUP)
Urban Planning Thesis
Advisor: Sai Balakrishnan

Urban planners and designers in Cameroon are faced with the incredible challenge of a rapidly increasing population without necessarily an increase in "formal" economic opportunities[1]—in fact, in the capital city of Yaoundé, 75 percent of the employment sector is informal.[2] Markets, as publicly owned parcels placed in key locations and assembling major actors, are a place of transaction where supply meets demand. Markets are the vital source of fresh food for the growing middle- and low-income population of Cameroon. They not only are a spatial representation of the food supply chain, but are also, as Amin and Graham say when discussing the Ordinary City, the spatial manifestation of the "diverse ranges of relational webs [that] coalesce, interconnect, and fragment" throughout time.[3] Yet these spaces suffer from a lack of basic services, obsolete amenities and structure, precarious vending, and poor hygiene. What is the role of public markets in urban food supply distribution throughout Cameroon? How can the market become visible with the view of the Global South?

Most studies of informal markets focus on the market as a unit of analysis, the market as the result of path dependency linked to frozen traditional ancestral customs, and the market at friction with modernity and development. This research uses Mfoundi Market (1,000–1,500 vendors) in Yaoundé as a case study. During January 2019, I administered 40 surveys with vendors in Mfoundi Market, designed a survey for 18 produce suppliers, and conducted three semi-structured interviews with Mfoundi Market authorities, in addition to several observational surveys and secondary source research. Through this work, I rescale beyond the boundaries of the market and situate the dynamics of the market in a wider food-supply chain within the region. I look at the market and urban food supply distribution as dynamic entities that change throughout time based on political interests and gendered relations. Finally, I look at the market not as a byproduct of failed attempts at modernity and development, but, because of its multiplex nature, as a catalyst in urban development through the southern urbanist dialogue.

Analysis of urban food supply distribution in times of rapid urbanization has primarily focused on the role of the monopolization of urban food systems by large multinational firms. For instance, we see this in the work of Karen Seto and Navin Ramankutty, who discussed the "potential [for] understudied linkages" of food security.[4] For them, rapid urbanization leads to the reduction of "wet markets" and the rise of large multinational firms that supply a considerable amount of food to urban areas. Yet, what's missing from this analysis is research into the opposite effect—that is, in which rapid urbanization has also led to the complexity of urban food supply systems. This occurs in Cameroon, where rapid urbanization has increased the use of wet markets and raised the complexity of food distribution systems. The reason we do not see the effect described by Seto and Ramankutty is in part due to the political and economic prioritization of export-oriented cash crops, such as bananas, cocoa (butter, powder, and paste), coffee, oils, and refined sugars.

1
Euromonitor International, "Cameroon in 2030: The Future Demographic" (Euromonitor International, October 2016).

2
"EMPLOIS ET REVENUS, 2014—Cameroon Data Portal," *Knoema*, accessed March 6, 2019, http://cameroon.opendataforafrica.org/fxobxedemplois-et-revenus-2014.

3
Ash Amin and Stephen Graham, "The Ordinary City," *Transactions of the Institute of British Geographers* 22, no. 4 (December 1, 1997): 411–29.

4
Karen Seto and Navin Ramankutty, "Hidden Linkages between Urbanization and Food Systems," *Science* 352, no. 6288 (May 20, 2016): 943–45.

Despite the inability to formalize the market structure and urban food supply distribution system, there have been interviews, research, and readings that suggest the marketplace is a dynamic entity due to its multifaceted role at various scales of urban food supply distribution. However, the organic and anarchic facade of public markets has intellectually and politically rendered them as urban spaces frozen in time and unaffected by development and urbanization. Paul Ulrich Elom, anthropology professor at the University of Yaoundé I, describes these informal vending spaces as the spatial representation of the inability of the native populations, to separate themselves from their "ancestral customs."[5] In this perspective Elom attributes the precarity of urban food distribution in markets to the "timelessness" of a culture that, he states, impacts the modern development of the capital.[6] By reducing a phenomenon to partial interpretation, Elom disregards the complexity and "the heterogeneity of economic, social, cultural, and institutional" factors that make the present conditions of public markets.[7] In fact, history has shown that the structure, use, and leadership of the market have changed throughout time.

The provision of low-cost food to the urban center has been the preoccupation of administrative leaders in Yaoundé since the colonial times of the late 1880s. In Jane Guyer's work, she shows the institutional power relations and the consequent effect on food supply distribution in Yaoundé.[8] Urban food supply distribution was used as a tool for political control, but also as a financial tool to generate property value in cities. Today, in times of weak bureaucracy, markets are mostly used to contain the urban population. This thesis aims to show that markets are not frozen in time and are the relics of ancestral customs—despite their chaotic and anarchic facade, they are the stages of current urban dialogues.

5
Paul Ulrich Elom, "The Privatization of Public Spaces in the City of Yaoundé, Cameroon: The Case of Business," *Africa Development* 36, no. 1 (January 1, 2011): 1–12.

6
Ibid.

7
Ibid.

8
Jane Guyer and the International African Institute, *Feeding African Cities: Studies in Regional Social History, International African Library* (Manchester: Manchester University Press for the International African Institute, 1987).

What would it mean to organize the way we live in China purely through agriculture?

Ting Liang (MLA I)
Landscape Architecture Thesis
Advisor: Sergio Lopez-Pineiro

This thesis uses agricultural fields as the medium to imagine an urban condition outside of the city. In opposition to the traditional centric-based urbanizing formula, "People's Agri-Topia" is a framework for an equitable field that allows for the continuous and even distribution of agricultural land with expressions of freely inserted urban conditions.

The implementation of the Great Leap Forward in the 1950s saw the birth of the People's Commune that structured China's countryside as we know it today. The original aim of the communes was to break the distance between the city and the countryside. However, since the 1980s, Chinese urbanization has shifted toward the celebration of metropolitanism. In the past 40 years, the process of urbanization has

Agriculture
Ownership
Utopia
Thesis

been the process of land transformation: the conversion of village-owned agricultural land into state-owned construction land. As a result, the countryside has gradually lost its spatial and cultural identity, producing a divide between "being in the village" and "being in the agricultural field."

In response to the contemporary urban-rural dichotomy, as well as the village-field division, "People's Agri-Topia" proposes a flexible system of evenly and equitably distributed agricultural fields with freely allocated services and communal space. In this proposal for a new type of commune, agricultural land is the only spatial organizer. "People's Agri-Topia" reinvents the cultural imaginary of China's countryside for the celebration of a new type of agrarian living.

Can the American culture of Autopia today be shifted toward a mobility culture centered around a Transitopia of tomorrow?

Evan Shieh (MAUD)
Urban Design Thesis
Advisor: Andres Sevtsuk
Recipient of the Urban Design and Planning Thesis Prize in Urban Design

This manifesto envisions a near future (year 2047) in which the Autonomous Vehicle (AV) catalyzes a mobility paradigm shift toward autonomous public transit as a model of regional urban growth in the city of Los Angeles, in order to combat many of the major negative externalities that the private automobile has imparted onto its urban realm: urban sprawl, traffic congestion, environmental unsustainability, and mobility inequality. The manifesto instrumentalizes automation as a revolutionizing force in the NextGen bus transit network of Los Angeles, introducing a new range of automated vehicle sizes that plug mobility gaps while simultaneously critiquing current Los Angeles transit agencies' obsession with the expansion of its light rail network. Methodologically, it proposes an alternative top-down, AV-incorporated transit planning model that is populated by a bottom-up narrative framework, a graphic novel that envisions this future world through the eyes of four distinct Angeleno archetypes as they experience this mobility paradigm shift firsthand. The manifesto offers a radical story that might convince the everyday Angeleno that alternatives to car culture can exist, as well as a set of concrete policies that would enable this potential Los Angeles of 2047 to emerge, and finally a set of urban implications and lessons-learned for the design and planning of the city of the future.

While the private car caused public transit to historically decline in the United States, we must now use the automated car to return us back to public transit as a model of urban growth. In envisioning this potential urban future and delineating the design, planning, and policy paths one might take toward achieving it, this manifesto contends that there is hope in transitioning from the Autopia of today to a Transitopia of tomorrow.

Automation
Infrastructure
Thesis
Transit
Utopia

ARCHETYPES
4 NARRATIVE PERSONAS

SUBURBAN NUCLEAR FAMILY

THE SMITH FAMILY

Configuration: 2 Parents (1 Working, 1 Home), 2 Children
Annual Income: $170,000
Daily Travel Budget: $30
Demographic: Caucasian
Residence Type: Single Family Home
Residence Area: Pasadena
Commute Type: Work-Home, Errands
Traditional Mobility: Single-Occupancy Car

COMPOSITE HOUSEHOLD

ROOMMATES ADAM & KI

Configuration: Group of 2 Friends
Annual Income: $70,000
Daily Travel Budget: $15.5
Demographic: Mixed
Residence Type: Mid-Rise Apt. Rentals
Residence Area: Koreatown
Commute Type: Work-Home, Work from home mobile schedule

EXTENDED WORKING HOUSEHOLD

THE PEREZ FAMILY

Configuration: 2 Working Parents, 1 Child & Grandfather in Wheelchair
Annual Income: $48,000
Daily Travel Budget: $10
Demographic: Hispanic
Residence Type: Multi-Family Home Townhouse
Residence Area: Leimert Park
Commute Type: Long Distance Commute

BUSINESS TRAVELER

MR. GIBSON

Configuration: Solo Traveler
Annual Income: $110,000
Daily Travel Budget: $20
Demographic: African American
Residence Type: Hotel
Residence Area: Downtown
Commute Type: Multiple Destinations need to be reached
Traditional Mobility: Rental Car

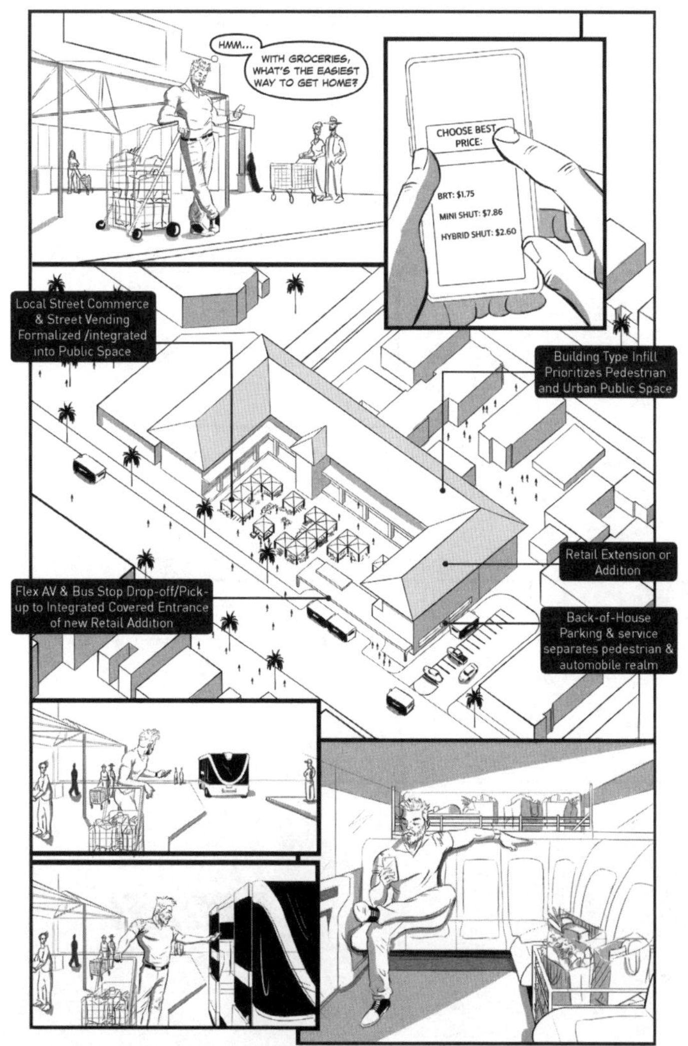

WHAT'S WRONG?
I HAD A NIGHTMARE. I WAS STUCK IN TRAFFIC WITH ZOMBIE CARS.
SOME DREAM YOU HAD.
LET'S GET OUR DAY STARTED AND YOU'LL FEEL BETTER
HELLO! TWO SEATS FOR A MINI SHUTTLE TO PASADENA DOWNTOWN EXPRESS RAIL IN FIVE MINUTES.
Dynamic Congestion Pricing Implemented in L.A.
HERE COMES THE A.V. BUS, KIDS!
BYE DAD!
BYE DAD!
MY RIDE'S HERE TOO.
SMOOCH
BYE DEAR.
REMEMBER WE HAVE RESERVATIONS AT SEVEN!
WOULDN'T MISS IT.

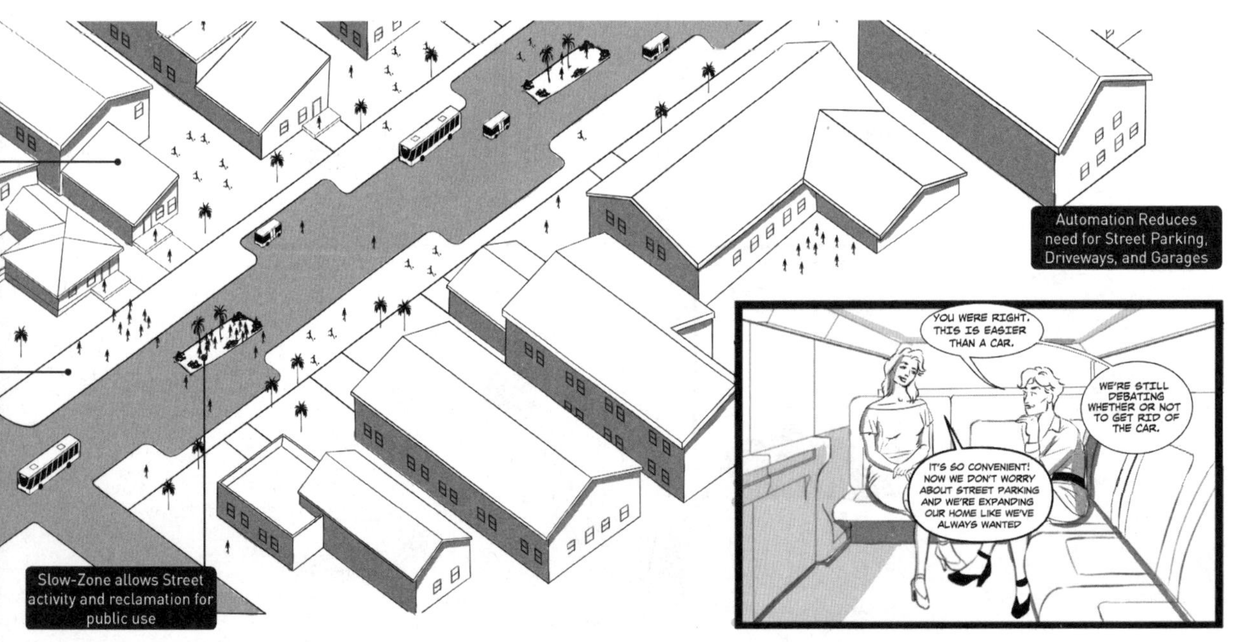
Automation Reduces need for Street Parking, Driveways, and Garages
Slow-Zone allows Street activity and reclamation for public use
YOU WERE RIGHT. THIS IS EASIER THAN A CAR.
WE'RE STILL DEBATING WHETHER OR NOT TO GET RID OF THE CAR.
IT'S SO CONVENIENT! NOW WE DON'T WORRY ABOUT STREET PARKING AND WE'RE EXPANDING OUR HOME LIKE WE'VE ALWAYS WANTED

"One is not certain what the architecture is. Is the place for bicycles architecture? Is a tree growing on a building architecture? Are the painted duct work and exposed mechanical unit architecture? Is the unit bare for functional reasons? For aesthetic reasons? The planes of interpretation always appear in a new light, and just as one thinks he has grasped the essence, it slips away and reappears in another place, mocking attempts at definition as timeless or immediate. Architecture, at best the result of process and situation, is ambivalent."

CTION

NOVEMBER 26

1963

Charles Jencks, "Polar Attitudes in Architecture," *Connection* (May 1964), 11.

How can the space between buildings perform as architecture?

Paris Nelson (MArch I)
Architecture Thesis
Advisor: Jon Lott

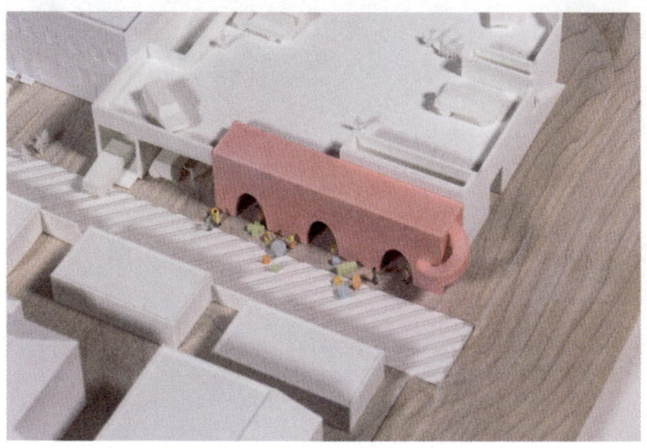

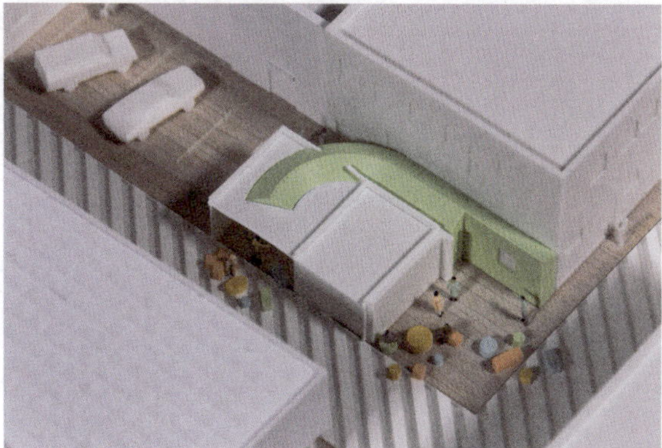

This thesis considers how the vast network of Los Angeles's largely obsolete alleys, an unused public space with an aggregate surface area twice the size of New York's Central Park, can serve as the grounds for a new, fine-grained urban condition antithetical to the city's current densification direction. The project proposes six architectural interventions—a public library, a greenhouse and community garden, a lap pool, a laundromat and cafe, a capsule hotel, and a ceramics studio—in investigating the potential of smallness in the odd lots of Los Angeles's alleys.

Odd Lots: A Case for Accumulative Architecture in LA's Alleys

Property
Public Space
Urbanism
Thesis

How can anexactitude in both form and program perform as architecture?

Khorshid Naderi-Azad (MArch I)
Architecture Thesis
Advisor: Jennifer Bonner

Architecture has historically given discursive priority to exact geometries and overlooked the anexact. In "San Giuseppe Ball Hall," an assemblage of faux cardioids brings etymological, formal, and programmatic rigor to the "bulbous": the anexact, or the essentially, rather than accidentally, inexact. The faux cardioid is defined by a convex surface with a single cusp—i.e., a point of indentation that produces equal tangent planes in the poked area. The anexact forms of "San Giuseppe Ball Hall" host the anexact program of a Bed Ball. During a Bed Ball, the ballroom's extravaganza is viewed from the platform of one's bed. San Giuseppe Ball Hall neighbors the perfectly symmetrical, disk-shaped Apple Inc. headquarters by Foster + Partners in Cupertino, California. As an irreducible and unrepeatable love child of Instagram culture and the Silicon Valley housing

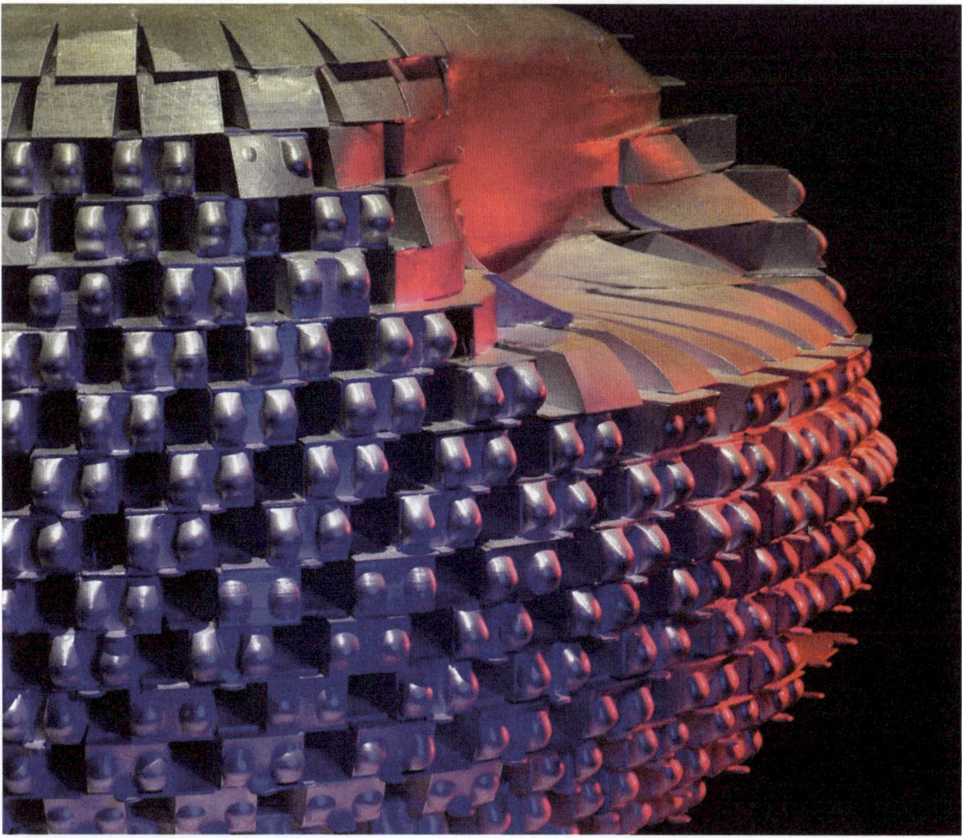

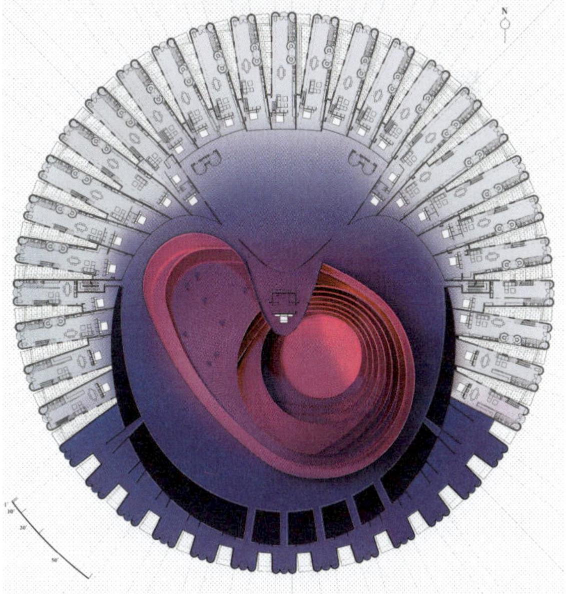

crisis, "San Giuseppe Ball Hall" is composed of equal parts preproduction and postproduction spectacle. Anchored in the dualism of luxury and affordability, of performance and routine, of spectacle and sleep, it bolsters the bed and the ballroom to confront the canon of Euclidean and Platonic architecture.

How can a building's interior infrastructure perform as architecture?

Keunyoung Lim (MArch I)
Architecture Thesis
Advisor: Oana Stanescu

This thesis seeks to change the relationship between architecture and infrastructure by reconstructing conventional notions of the architectural elements that define a living space. "This is Not a Pipe" disrupts the traditional perspective of infrastructure by negating the distinction of architectural dichotomies: structure and ornament, superstructure and infrastructure, front and back, servant and served.

Infrastructure
Performance
Structure
Thesis

How can sanitation infrastructure organize and upgrade communities and integrate them with the city more broadly?

Soledad Patino (MAUD)
Extreme Urbanism 6: Designing Sanitation Infrastructure
Instructor: Rahul Mehrotra

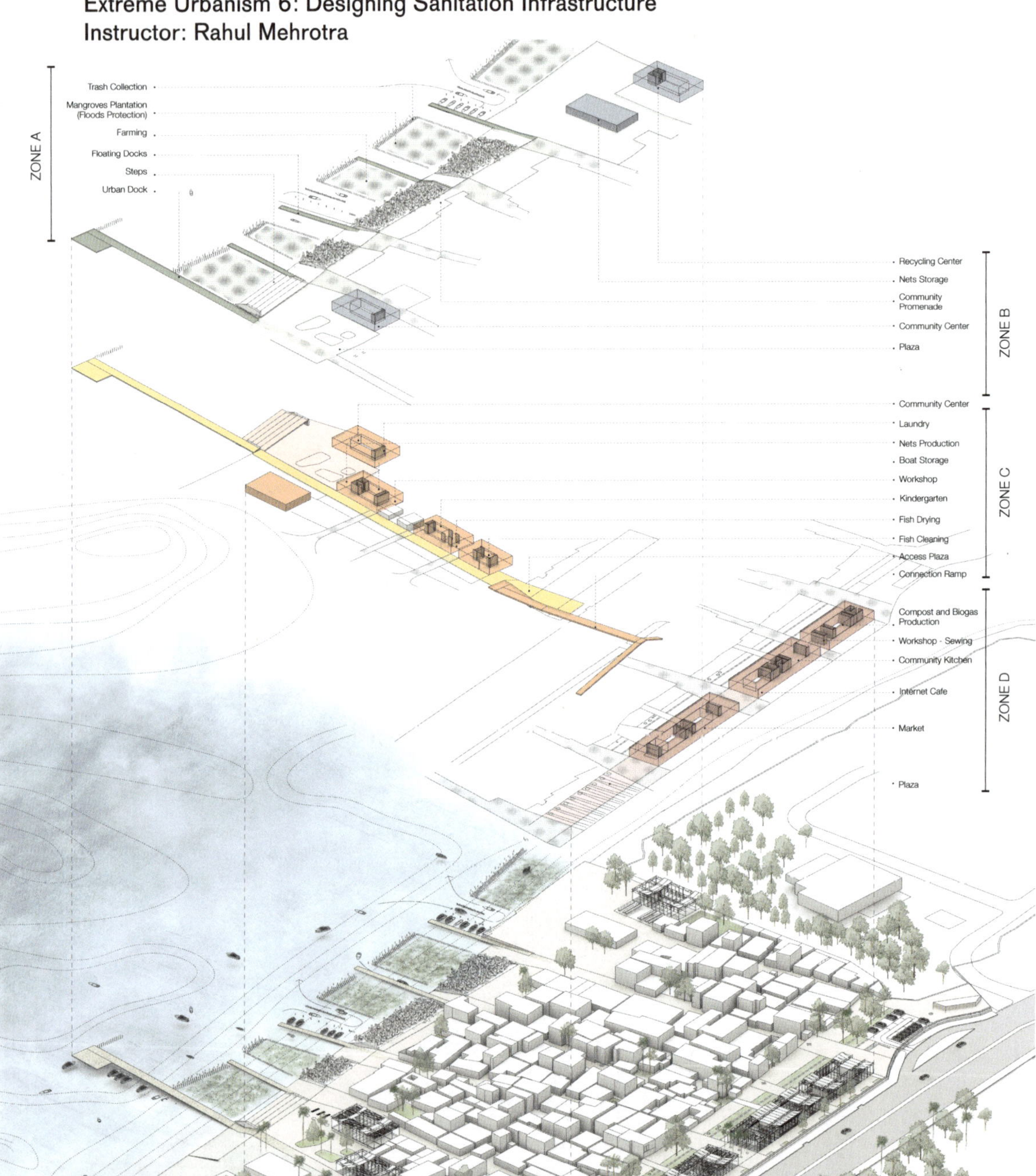

The Koliwadas fishing villages are indigenous settlements at risk of losing their cultural identity and space in Mumbai. This project explores ways to help integrate these communities, allowing the fishing villages to acquire recognition and legitimacy while strengthening their economic role and improving basic infrastructure.

This project reconfigures fishing activity to improve infrastructural capabilities and adds function and programming to new multiuse systems. At the urban scale, the Koliwadas creates connections between Mumbai's central mobility railway spine and the city's western waterfront.

Can the bathroom be the new clinic?

Anesta Iwan (MDE)
Independent Design Engineering Project I
Advisors: Martin Bechthold; with Rachel Carmody, Curtis Huttenhower, Peter Stark, Mary Tolikas (Harvard John A. Paulson School of Engineering and Applied Sciences)

In designing "Smart Toilet Paper," it is critical to understand the processes involved in taking fecal matter and interpreting data to know which bacteria are present. In general, (1) the microbial DNA from the fecal sample need to be extracted, then (2) specific targeted DNA sequences need to be amplified/multiplied, and finally (3) a determination will be made whether those targeted sequences are present in the sample or not; the final DNA then dyed and visualized on a paper pad.

"Smart Toilet Paper" integrates these processes into one device made of disposable materials.

Data
Health
Independent Study
Waste

How can reimagining the building membrane lead to new passive vent strategies?

Pamela Cabrera (MDes EE)
Design Studies Thesis
Advisor: Jonathan Grinham

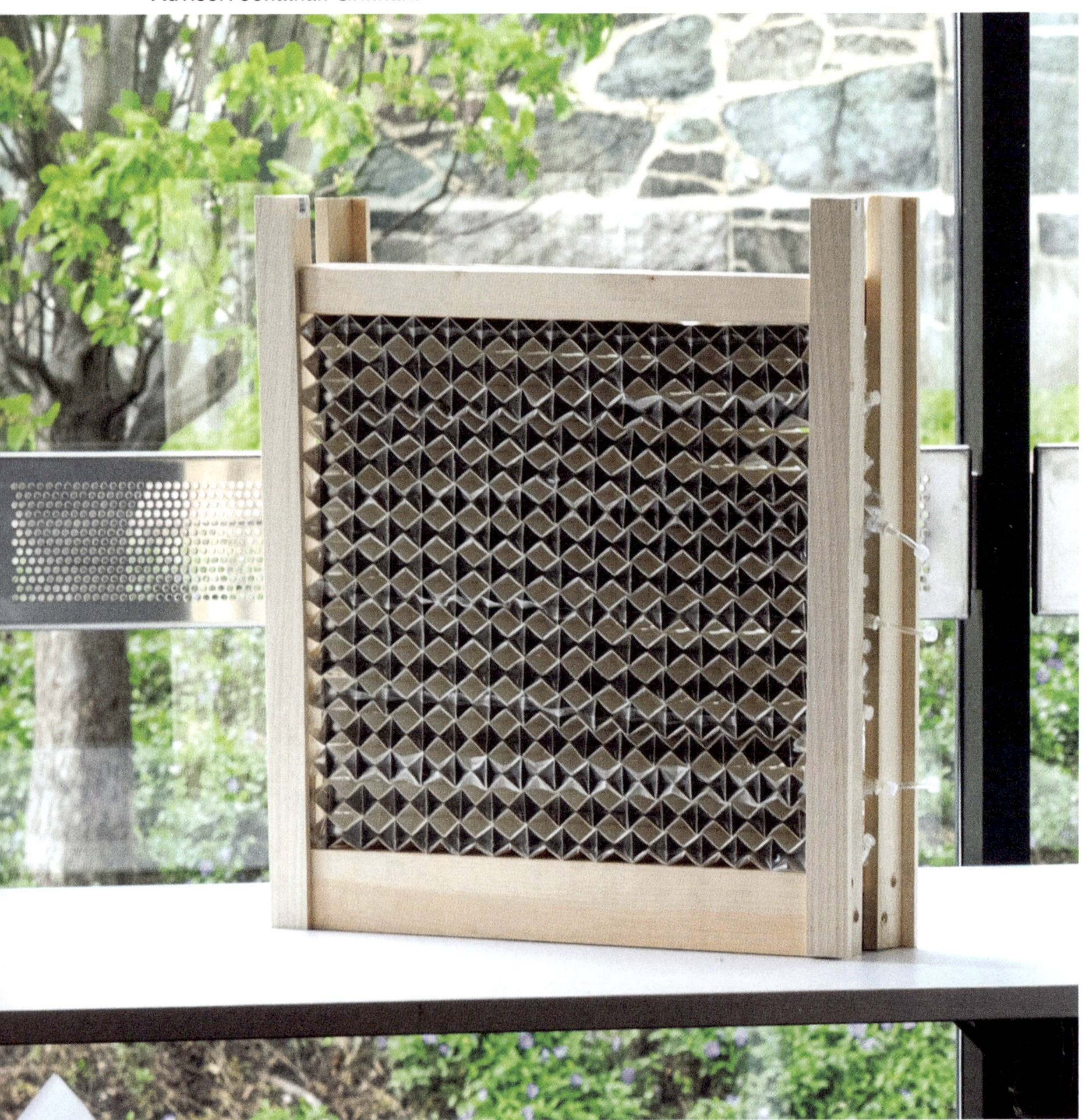

While membrane selectivity is a well-known field of study throughout nature and applied across industries, architecture has regarded membranes only as barriers rather than as selective screens. Through a mixed-method study that includes experimentation, design prototyping, and simulation, the thesis concluded with a membrane assembly using Miura fold geometry to increase surface area and flow turbulence for higher mass transfer flux. Two membrane materials are tested under different form configurations: a dry membrane (PVA with LiCl) and a supported liquid membrane (PTFE and CA with PEG400), and the results show a high impact on performance. This new passive form could reduce the need for vapor compression mechanical systems and the operational energy of buildings, and therefore create more resilient spaces by allowing natural ventilation design strategies.

Building Science
Fabrication
Facade
Technology
Thesis

The Humid Threshold: Cooling Hot, Humid Climates via Membrane Dehumidification

How can the materiality of air and our human entanglement with it be made visible?

Isabel Preciado (MLA I)
Landscape Architecture Thesis
Advisor: Danielle Choi

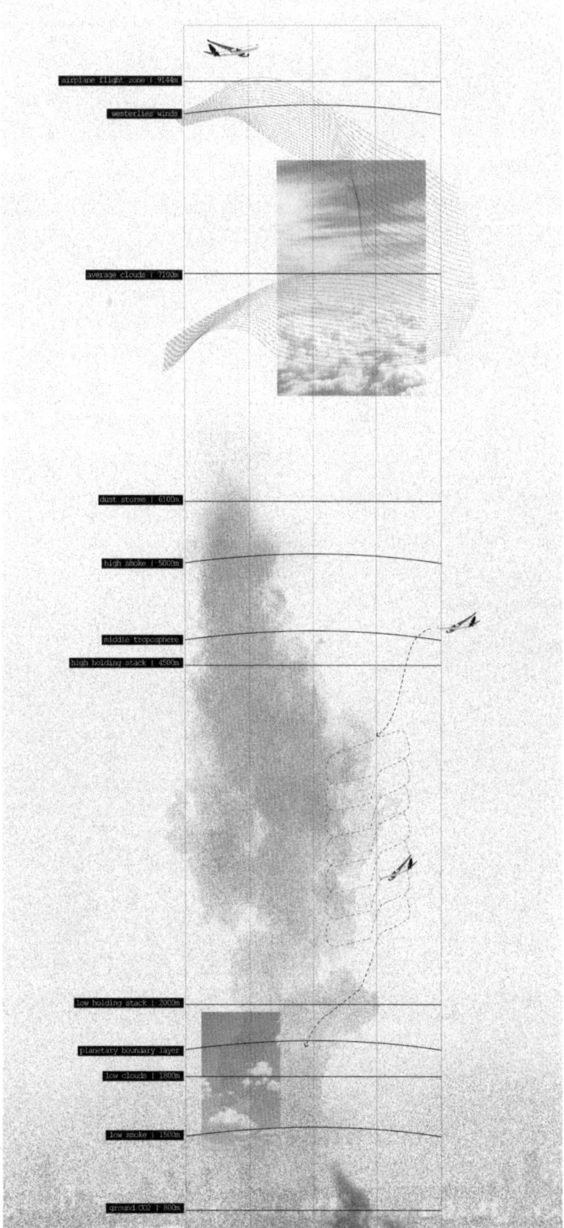

This thesis speculates on the landscapes of a post-Brexit world, where new environmental protection agencies have failed to settle and air quality regulations have been voided. As a result, a new thick atmosphere—composed of earthy particulate matter—is the new normal. By studying two sites at two different air stratas, "Airscapes" questions the difference between the emission and the dispersion of particulate matter and their impact.

This is the story of air becoming earth—where personal and political claims are scaled up to global environmental politics and scaled down to the politics of health.

Climate Change
Health
Territory
Thesis

How can we design a conversation around retreat and climate change?

Simon Escabi (MLA I AP), Carson Fisk-Vittori (MLA I), Camila Huber (MLA I AP, MAUD), McKenna Mitchell (MLA I)
Landscape Architecture III: Third Semester Core Studio
Instructor: Rosetta S. Elkin

As changing climate brings increasing instability to shoreline communities, the processes of retreat and rebuilding are becoming a more urgent reality. To where does a community retreat? How do neighborhoods and individuals decide when to leave? And to what extent do landscape architects facilitate the process of rebuilding?

This project addresses these questions by challenging current conservation practices and presenting an opportunity for the vulnerable island of Hull, Massachusetts, to move to the neighboring, unoccupied, and conserved land of World's End. World's End sits on higher ground, on a drumlin that was shaped by the geologic forces that produced Boston Harbor's characteristic islands. An alternative form

of conservation is proposed, asking conservation agencies to exchange their higher and unoccupied ground for threatened low-lying regions. The proposal is presented with an interactive hand-built display that intends to bring the community to the table for participation in design strategies for climate-induced community retreat. The result is a conversation that brings hope and imagination to the challenge of retreat.

How do we design a toolkit that starts a conversation about sexual harassment, gender-based discrimination, and protocols?

Carolina Sepúlveda (MDes ADPD) and Daniela Terán (MDE)
Spaces of Solidarity
Instructor: Malkit Shoshan

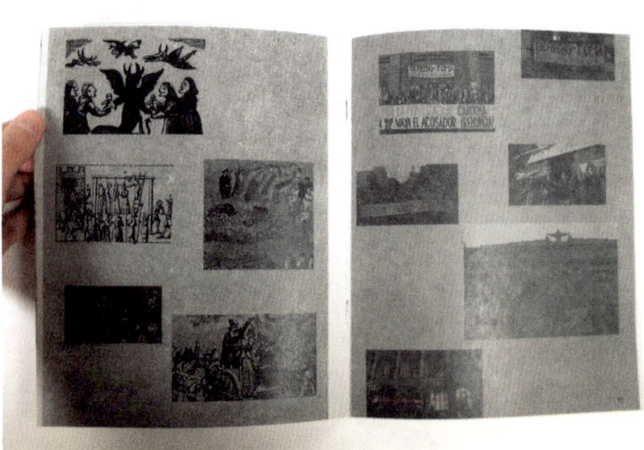

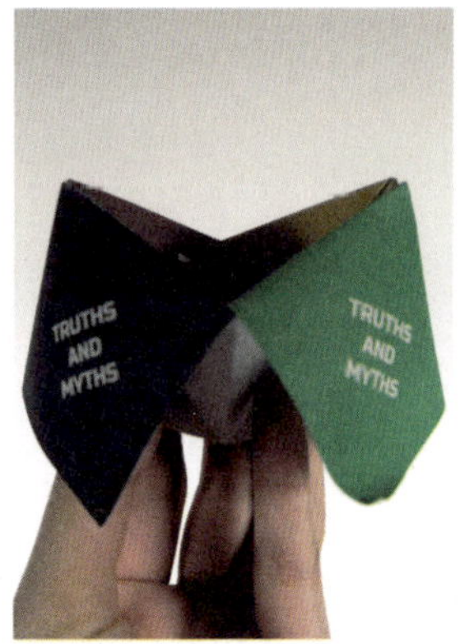

In 2018 a wave of feminist demonstrations in several countries and contexts denounced violence and sexual harassment toward women. These included the #MeToo movement in the United States and the #NiUnaMenos movement in Latin America. This wave not only exposed the ubiquity of gender violence, but also questioned educational institutions' protocols that protect women from sexual violence and harassment.

This project is an object-kit that provides tools to start a conversation about sexual harassment, gender-based discrimination, and associated protocols. This object is aimed at women's movements within educational institutions to learn how a protocol on sexual violence and harassment in schools and universities should be built.

Based on Chilean universities and Harvard's efforts, successes, and obstacles, the kit will propose simple ways to recreate safe spaces of conversation and exchange for clear petitions that can later become protocols, policies, or laws.

This kit can be used by communities that have not started a conversation about sexual harassment protocols, but may also be useful in contexts like the United States, where there are clear policies and a federal law—Title IX—but whose student organizations still need an easier, more interactive, and more compelling way to talk about these issues.

The purpose is not only to educate a community on the subject but also to provide tools that will allow policy-building to be an easy and straightforward matter, as policy-building needs to be followed by a process of negotiation and approval, and then by a process of teaching and promoting the new protocol.

How can we conceptualize and design spaces capable of promoting cultural diversity, social acceptance, and individual spontaneity?

Natalie Wang (MDes RR)
Experiments in Public Freedoms
Instructor: Sergio Lopez-Pineiro

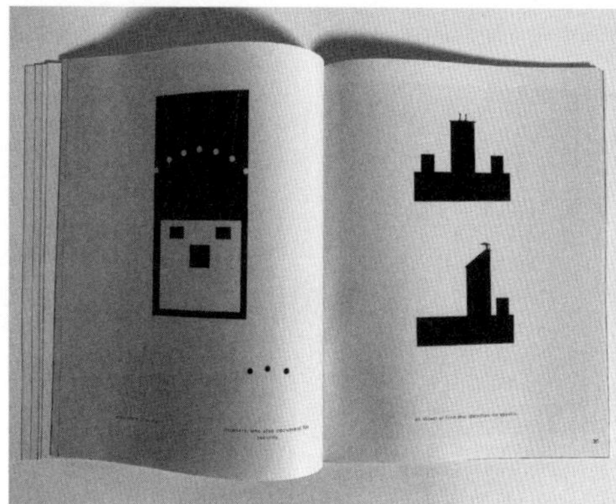

As part of a design theory seminar, Professor Sergio Lopez-Pineiro provided six provocative terms for students to engage while guided by a theme of the student's choice. The terms provided were "containment," "neutral," "blank," "normal," "anarchic," and "amnesia."

"PF:6" illustrates the unique qualities of spatial conditions from a range of different scales of design and design practices, all of which coalesce around the theme of political public freedoms—for it was difficult to separate the political nature of public freedoms whether they are implicit, explicit, or both.

Each case study includes an essay of analysis, graphics distilling essential design properties, and images of the public freedoms it afforded.

Through design analysis, "PF:6" surveys the infrastructure, strategy, and social conditions of Freedom Day in Selma, Alabama; the set of Cuban performing artist Tania Bruguera's *Tatlin's Whisper #6* (2009); the installation of *A Volume, within which it is Not Possible for Certain Classes to Arise* (2015) at the Institute of Contemporary Art by William Forsythe; the everyday qualities of church parking lots in the American South; the branding and communications strategy of "For Freedoms," an on- and offline creative civic engagement platform; and the indigenous and colonial relationships to the Pacific Ocean.

While each of these case studies may stand alone, their compilation as a book is meant to act as an accessible tool, for the designer and non-designer, to expose the political opportunities in design, art, and the public, and to further critical conversations.

How can design address toxic speech on the Internet?

Jenny Fan (MDE)
Independent Design Engineering Project
Advisors: Robert Pietrusko, Krzysztof Gajos (Harvard John A. Paulson School of Engineering and Applied Sciences), Amy X. Zhang (Massachusetts Institute of Technology)

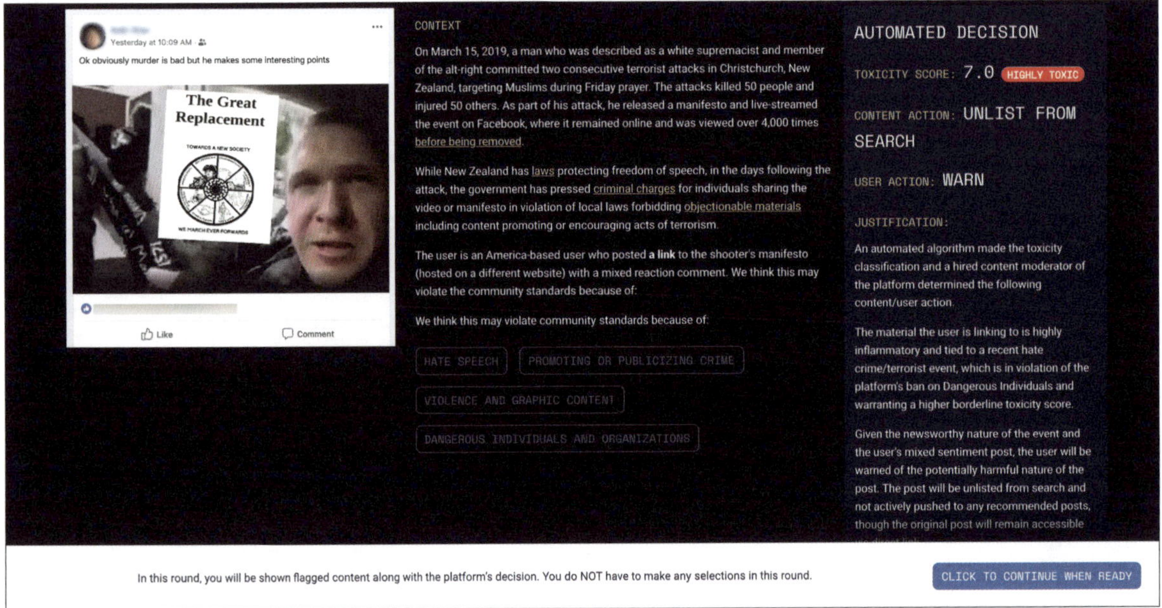

All votes are in! Below you can continue discussion, and you can also change your vote. Your changes are reflected in real-time above. Click Continue when you are ready to move on. CONTINUE

Doug I agree it is offensive and needs deleted
vs so deletion and a warning, right?
Doug yea I agree warning as well
a yeah and unlist
d p
a hello?
Post a public message

DRAG CURSOR TO SELECT TOXICITY SCORE: 9.50
WHAT ACTION (IF ANY) SHOULD THE PLATFORM TAKE ON THE CONTENT?
UNLIST FROM SEARCH | DELETE | REPORT TO AUTHORITIES
WHAT ACTION (IF ANY) SHOULD THE PLATFORM TAKE ON THE USER?
WARN | BAN FOR 1 WEEK | PERMANENTLY BAN

Increasing concerns about the harms of misinformation, dog-whistling, and hate speech that are spread on social media platforms cast new light upon the challenges of content moderation. In particular, large-scale platforms lack sociotechnical processes for users to contribute democratically on platform governance issues. This paper proposes "digital juries" as a civics-oriented, decision-making approach for adjudicating online content moderation questions at scale. Digital juries for content moderation draw inspiration from the constitutional jury system as a democratic, digital governance system. Building on existing theoretical models of jury decision-making, we outline a five-stage model characterizing the space of design considerations when developing a digital jury process. We conduct an experimental study of two prototype jury duty workflows involving blind voting and deliberation, comparing both to an automated decision. In our empirical analysis, we find that digital juries are perceived as being more procedurally just than the control on all attributes measured, with the exception of "effectiveness." Both jury conditions are ranked as being more preferable to the control, though there is a conflicting opinion on whether jury decisions should be enforced as-is or passed on to platforms as a recommendation. We conclude with a discussion on the feasibility and design criteria for such a jury system in moderating toxic speech at scale.

How can design address the illegibility of the U.S. benefits system?

Taylor Greenberg Goldy, Jacob Schonberger, Mengxi Tan, Mia Zaidan (all MDE)
Collaborative Design Engineering Studio II
Instructors: Sawako Kaijima and Jock Herron; Julia Lee and Arianna Mazzeo (Harvard John A. Paulson School of Engineering and Applied Sciences)

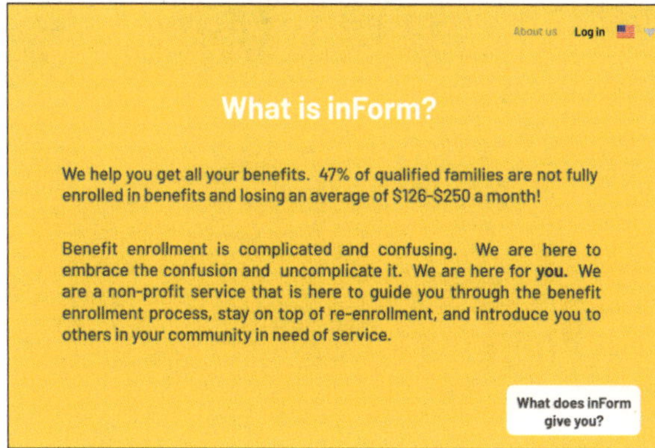

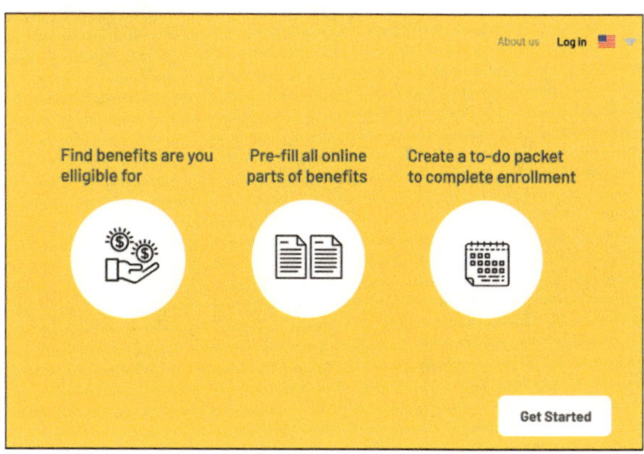

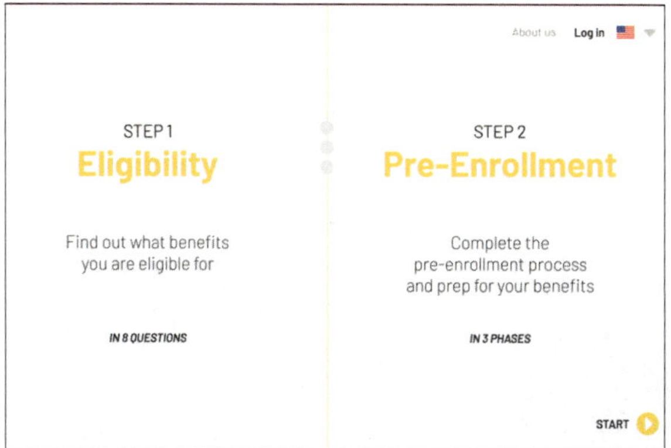

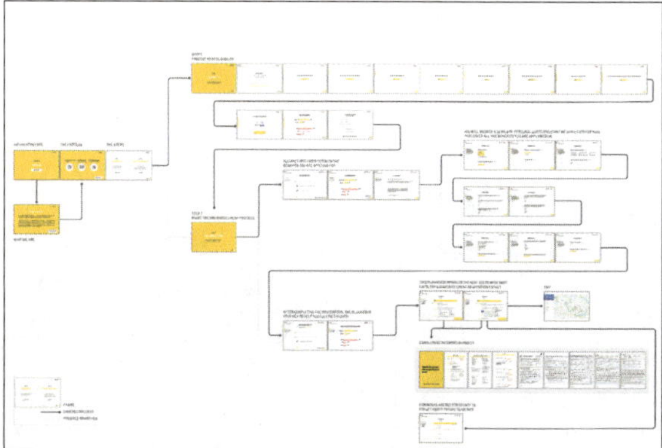

The United States benefits system exists to support the lives of thousands who struggle to provide for their families. The application process should be easy, but in reality, it requires a massive amount of research into exactly what one qualifies for, filling out complex forms, scheduling appointments, and locating the correct offices to seek. Twenty websites, 126 pages, and 67 hours later, you might end up receiving the benefits you qualify for. But it doesn't need to be this way: "inForm" is a website that serves as a platform for low-income benefits enrollment. This platform allows users to (A) learn about benefits they might be eligible for; (B) pre-populate all documents needed for the preenrollment stages; and (C) consult interview preparation guides and maps of locations where they can finish in-person enrollment.

Computation
Core Studio
Infrastructure
Justice

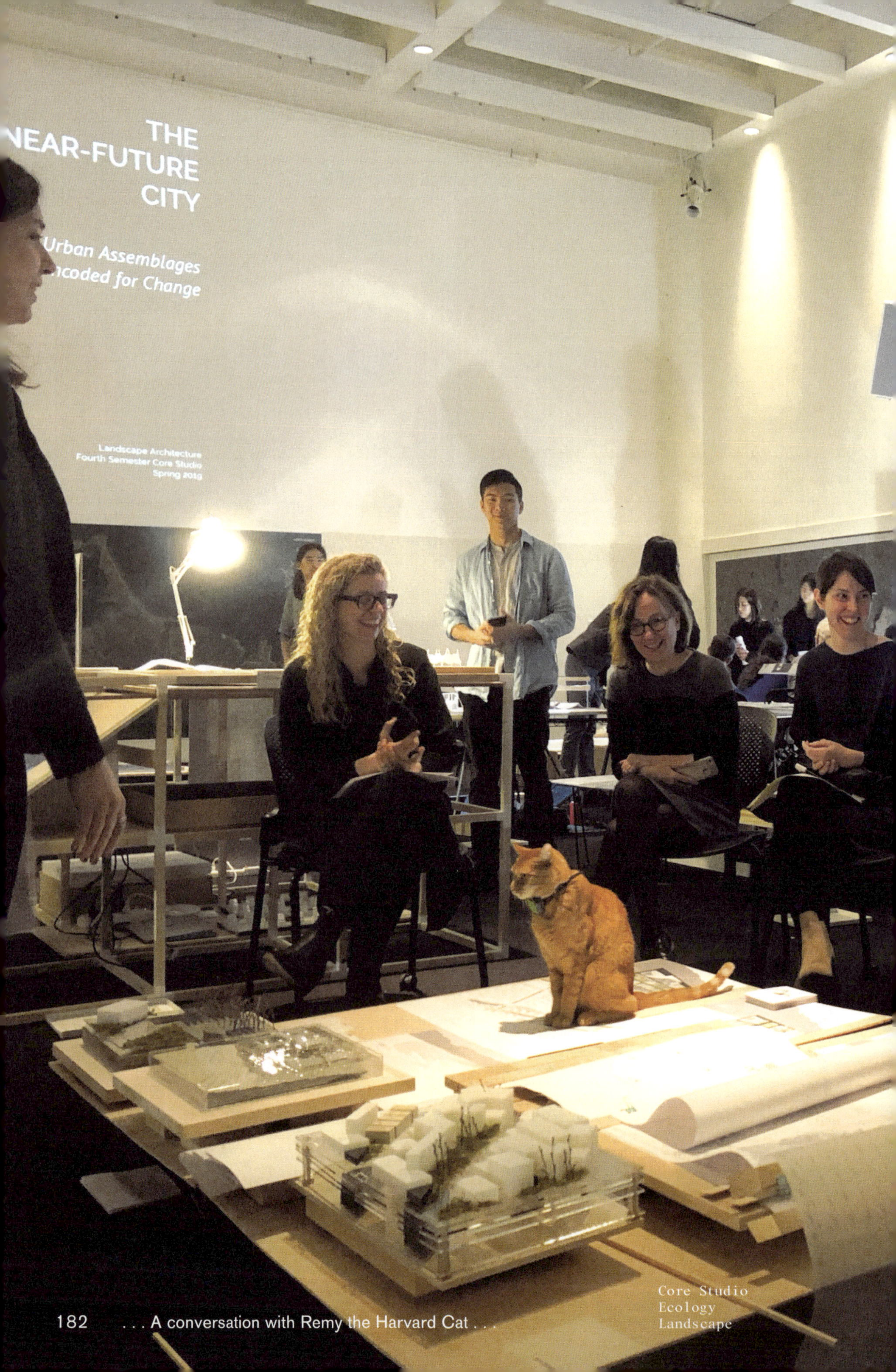

Core Studio
Ecology
Landscape

"Landscape Architecture Core Studio IV: Fourth Semester Core Studio," Final Review, Spring 2019

"Field Methods and Living Collections," Review at the Arnold Arboretum of Harvard University, Fall 2018

How does philanthropy shape the built environment, both urban and territorial alike?

Steven Austin Ward (MAUD)
Urban Design Thesis
Advisor: Rahul Mehrotra

"While philanthropy is a more competitive and fractured field, it is also potentially a more powerful force than at any other time in history."
–Justin W. Cook (2008)

Throughout the latter half of the 20th century, philanthropy emerged as a ubiquitous practice in the landscape of contemporary urban and territorial development—both as an institutional figure and as an infrastructural actor. The ascendancy of philanthropists of the Carnegie-Rockefeller generation has given way to new formations in contemporary civil society. Practices of strategic philanthropy and catalytic investment have signaled a shift in the landscape of philanthropic capital.[1] Philanthropy persists within the backdrop of increasing fiscal austerity by federal, state, and local scales of governance—which marks, as some scholars have suggested, the complete erosion of the public sector. The terrain of philanthropic action represents a network of institutional actors, strategic investment, and multi-sectoral coordination, which has to this point been given marginal scholarly attention outside the fields of education and business.[2] This thesis aims to interrogate engagements and practices of strategic philanthropy[3] in the production and formation of the built environment—to probe the intersectionality of processes, investments, and their spatial formations. Acknowledging that philanthropy is active in shaping the built environment, this thesis asks: How then does it define, create, and transform space, both urban and territorial alike? In order to study this tenuous relationship between philanthropic capital and urban formation, this research focuses on a singular case: the region of Northwest Arkansas, and the influence of the Walton Family Foundation. In so doing, this thesis interrogates the impacts of the visible products of philanthropy and expose the latent realities of what remains largely an invisible infrastructure in the process of urban formation.

1
See Mary Rocco, "Partnership, Philanthropy, and Innovation: 21st-Century Revitalization in Legacy Cities," Dissertation, Order No. 10134975, University of Pennsylvania, 2016.

2
Ibid., 11.

3
Peter Frumkin, *Strategic Giving: The Art and Science of Philanthropy* (Chicago: University of Chicago Press, 2006).

American City
Ownership
Philanthropy
Property
Thesis

Urban Formation: Northwest Arkansas.

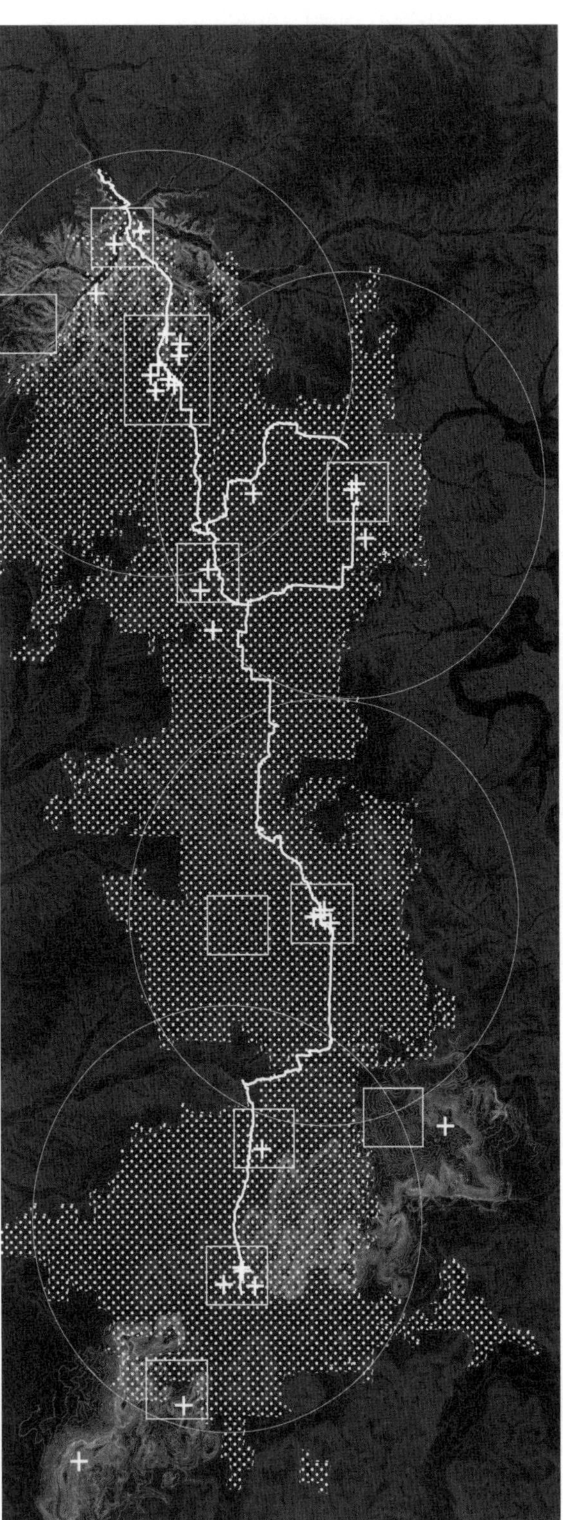
Philanthropic Infrastructure: Northwest Arkansas.

How can designers consider toys as a tool for expanding a child's spatial thinking and imagination?

Stella Rossikopoulou Pappa (MDes Tech)
Design Studies Thesis
Advisor: Allen Sayegh

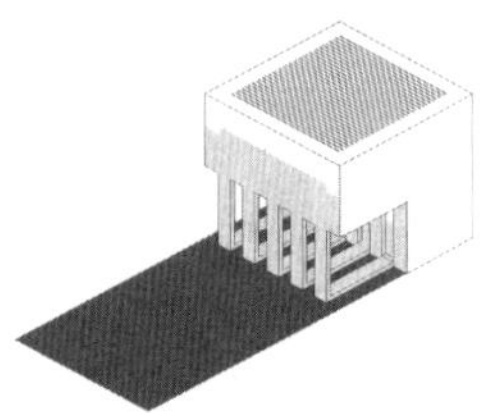
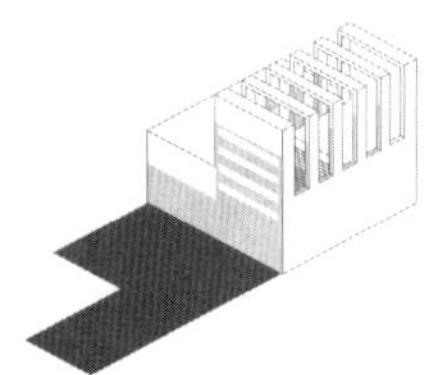
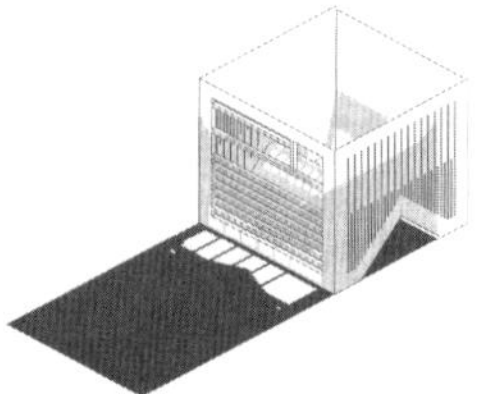
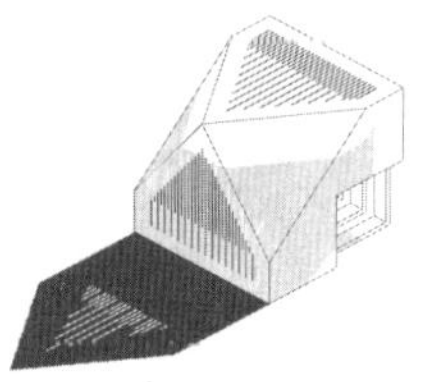
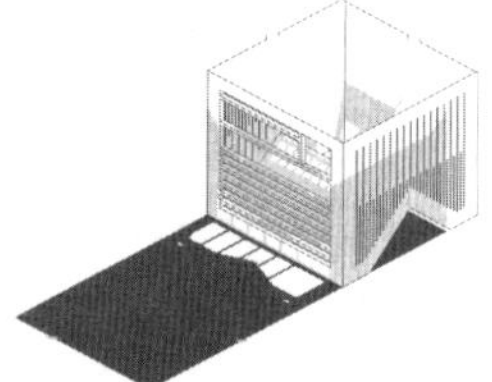
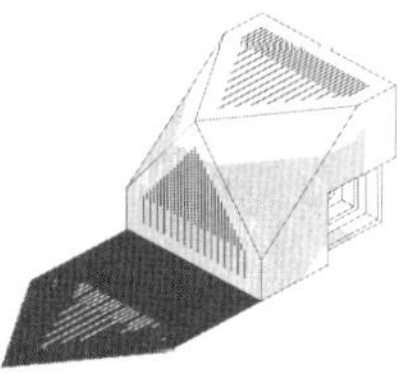

What constitutes the nature of children's toys today? "Dēmiourgós" is a construction-based toy for children that aims to bridge the gap between 2-D drawings and 3-D spatial relations through the use of algorithmic, interactive 2-D projection. The game requires children to draw shapes that are then scanned and processed in order to generate a 2-D projection of a series of simple physical blocks included with the game. The child then combines the physical blocks with the 2-D projection in order to discover connections between the shapes they have drawn and the physical blocks included with the game.

The primary goal of "Dēmiourgós" is to facilitate an ongoing interest in, and skill for, both spatial experimentation and transformational awareness in symbolic thinking by working

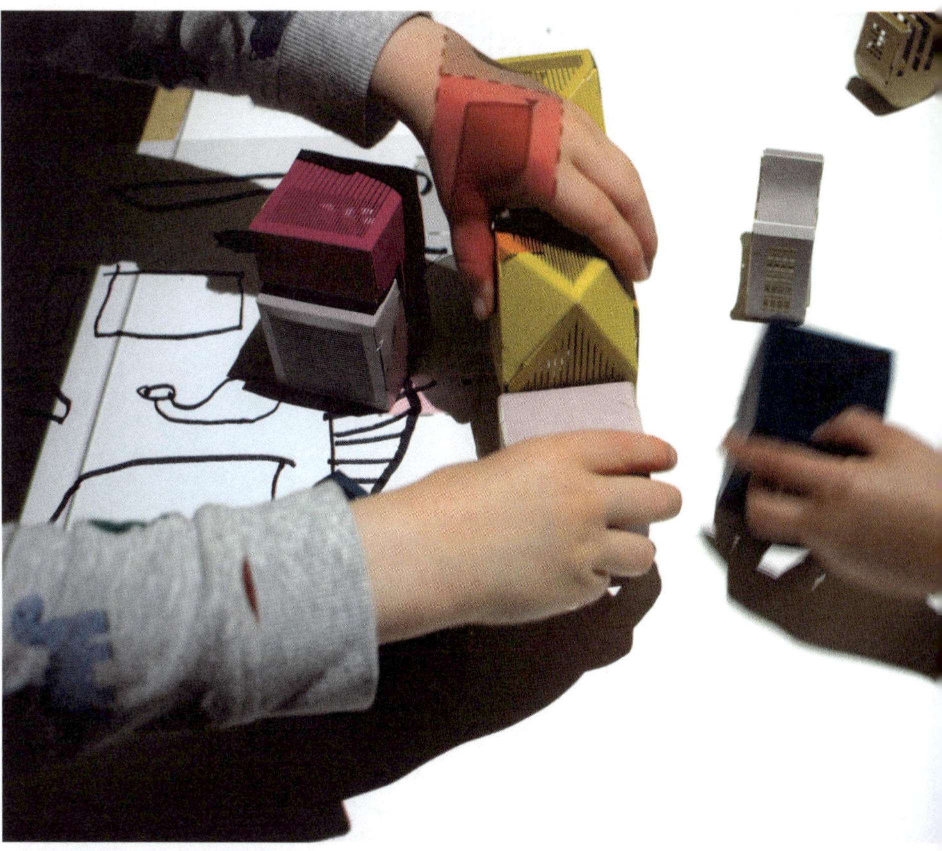

between two distinct forms of spatial thinking: two-dimensional and three-dimensional. In "Dēmiourgós," the toy is the process—not merely a static object or a predefined objective that, once completed, ends the game. This puts the child and their imagination at the center of the event of play. The result is a constant dialogue and feedback loop between the imagination of the child and the sorts of effects that imaginative thinking might have in the world. This invites the child to posit an idea and then respond to the consequences or effects of how that idea interacts with the world, but in a timeframe short enough to maintain the child's attention and interest.

What could emotional planning look like? How might it scaffold a climate relocation process?

Emily Duma (MUP), Emily Klein (MUP), Jana Pohorelsky (MPP)
Community Development: History, Theory, and Imaginative Practice
Instructor: Lily Song

What are dominant **planning responses** to climate crises?

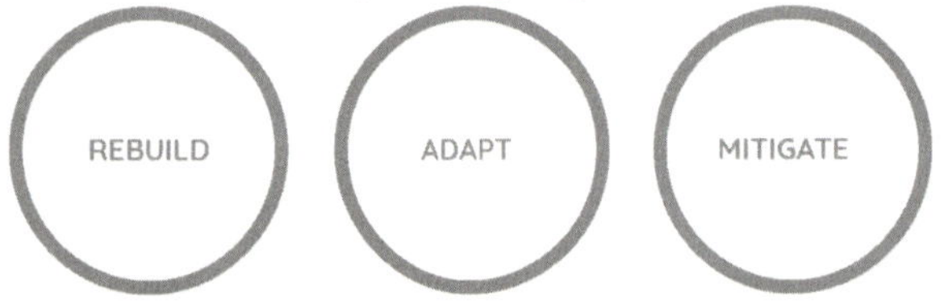

WHAT ABOUT RETREAT AND RELOCATION?

What are dominant **emotional responses** to climate crises?

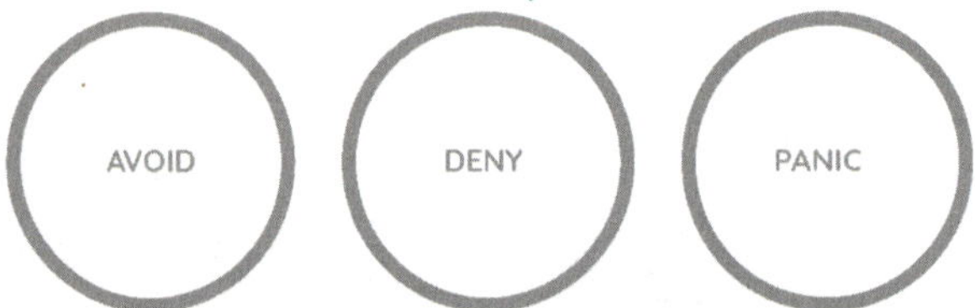

WHAT ABOUT GRIEF, MOURNING, AND OUR EMOTIONAL CONNECTION TO PLACE?

It is increasingly likely that humankind will need to adapt to a new environment in which certain places become uninhabitable. This adaptation is imminently demanded of coastal communities, who face dual risks of rising sea levels and increased frequency of destructive storms. While we know that spaces of home are sites of powerful emotional tethering and connection, the economic and emotional costs of rebuilding coastal communities may soon outweigh the benefits of staying. This project builds the case for retreat and relocation as tools in the arsenal of climate-focused community development, and particularly considers a planning framework that centers emotions.

As climate change makes places uninhabitable, how can proactive community-planning strategies help people and communities navigate grief, face the loss of their traditional homes, and relocate together? What could "emotional planning" look like? How might it scaffold a climate relocation process? To answer these questions, we reviewed literature on the environmental and emotional impacts of climate change, investigated precedents for planning with consideration of emotions, and examined ongoing and completed climate relocations. We synthesized these learnings into an emotionally sensitive planning process and framework that honors connection to place, incorporates space for communal grieving, and ultimately produces a plan for relocation that is driven by and responsive to community. Interwoven throughout our analysis is explicit consideration for how multiple supremacies manifest in the built and natural environments, and how they may obscure the path toward design justice within the context of climate change.

Climate Change
Empathy
Community
Seminar
Trauma

Framework for Emotional Planning

Community-led decision-making and timing

While it is important to acknowledge that many communities currently at climate risk may have no desire to relocate, and this decision should be respected, a proactive approach to relocation can reduce physical and emotional loss and benefit a community, and the design of the process should help to change hearts and minds. The ideal process should be led by community members, and on a time frame adaptive to their community needs. This may require extensive time for the community to arrive at the decision to relocate, and also requires that governmental policies and programmatic structures be nimble enough to respond to relocation requests when communities do decide to move.

Include practices for collective mourning by incorporating ceremony, celebration, and ritual

In order to emotionally honor the place that the community is leaving behind, it is necessary for community members to undertake a grieving process together, which may lead to a better collective imagination of a future on new land. A community may consider grieving in a public and communal way: by allowing for the full experience of sadness and mourning, and celebrating the place they are departing in preparation for affirming life in a new one. The formulation of such traditions should be consistent with the local social and cultural context.

Use storytelling as a tool for collective feeling; weave a community story of the relocation process

Storytelling is a powerful tool for collective processing. Storytelling and documentation practices could be used to record real experiences of pain and loss in the relocation process, as well as the ways such relocation has enabled community vibrancy and resiliency.

Memorialize the places that people are leaving, and consider the right to return

The community should think through ways their old place can be memorialized, who can return, if/when that can happen, and how. There may be physical limitations, but the ability to personally visit places with emotional significance can aid in the healing process.

Preserve livelihoods, community fabric, and economic opportunity

Successful past relocations have intentionally approached the economic and physical components that can be preserved through the move. Often, people's vocations are site-specific, and relocation may disrupt their ability to continue to sustain their livelihoods. Whenever possible, relocation sites should seek to mirror positive economic characteristics of the existing community, and investments should be made to enable economic activity in the new site.

Collective mourning to collective action

It is important to consider that collective grieving can also give way to collective mobilization. Similar to the Black Lives Matter movement, which is mobilized by collective mourning rather than through a leader or figurehead, it may be possible to collectively mourn the loss of place to spur collective action toward a more environmentally sustainable future.

What are the stories held in the soils in our front- and backyards, in the plants that feed us, in the waters that sustain us?

Katie Gourley (MUP)
Urban Planning Thesis
Advisor: Lily Song

Quotes and dialogue are from the following interviews with seed savers and seed library managers:
David, January 12, 2019;
Neil, January 9, 2019;
Sara, January 5, 2019;
Minna, January 8, 2019; and
Maya, February 20, 2019.

Humans have sowed, saved, and shared seeds for millennia. Maintaining relationships with seeds allows food growers to influence yield, taste, and nutrition, as well as adapt to uncertain and changing climatic conditions. Yet, in the last half-century, legal and policy regimes of biotechnology, intellectual property rights, and corporate consolidation have threatened rights and freedoms to save seeds, and the knowledge of how to do so. In turn, resistance efforts seeking to get seeds into the hands of the people and protect the ability to grow out and save open-pollinated, heirloom seeds through living conservation practices (in situ conservation) have sprouted up from the global to hyper-local scales.

With emphasis placed on the need for scholarship to make uncompensated acts of care visible and to foreground non-dominant worldviews, this thesis explores particular trends in community seed-saving and the seed sovereignty movement in North America through the lens of feminist political ecology. This multi-site case study of public seed libraries in the San Francisco Bay Area investigates seed-saving as a material and discursive practice of place-based socioecological care, as well as public libraries as sites of alternative sharing economies.

Ultimately, seed-saving can be seen as an antithesis to commodification of place, hyper-individualism, and the human will to dominate nature. It is an example of communities building lived examples of other worlds and suggests a significant contribution to feminist understandings of post-capitalist, care-centric, and eco-centric modes of living. Many seed-savers reject the notion that private property logics can be extended to seeds. They express a belief that seeds should not and cannot be owned by anyone, but rather belong in the public commons. As Neil remarked: "It is important to recognize seeds, like other resources, are things that don't belong to any one person. Same as land, air, and water." Sara also asserted that this belief is what motivates her work to grow and share seeds for her community: "We believe that seed is part of the commons. This quinoa is not something that I grew and is mine. This quinoa goes back 7,000 years and was developed by people in Peru and Bolivia. It's not something I have any right to own."

Therefore, one significant conceptual contribution of seed-saving is the way it can stoke imagination for post-capitalist and post-growth modes of governance. Seed sovereignty advocates commonly express a belief that their practice is a way to reclaim community control and take power away from corporations. David noted, "Seed-saving is devoid of feeding into consumer capitalism. With seeds, you can grow more food for yourself and your family and your community. Seed-saving can be a revolutionary act, if even just for a moment." These sentiments gesture towards the political economic implications of seed-saving. Minna articulated a particular awareness the direct ways that seed-saving challenges hegemonic Western economic assumptions and practices: "All of the things capitalism does—exploiting the planet, exploiting labor, forcing things into the cash economy—seed-saving is literally the opposite of all of that. It is about

Colonialism
Empathy
Food
Indigeneity
Thesis

sustenance. You are also actually regenerating the environment. It stands counter to the tenets that make up the profit structures of capitalism." This suggests the link between seed-based acts of care and radical economic reconfiguration.

The acts of seed-saving also present a challenge to temporal binaries upheld by Western rationalist ideologies. By keeping seed alive and continuously grown out in a community, a grower is not just caring for the people alive now, they are also expressing care for the people who came before them and honoring the past steward who grew and saved those seeds, ensuring survival and adaptation. Within their respect for the past, however, is interwoven considerations of futurity, expressing care for future generations by working to protect important food crops and to mitigate climate change. In this way, seed-saving instills a felt responsibility to be both a good descendant and a good ancestor.[1]

Revitalizing traditional gardening methods and knowledge reframes a conversation about sustainability to better involve recognition of that past. As Maya explained: "I have spent a lot of time in food justice and urban agriculture, and the definition or framing of sustainability is always lacking in those spaces because it never embeds it in the past. This is what our work is about. Re-embedding sustainability in traditional and generational knowledge." The blurring of temporal binaries allows for a conception of sustainability that becomes rooted in the past. This requires a new understanding of the past as not static, "primitive," or unevolved, but rather, fluid, ever-changing, and living.

Maya further explained how seed-saving practices require us to hold space for this nuance: "Especially in native communities, in both seed-saving and any other aspect of cultural revitalization, this tension exists. It is about the balance of connecting to the past while understanding that we are a living culture that adapts. It is this adaptability and resilience that got us here not. When seed-saving is a living practice, not like the Svalbard seed vault, you are taking that seed memory and allowing it to continue to create new memories and new opportunities to adapt and best be resilient. That takes constant experience. That constant experience comes from growing out the seed every year in every condition." Here we see how seed-saving as place-based socioecological care blurs the often pejorative conceptual lines drawn between the past and the present and contributes to a more radical understanding of its role as practice of counter hegemonic resistance.

With stories such as these, this thesis provides a brief glimpse into the world of community seed-saving to illuminate everyday struggles and resistance against systems of control and manipulation in the capitalist food system. Our contemporary era is defined by multi-scalar environmental and social crises. These crises are deeply interwoven with an industrial agro-food system built on dominance and exploitation. It is important to consider how can we choose to pursue place-based community-making efforts which support culturally sensitive policies and projects[2] and which promote inter-cultural, inter-species alliances. We do not have to—nor can we—accept the food system for what it is any longer. We can choose to redefine a care-based ecological economy with the capacity to protect and preserve our collective biodiversity and cultural liberation. The stories presented here suggest that seed-saving and sharing—within and across place-based communities—can stoke transformative imaginations, spur collective action, and nurture hope for dealing with the multiple crises and injustices perpetuated by the industrial agro-food system through enacting an ecological-economy of care. It starts with a seed, mind you.

1
The phrase, "be a good ancestor," is deployed in many social justice spaces, and is often attributed to Marian Wright Edelman who founded the children's defense fund.

2
Tirso Gonzales, ed., "Sense of Place and Indigenous People's Biodiversity Conservation in the Americas," *Seeds of Resistance, Seeds of Hope: Place and Agency in the Conservation of Biodiversity* (Tuscon: The University of Arizona Press, 2013), 85–106.

How can food shape the landscapes we inhabit?

Christina Graydon (MArch I AP) and Olivia Hansberg (MUP)
The Landscape We Eat
Instructor: Montserrat Bonvehi Rosich

This project examines the anchovy in relationship to its geomorphology, natural ecosystem, and historical and economic character as a local and global food product. This study compares two ports considered optimal for the anchovy: Saint-Louis-du-Rhône, France, which fishes the anchovy in an industrial manner, and Kalaat el Andalous, Tunisia, which carries out its fishing in a much more traditional and local scale.

The initial exploration was an investigation into how each landscape provided exceptional conditions for the anchovy. The next explored how the anchovy, and the methods of fishing and farming, influenced those landscape conditions. Today, the anchovy trade is part of a globalized production and consumption system that is variable and inconstant, generating a constant variation in the world price of anchovy.

Agriculture
Economy
Food
Representation
Seminar

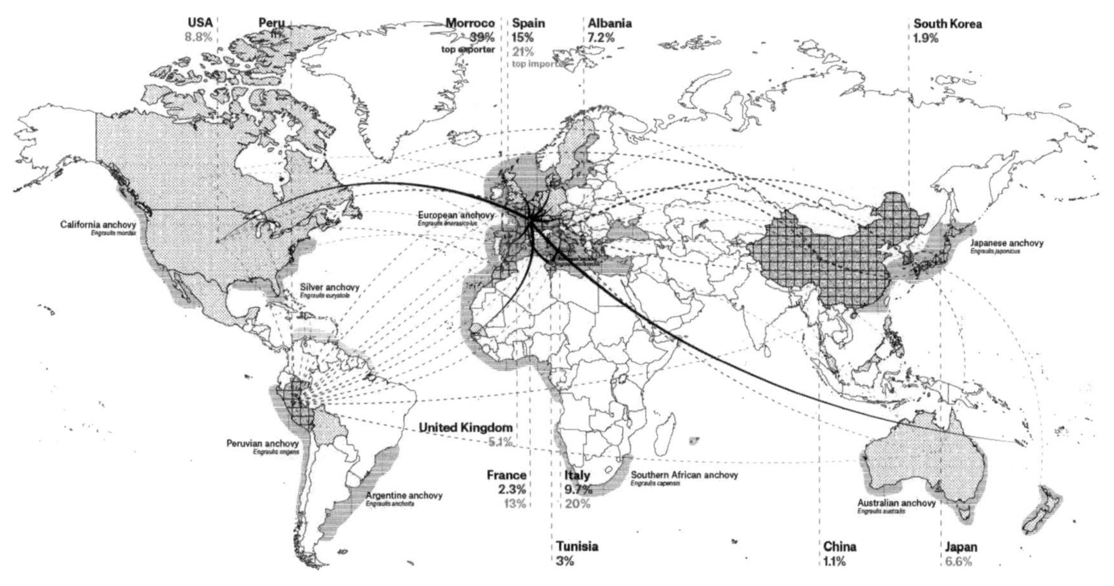
USA
8.8%
Peru
Morroco
39%
top exporter
Spain
15%
21%
Albania
7.2%
South Korea
1.9%
California anchovy
Engraulis mordax
European anchovy
Silver anchovy
Engraulis eurystole
Japanese anchovy
Engraulis japonicus
Peruvian anchovy
Engraulis ringens
United Kingdom
5.1%
Argentine anchovy
Engraulis anchoita
France
2.3%
13%
Italy
9.7%
20%
Southern African anchovy
Engraulis capensis
Australian anchovy
Engraulis australis
Tunisia
3%
China
1.1%
Japan
6.6%

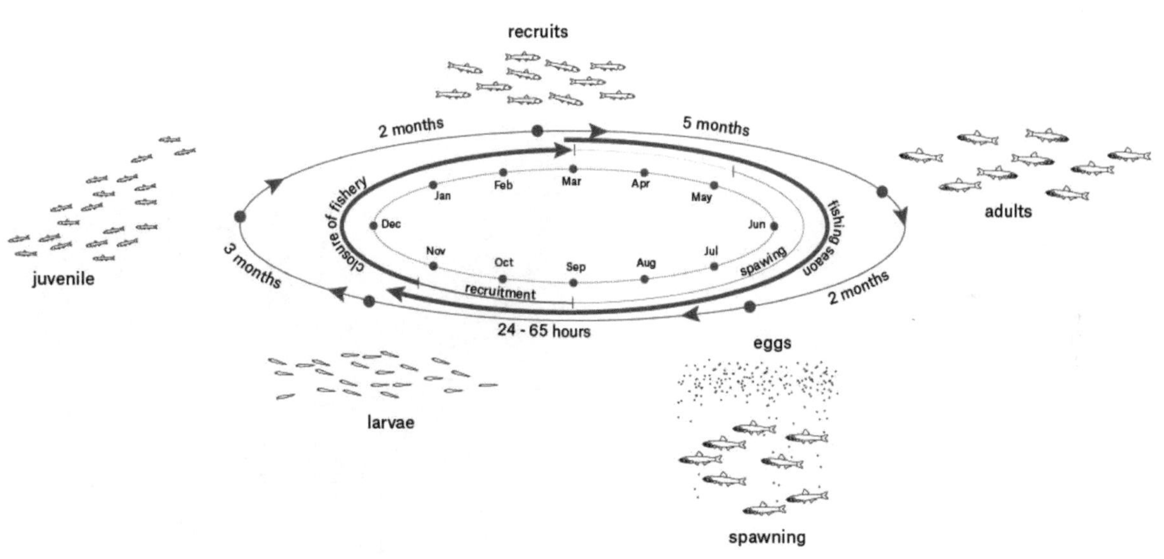
recruits
2 months
5 months
adults
juvenile
closure of fishery
fishing season
spawing
recruitment
Jan
Feb
Mar
Apr
May
Jun
Jul
Aug
Sep
Oct
Nov
Dec
3 months
2 months
24 - 65 hours
eggs
larvae
spawning

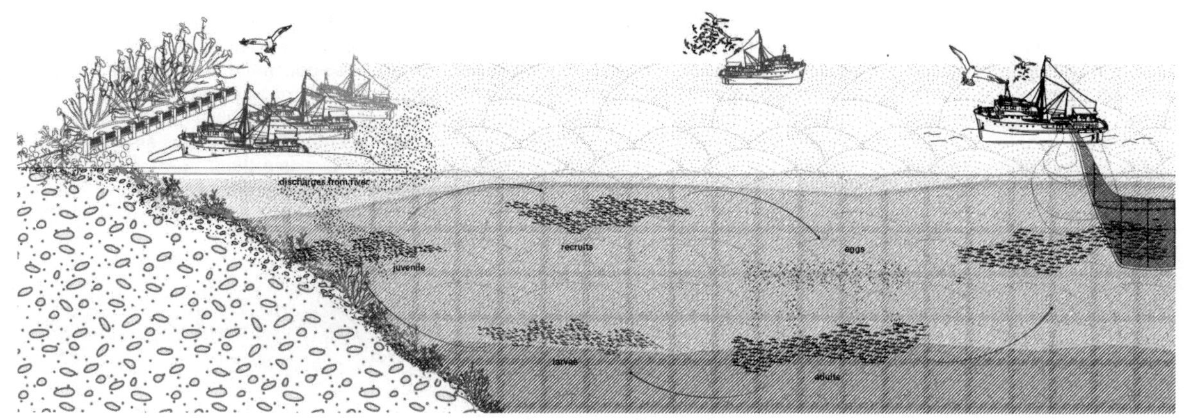
discharges from river
recruits
eggs
juvenile
larvae
adults

How can a more empathic form of representation make visible the links between climate change, resource scarcity, and migration?

Tessa Crespo (MDes RR)
Experimental Infrastructures
Instructor: Abby Spinak

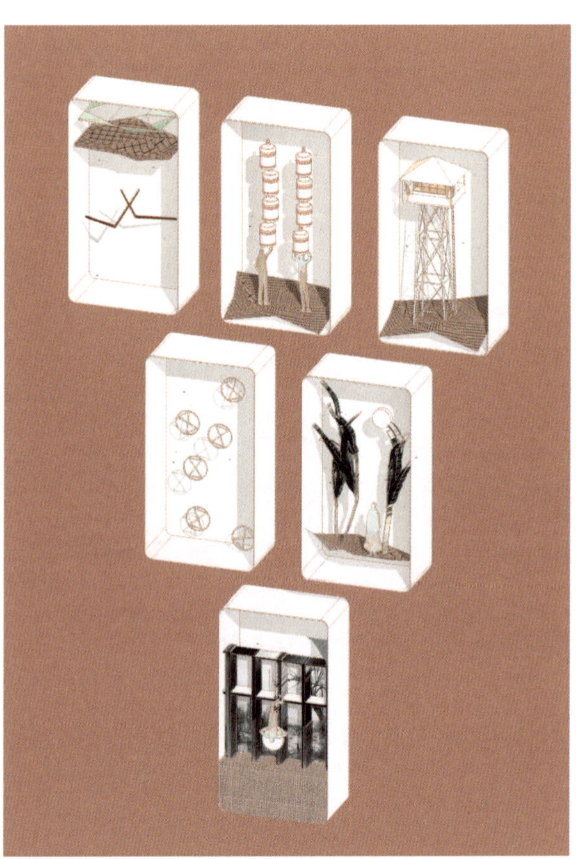

As an experimental infrastructure, I reimagined the classic archetypes of tarot as a means to reconstitute the human condition and our perceptions of boundary and territory. This required a reexamining of our understanding of being as well as challenging the constructed myths of scarcity and abundance that justify violence toward both human and nonhuman entities in modern societies. For this project, I reinterpreted a six-card spread for our collective climate, where we can look to tarot not as a fortune-telling device, but rather a conduit between unconsciousness and consciousness. I believe that alternative modes of representation could empower the disenfranchised and lead to new forms of legitimacy. Acknowledging that neither frameworks nor facts are static, but are rather continuously being reconstituted, may lead to a form of representation that is more event-based than object-based. Understanding symbols, such as the border wall, as a phenomenon rather than an object will help us think outside the constraints of geographic space to speculate alternative realities or ways of seeing. Experiences constitute our understanding of the world, yet many of the hard sciences avoid the experiential as a legitimate form of knowledge. For this project, I was interested in the idea of tarot as an alternative technocratic device that subverts orthodox projection methods and furthermore questions how an empathic form of representation could make visible the links between climate change, resource scarcity, and migration.

THE HANGED MAN

The Hanged Man depicts a figure suspended from the border wall - their right foot bound, the left leg free, bent at the knee and tucked behind their right. Arms crossed behind the back, halo around their head. A symbol of insight, awareness, and enlightenment.

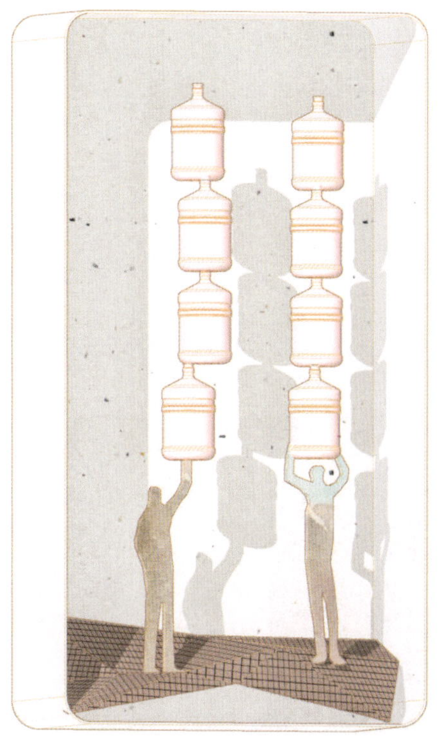

VIII OF CUPS

The 8 of Cups depicts two figures precariously balancing jugs of water, symbolizing water scarcity due to global shortages and lack of adequate infrastructure. The United Nations Convention to Combat Desertification predicts that by 2025, 1.8 billion people will experience absolute water scarcity, and 2/3 of the world will be living under water-stressed conditions (9). Alternative irrigation and distribution systems need to be imagined if we are to mitigate these risks.

VI OF PENTACLES

The pentacles represent the onset of the Holocene -- the 6th mass extinction period on earth -- with the highest rate of species die off since the loss of dinosaurs (14). Although extinction is a natural phenomenon, it occurs at a natural "background" rate of about one to five species per year (14). Scientists estimate we're now losing species at 1,000 to 10,000 times the background rate -- this means dozens are going extinct every day (15).

THE TOWER

This card depicts a fire lookout perched above a forest with a single figure keeping watch. In the context of recent record wildfires, and specifically the Camp Fire, it is underscoring the impact of slow disasters (land degradation) versus fast disasters (wildfires) that can be attributed to climate change, and the different ways their timescales occupy our imaginations. Within the practice of tarot, the tower represents ambitions and goals made on false pretenses, and in this interpretation the fire represents insight that (hopefully) leads to a revelation (12).

“Where then would you place ‘history’ in the education of an architect?” [. . .] “There has been a lot of talk lately about the New Economy, new modes of production, and virtual reality. How much are these things ‘new beginning’? How are we to interpret all this?”

Editors of *Gamut*, “Interview with Eduard Sekler,” *Gamut* (Spring 2000), 22–23.

How is landscape practice simultaneous with memory practice?

Sarah Diamond (MLA I)
Landscape Architecture Thesis
Advisors: Emily Wettstein and Edward Eigen

"Her Home" is a project about representation, memory, and maintenance as landscape practice, and it designs a way of seeing the landscape to remember Gramma. Gramma is the subject: her place in the world, memories of her, her memories, her sense of herself. Gramma has no tomb. The material of her being continues to exist in the form of the place she was. Representation of this place is the process by which she is remembered. "Her Home" follows the arguments of scholars like Edward Casey, John Berger, and Doreen Massey to assert that landscape—and memory—exist only through some form of representation, especially, in this case, representation as remembering and representation as maintenance process: (A) Representation is a spatial practice. Through practice, an idea is manifested in material, in space. (B) Remembering is a spatial

Herstory
Identity
Maintenance
Memory

practice. Memories, like landscapes, can be actively maintained, nurtured, and evolved through material operations, which are representational. (C) Remembering is an act of maintenance and simultaneously an act of representation. Thus, representation is a maintenance of memory and landscape.

Representation of time-space, often imagined as four dimensions of related units, becomes representation of memory-landscape—numerous dimensions of varying and fluid values. The oil paintings are the land as I remember it, but also as it has been described to me by others, as I imagine Gramma saw it, and as it could be in the future. Painting is the classical method for representing the memory-landscape relationship as it involves the layering of material to create tonal variations. This tonality expresses the material and spatial qualities of the

From Fall of 1999 – Fall of 2016, she lived here alone.
Not isolated, surrounded by life, memories, + friends. 160
→ ALL EMBEDDED IN THE PLACE 205

landscape, all filtered through memory. The ground itself is variable, but the ideas, the imagined, are represented. The paintings are a highly mediated act of maintenance as both material and projective practice and a material manifestation of memory. Memories are constructed, and they make meaning. Thus, to maintain memories is to construct meaning.

This maintenance manual is the representation of the memory-landscape maintenance process. The manual itself is a representation of memory and a method for maintaining memory. The manual is premised on the tension between the personal and the structural or abstract. The construction (and representation) of identity and place exists in that tension.

How do designers inscribe social, political, and culture histories into the objects they make?

Jiho Sejung Song (MArch II)
14 Things (A Secret History of Italian Design)
Instructor: Jeffrey Schnapp

The project approaches the 20th-century Italian design history from an aesthetic, historical, and socio-anthropological point of view. "Passeggino Beluga / Beluga Stroller" is the fictional baby stroller manufactured by Piaggio during the 1950s global baby boom.

In the fictional design narrative, the 1953 film, *Roman Holiday*, first featured "Passeggino Beluga" in its alternate ending scene. The product was as successful as a Vespa scooter in a market, and quickly became an iconic object for the fun and liberated lifestyle of young families in the postwar era.

Fabrication
History
Play
Seminar

For designers, what has been inherited through the terms 'site' and 'shelter'?

Charlotte Leib (MLA I, MDes HPDM)
Design Studies Thesis
Advisor: Sonja Dümpelmann
Recipient of the 2018–2019 Best Paper on Housing Prize from the Joint Center for Housing Studies

An excerpt from the introductory text of "Site and Shelter: Design for the 'Whole Landscape'"

"Fair housing." "Better homes for all." "Shelter."[1] These were the calls for reform being aired in the United States during the 1920s and '30s in response to a massive housing shortage—and now Walter Gropius and Martin Wagner, who had worked to improve the quality and quantity of housing in Weimar Germany, were confronted with the challenge of finding shelter and stability in their adopted home country. Though the architects-in-exile experienced a kind of homelessness different from that of the farmer displaced by the Dust Bowl, or of the tenement resident evicted for failure to pay rent, they shared the same general problem: how to secure shelter and locate a sense of belonging in an increasingly mobile, mechanized, and volatile world.

For Wagner, the ramifications of the machine age and total war demanded not only "total architecture" as outlined by his colleague Gropius, but also design for the "whole landscape." Wagner invoked this phrase repeatedly in his lectures for "Site and Shelter," a course he taught at the Harvard GSD from 1939 to 1941.[2] Wagner's course and "whole landscape" idea is situated within a broader transatlantic discourse that developed during the 1930s and '40s concerning the terms "site" and "shelter," arguing that during these years, many architects, landscape architects, and planners began to see their work as part of an interconnected, holistic system. As designers developed rational approaches to regional planning and aimed to solve the housing shortage by standardizing building construction into component parts, they simultaneously conceptualized living environments as irreducible wholes.

Recognizing that defining the designer's task in terms of "site" and "shelter" aided in this epistemological shift, this thesis begins by tracing how these terms gained currency in modernist architectural circles during the first decades of the 20th century. It then considers how Gropius and Wagner furthered the site and shelter discourse through their teaching and practice in the United States, first working together and then splitting ways as they developed their "total architecture" and "whole landscape" concepts. The final section of the thesis examines how several of Gropius and Wagner's students went on to create the non-profit "Site and Shelter Corporation" in 1950 to experiment with the communitarian and proto-ecological housing design ideals that they had learned in Gropius's design studios and Wagner's eponymous course. By examining the synthesis of site and shelter in discourse, teaching, and practice, this thesis aims to contribute to the small but growing body of scholarship that attends to the political, environmental, pedagogic, and interdisciplinary aspects of modernist building projects that have been overlooked or glossed in scholarship focused more exclusively on their formal and aesthetic qualities.

1
See, for example, *Guidebook for Better Homes Campaigns in Rural Communities and Small Towns; Guidebook for Better Homes Campaigns in Cities and Towns,* (Washington DC: Better Homes in America, 1927); and Simon Breines,"The Emergencies: Structural Study Associates' Emergency Shelter Plan. Part I" *Shelter* 2, no. 4 (May 1932): 18–23.

2
Official Registers of Harvard University and Harvard Graduate School of Design Summer School Bulletins (1938–41), Special Collections, Frances Loeb Library, Harvard University, Rare Ref H261f v1.

For Wagner, the ramifications of the machine age and total war demanded not only "total architecture" as outlined by his colleague Gropius, but also design for the "whole landscape."

How can revisiting Bauhaus principles continue to change our relationship to space and architecture?

Entanglement of Movement and Meaning: The Architect, Spatial Perception, and the Technological Body
Instructors: Krzysztof Wodiczko and Ani Liu

Marking the 100th anniversary of the Bauhaus School of Design, this special seminar-workshop continued the historic work of painter, sculptor, designer, and choreographer Oskar Schlemmer, and invited students to investigate the body as a medium for design. This seminar examined how contemporary technologies and scientific discourse surrounding the body, the mind, and perception can change our relationship to space and architecture. Integrating design, fabrication, movement, and performance, the course explored new bodily and spatial interfaces and culminated in a public performance at the Harvard GSD for the Harvard Art Museums in celebration of the Bauhaus.

What can non-linear documentation methods reveal?

Nicolás Delgado Álcega (MArch II), Inés Benítez (MDes ADPD),
Mariel Collard (MLA I AP, MDes ULE)
Field Methods and Living Collections
Instructor: Rosetta S. Elkin

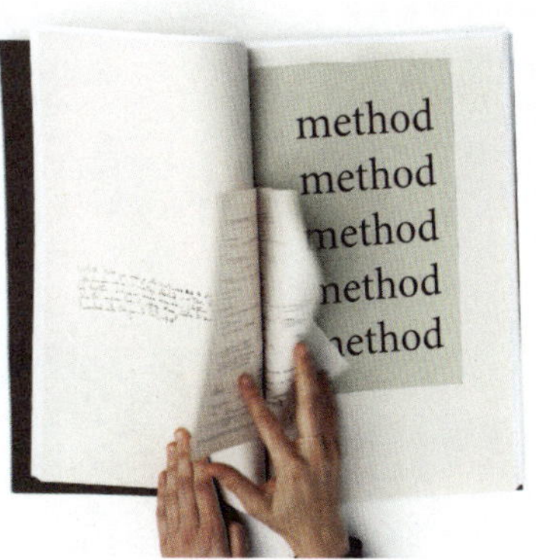

This book reveals a non-linear path where experiences, ideas, questions, methods, and answers emerge seemingly out of order, concurrently through a process of back-and-forth. Rather than organize the documents as one would in an archive, they are arranged like one would a journal. The aim has been to collect the work in a way that allows for constant questioning of the way we truly arrived at a conclusion—not chronologically or through the application of standardized procedures independent of the questions. "For Holly" represents relevant references, encounters, and exercises—if not in their entirety, at least one-to-one scale. It seeks to communicate the value of working in the field, with specimens rather than categories, paying attention to what can be perceived and understood then and there before resorting to cameras, microscopes, or model spaces.

Archive
Ecology
Plants
Seminar

How does a significant change to the landscape—the death of the olive tree—affect the community and culture intertwined with it?

Danica Liongson (MLA I, MDes ULE)
Landscape Architecture Thesis
Advisor: Montserrat Bonvehi Rosich

The cultivated olive tree, *Olea europaea*, has thrived for millennia, yet now it is a victim of its own prosperity. What was once a sacred object has been commodified in the global market, and along with it came spatial consequences in the form of olive tree plantations. The emphasis on speed and efficiency in this agricultural landscape has fostered the conditions for "olive quick-decline syndrome" to spread. Desiccating trees and devastating orchards in the Italian province of Puglia, the blight is the catalyst for significant landscape change. This thesis contemplates not only the olive tree, but also the medium in which it grows. Using the olive tree as a point of entry into the landscape, this project calls for an alternative model of land-based management with the construction of a territorial common in Puglia. The common would be dedicated to the care and renewal of an undervalued, overlooked resource: the soil.

A framework of ecological succession relies on site-scale strategies to build soil layers, introduce new plants into the monocultural groves, and provide opportunities for human and animal cohabitation. To build a territorial common for soil-building is to serve the interests of the environment and of future generations. As such, this eulogy is not only a celebration of the olive tree as a symbol of people's relationship with the environment in the Mediterranean cultural sphere, it is also a call to engender a new attitude, to envision a different system to work within, and to reorganize the landscape.

Agriculture
Ecology
Economy
Public Space
Thesis

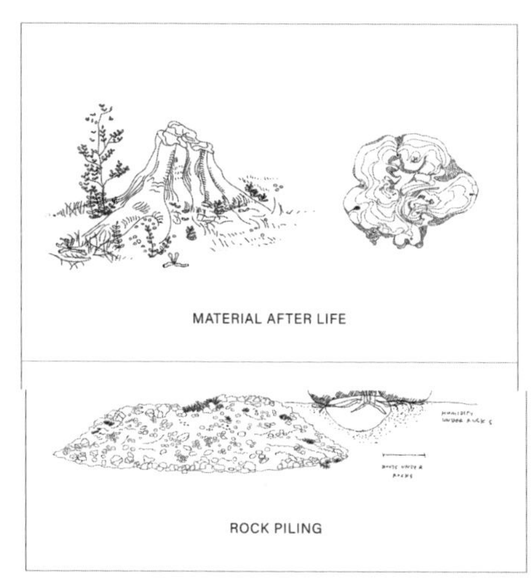
MATERIAL AFTER LIFE
ROCK PILING

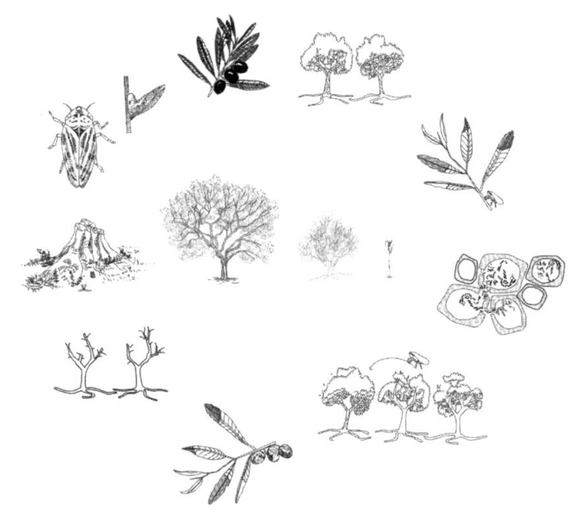

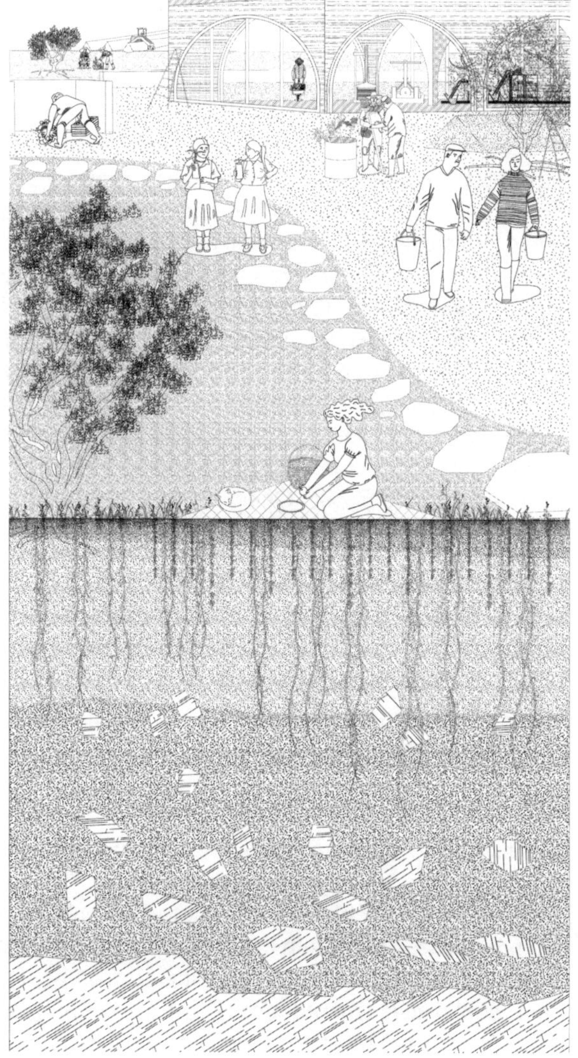

What are the afterlives of orbital infrastructures?

Rajji Sanjay Desai (MDes ULE)
Design Studies Thesis
Advisor: Neil Brenner

At present, the global space industry generates approximately $350 billion in revenue, and according to a recent report published by Morgan Stanley, it is estimated to become a $1.1 trillion industry by the year 2040, with over 500 satellites currently being launched into orbit every year.[1] From the first Soviet satellite, Sputnik, which was launched in 1957 during the Cold War, and continuing over the past 62 years, over 8,378 space objects have been launched into outer space.[2] Of these 8,378 space objects, 4,994 are still in Earth's orbital field.[3] This is unsurprising considering that the global scale of consumer commodities trading and production is primarily facilitated through the use of satellites. In large part due to the growing prominence of satellite-related activities, such as communication networks, remote sensing systems, weather, climate analysis hardware, and much more, the space industry has also come to be known generally as "the satellite industry."[4]

Less well known, though, is that these satellites have a life span of only five to eight years.[5] This is mostly due to the economics of satellite profitability and distribution, which are primarily linked to the fuels that make the transport cheaper and more frequently possible. Even lesser known is what happens to these satellites at the end of their use cycle. What starts as a feat of complex engineering and precision material-craft, designed to facilitate the day-to-day workings of our information and data-driven age through the commodities they create, eventually ends up decommissioned in two principal ways. In the first instance, at about 22,400 miles above the Earth, there is a "Graveyard Orbit" at the outer edge of orbital space, which is routinely stocked with the dead and decaying space artifacts.[6] By disposing of obsolete satellites in this way, less fuel is required and the risk of unburned parts landing back on Earth is considerably reduced.[7] The second method of decommissioning has developed to deal with the increasing unpredictability and uncertainty of these derelict space objects landing on Earth. As a result, space agencies are increasingly dumping their techno-fossils into a remote area of the South Pacific Ocean. In this "Space Graveyard," defunct space objects typically occupy depths of about two miles below the ocean's surface.[8]

Naturally, the making of waste spaces such as these raises a number of critical social, political, and environmental issues. In order to answer these questions, this thesis aims to investigate the various forces that drive the space waste metabolisms as they emerged in the context of the afterlives of their orbital infrastructural operations. Toward this end, this work explores two of the world's largest sites of space waste disposal—namely, the Earth's hyper orbits and its high seas.

These sites present two limit cases of extreme environments—one operating at the outermost edge of orbital space and the other diametrically opposite in the depths of the South Pacific Ocean. Together they form the highest and the lowest boundary conditions of extreme environments, which, as Steve Pyne describes, are "remote, uninhabited, and unruly natural places that nonetheless constitute compelling sites of human practices and politics." Moreover, much like Pyne's "extreme environments," these waste zones "represent places where humans can go, but only by using life-sustaining technologies, and only temporarily. In these places life either does not exist

1
Michael Sheetz, "Morgan Stanley Predicts Space Travel Will Triple in Size: Here's How to Invest," http://cnbc.com; Morgan Stanley, "Space: Investing in the Final Frontier," http://morganstanley.com.

2
"How Many Satellites Orbiting the Earth in 2019?" Pixalytics Ltd., https://pixalytics.com.

3
"NASA Major Launch Record," https://history.nasa.gov/pocketstats/sectB/MLR.pdf.

4
OECD, *The Space Economy at a Glance 2007* (Paris: OECD Publishing, 2007).

5
Stason.org, Stas Bekman: stas (at). "39 How Long Does A Satellite 'Last' And Why Do They Get Regularly Replaced?" Accessed May 8, 2019. https://stason.org/TULARC/entertainment/satellite-tv-faq/39-How-Long-Does-A-Satellite-Last-And-Why-Do-They-Get-Regu.html; aijun Shen and Panagiotis Tsiotras, "Peer-to-Peer Refueling for Circular Satellite Constellations," *Journal of Guidance, Control, and Dynamics* 28, no. 6 (2005): 1220–30.

6
"Orbital Debris Management and Risk Mitigation," http://nasa.gov/pdf/692076main_Orbital_Debris_Management_and_Risk_Mitigation.pdf.

7
L. Anselmo and C. Pardini, "Space Debris Mitigation in Geosynchronous Orbit," *Advances in Space Research* 41, no. 7 (January 1, 2008): 1091–99. 8 "Making Sure ATV Reentry Is Safe," *Orion Blog*, October 30, 2013, http://blogs.esa.int/orion/2013/10/30/making-sure-atv-reentry-is-safe/.

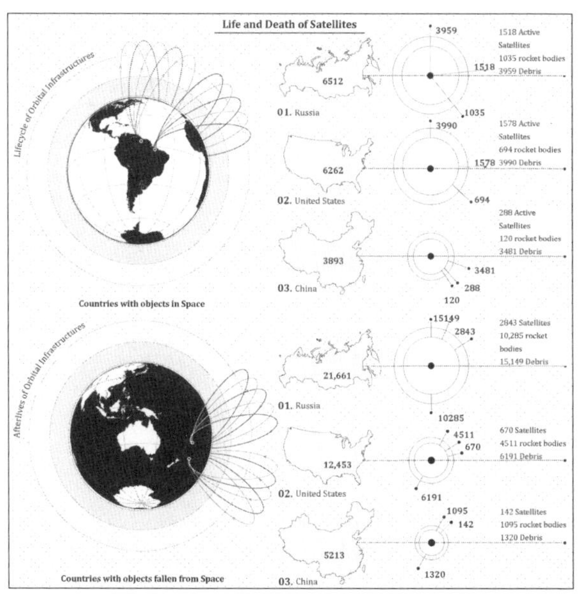

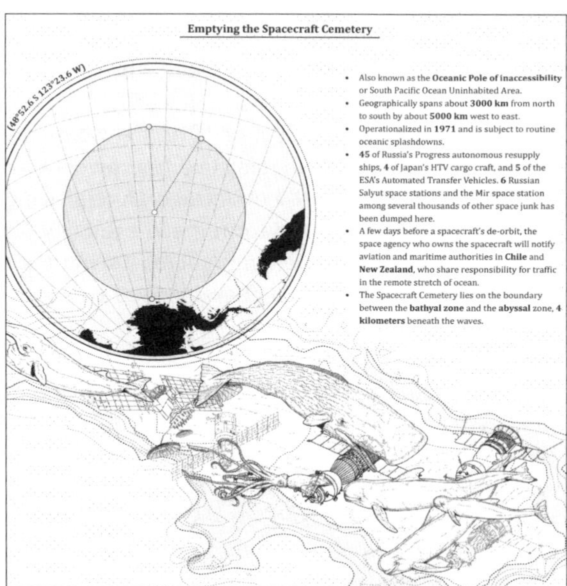

or exists only at the microbial level and at the margins."[9] Given the peripheral location and inaccessible character of these extreme environments, the study of the frontier conditions they represent is instrumental, as the "lack of other humans and even biota to resist or conquer has translated to a lack of urgency in examining the environmental histories of extreme environments."

As a result of their marginality, both the Graveyard Orbit and the Space Cemetery are subject to processes of geographical distancing and displacement of hazardous waste (defunct space objects, mainly dead satellites). These sites have taken on a specific character of invisibility to not merely obscure such waste proceedings from public view, but to eventually drive into oblivion the contested nature of their environmental repercussions. However, both these sites entail not only the externalization of large-scale techno-communication infrastructures into the Earth's orbits, but they also feature the internalization of their wastes back here on the surface of the Earth.[10] More meaningfully, their waste exchange also features the internalization of the embedded environmental and socioeconomic ramifications onto less-regulated international, shared waters that are circumvented through obscure legal and political frameworks.

In light of the "internal" and "external" dialectic these sites engage and rely on, I propose the concept of "false externalization" to characterize and document the current practices of space corporations, businesses, and other profit-driven organizations in which the environmental responsibility for techno-waste is ostensibly externalized in their use of sites outside of their own visible spheres of responsibility. Despite beliefs and claims to the contrary, these so-called externalizations fundamentally remain internal to the Earth's life-supporting and self-sustaining systems—the ramifications of which are profoundly socially and environmentally destructive. Driven by larger questions of environmental ethics and geopolitics, I argue that this strategy of "false externalization" is exploited by various powerful, economically-vested political actors in order to circumvent not only their economic and environmental responsibilities, which are a part and parcel with the proper decommissioning and disposing of these hazardous forms of infrastructural waste, but how externalization is also used to evade the legal repercussions that would follow if such activities came to light.

9
Steve Pyne, "Extreme Environments," *Environmental History* 15, no. 3 (July 1, 2010): 509–13.

10
In this regard, I employ the formulation of *Design Earth*, with regards to the extra-planetary scaling up of environmental externalities, which they define as follows: "Inscribed through technological systems, such metabolism of the Earth differentiates between (economic) value that is attributed to desired resources and by-products costs such as pollution, spills, and the degradation of public health. Economists commonly employ the term "externalities" to refer to such unpaid costs, unpaid in so far as a substantial portion of the actual costs of production remains unaccounted for in entrepreneurial outlays. Instead, these are shifted to and, ultimately borne by, third persons, the community as a whole."

In an attempt to demonstrate the prevalence of this practice in the context of orbital development today, I pursue two lines of inquiry. First, I trace the legal landscape of orbital waste, foregrounding the inextricable link between the spatial politics of orbital waste and the indeterminacies that exist within the legal and legislative frameworks that govern the production of orbital space. Second, I undertake an analysis of the visual and aesthetic regimes that have resulted from these orbital waste processes in order to document how these legal ambiguities permit the materialization of uneven geographies of distribution characterized by widespread environmental and humanitarian injustices.

Given the emergence of spaces such as the Graveyard Orbit and the Space Cemetery, it is indeed timely that, as the authors of *Two Cosmograms* state, "We should embrace a notion of the Environment in which there is no reserve outside which the unwanted consequences of our actions could be allowed to disappear from view; 'no zone of reality in which we could casually rid ourselves of the consequences of human political, industrial and economic life.'"[11] As a means of rendering visible the socio-environmentally contested nature of these "zones of reality," I adopt a largely interdisciplinary research methodology. On the one hand, I make use of several theoretical frameworks to position, ground, and inform my research. And on the other, I propose the use of artistic cartography as a graphical tool to capture waste sites such as the Graveyard Orbit and the Space Cemetery.

With respect to artistic cartography, I contend it is useful to not only illuminate the contested environmental realities that remain mostly out of visual bounds for most citizens, but it also serves as a powerful archival tool of the temporalities of sites such as these that are in a perpetual state of decay and degradation. To do so, I use data visualizations and cartographic representation (drawing upon the works of artists such as Trevor Paglen and Tom Sachs) as an attempt to foreground the visual and aesthetic regimes that are deployed in the service and production of these waste sites.

Salient among this analysis is the fundamental technique of late capitalism adopted by some of its most powerful actors (characterized here by the main drivers of the paradigm of the privatization of orbital space), to simultaneously ecologically degrade as well as render invisible the continual destruction of the global commons into environmental sacrifice zones. In the pursuit of a fictitious infinite growth, it not only sacrifices the environment through the slow death and invisible violence it inflicts upon some of its most nascent and virgin territories, but also, how it systematically excludes and disempowers the less powerful actors from the ostensible benefits of the services it claims to provide.

This thesis aims to grasp the obscure—and often invisible—mechanisms through which the current paradigm of privatized orbital space immutably transforms these transnational territories which belong to all of humankind into environmental sacrifice–zones, both internal to the confines of our planet as well as the radically tiny region of space we are presently capable of operating in. Ultimately, it is my hope that this study can contribute to the spatial understanding of the knowledge production pertaining to the frontiers of waste disposal operating both on and beyond the boundaries of the planet.

11
Rania Ghosn and El Hadi Jazairy, *Two Cosmograms* (Cambridge, MA: MIT School of Architecture and Planning, 2016).

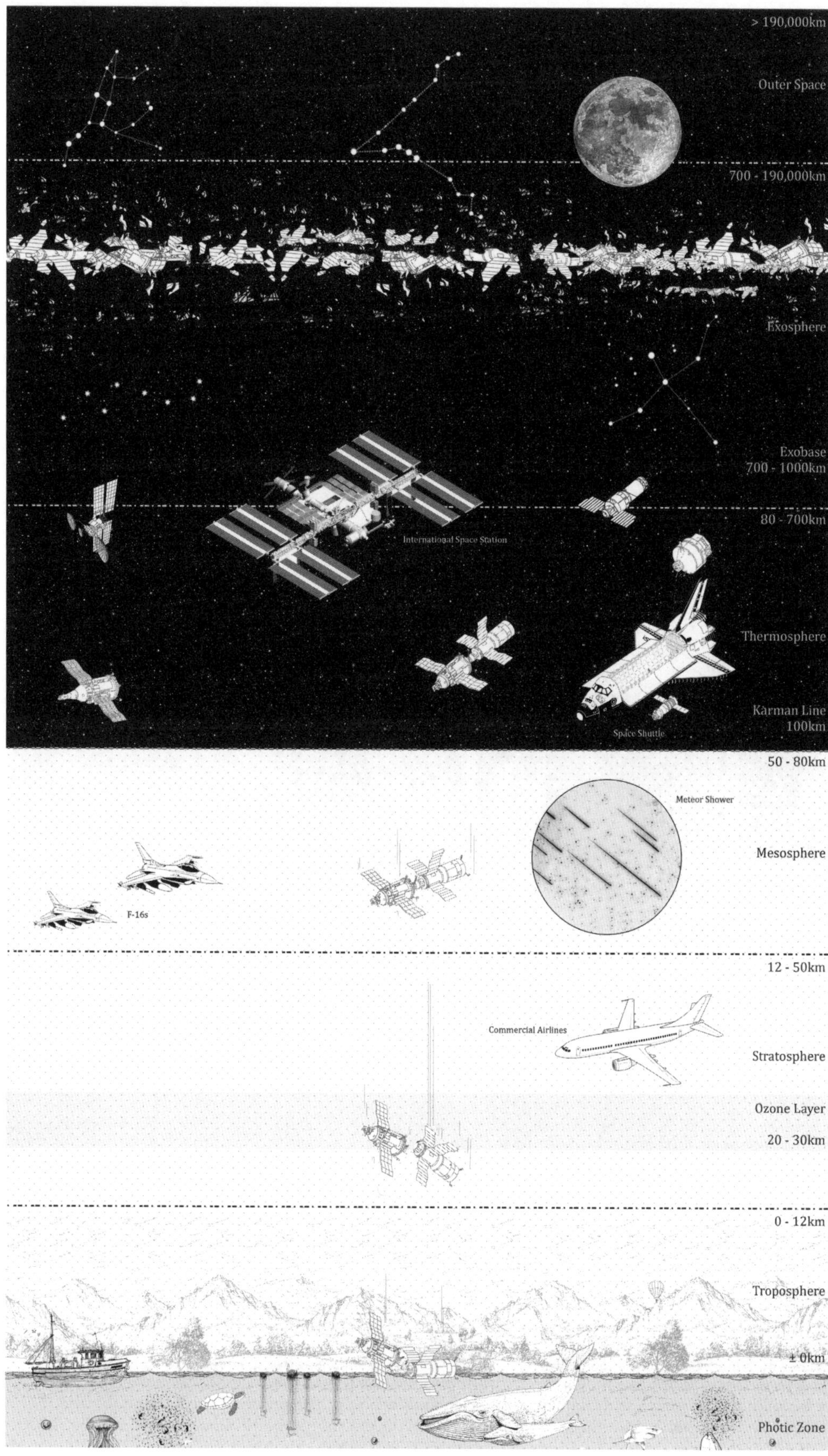

> 190,000km
Outer Space
700 - 190,000km
Exosphere
Exobase
700 - 1000km
80 - 700km
International Space Station
Thermosphere
Karman Line
100km
Space Shuttle
50 - 80km
Meteor Shower
Mesosphere
F-16s
12 - 50km
Commercial Airlines
Stratosphere
Ozone Layer
20 - 30km
0 - 12km
Troposphere
± 0km
Photic Zone

What is the material culture of death?

Lindsey Krug (MArch I)
Architecture Thesis
Advisor: Sergio Lopez-Pineiro

A look into the history of architectural manuals for bodily accommodation, authored throughout history by the likes of Vitruvius, Le Corbusier, and Neufert, reveals a disciplinary disinterest in indulging an excess of physicality or identity. Architecture and the systems of governance and commerce that produce it appreciate bodies at their most acquiescent, standardized, and "good."

What happens when bodies come to stay awhile? The corpse may be the most acquiescent subject, or perhaps the most radical as it is freed from our lived standards of comfort. But typical spaces for housing the dead are standardized, rigid, and austere. Even in death, bodies are opted-in and conformed to structures and systems of hierarchy and power.

Body
Death
Monument
Thesis

This is the material culture of death. In these objects are traces of gender, race, and class—the cleavages that are typically smoothed over in the planning of dead communities. In the spirit of the hodgepodge of commemorative objects, this thesis makes a case for the idiosyncratic, the subjective, and the mess in the realm of the institutional processing of the dead.

In Chicago, a city very aware but often indifferent to the mortality of its citizens, the institutional machine for the processing of dead bodies can be found at the Cook County Medical Examiner's Office—the morgue. To reconcile the individual body and the masses, this thesis proposes a new site in the Illinois Medical District that simultaneously accommodates the deconstruction of the animate body and

the reconstruction of the inanimate body. A mess amid the sterile, agglutination adjacent to disaggregation, the county morgue becomes a permanent abode for the registration of bodies and objects, rescued from material oblivion.

"SUPERBLOOM: Shelter, Drought, and Sculpture in the California Desert," Studio Trip, Spring 2019

How can a game be a site of public memory? What and who is or is not represented in public spaces?

Eric Moed (MDes ADPD)
Design Studies Thesis
Advisors: Krzysztof Wodiczko and Malkit Shoshan

"Memory Monument," a lexiconic system that invites exploration into the representation of memory in public space, engages questions of the historical and cultural value of monuments. Composed of a card-based compendium for users to contribute to, edit, and ultimately take ownership of, "Memory Monument" treats historical and contemporary monuments as unfixed and nonhierarchical. "Memory Monument" contains dozens of monuments and memorials within its walls, and invites participants to probe the complexities and possibilities of this new era of monuments and memorials. The open system can be engaged in multiple ways. When dormant, monuments and memorials can be added or taken away. Cards contained in its stone interior enable participants of all ages to form connections between the histories, intentions, and forms of monuments and memorials.

Memory
Monument
History
Thesis

How can artistic and design methodologies bring new meaning to public space?

Aleiya Evison (MDes ADPD) and Nadia Asfour (MDes ADPD)
Art, Design, and the Public Domain Proseminar
Instructor: Krzysztof Wodiczko

One cold November night, the Harvard Law School yard was awoken to a silent and illuminated orchestra of testimonies; footage of students who had come forward with their own experiences. These are their faces.

This is a memorial to all the women who have given testimony, defied the shackles of misogyny, and told their truth while knowing the physical, social, and political consequences they would face. Their stories intersect with our stories, and with the women and men across the world who have also faced the terror of sexual assault.

Identity
Public Space
Seminar
Trauma

How can ephemeral qualities of space be monumentalized?

Sunmee Lee (MLA I AP)
Now Arriving: A Manhattan Transit Landscape
Instructor: Gary Hilderbrand

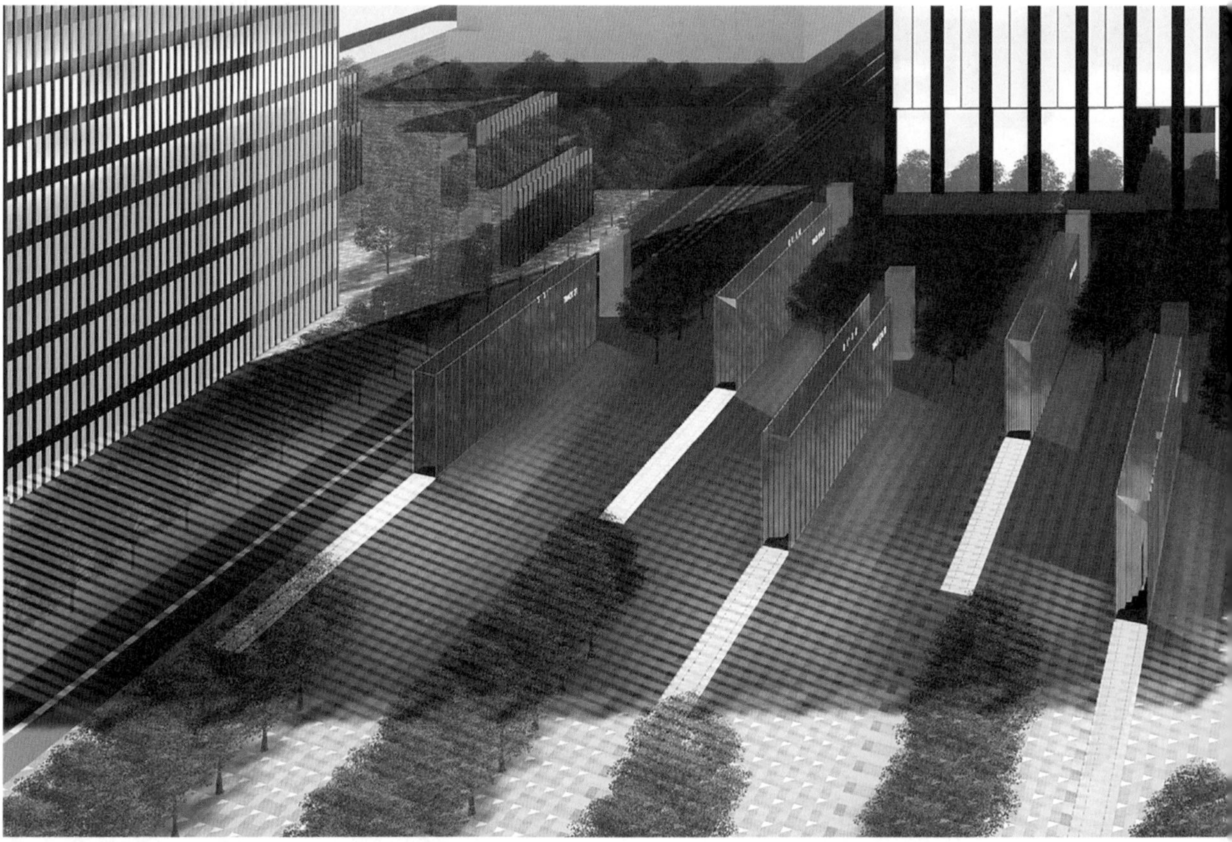

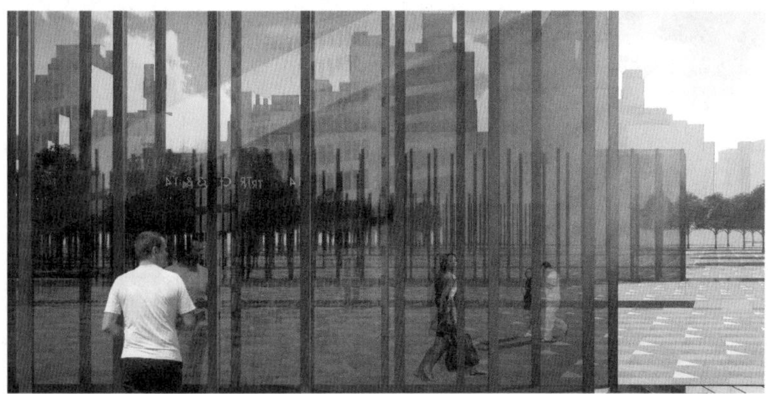

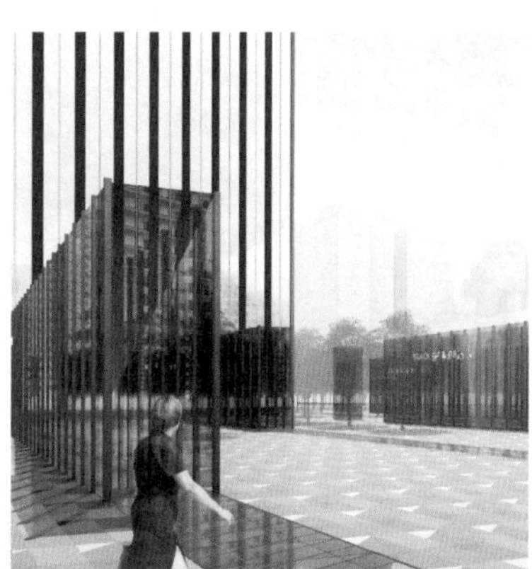

There has been a radical shift in memorial strategies in the public sphere. Once ubiquitous tools for reinforcing power structures and hegemonic state narratives, sculptural monuments and memorials have been reconsidered.

New York's Pennsylvania Station was at one time Manhattan's crowning glory. But, in 1963, only 54 years after its completion, Charles McKim's original station was demolished, replaced by Madison Square Garden and Two Penn Plaza. Understanding ongoing and future development, "Angle of Incidence" proposes a personalized arrival experience using materials embodying light and time.

One's arrival or departure through Penn Station is marked by reflection and shadows. Omnipresent daylight, incident light, is reflected when it meets the ground pavement

Monument
Performance
Option Studio
Transit

and the skylights. The glass staircase boxes extending from the train tracks to the street level create reflections and shadows on the ground. Each stairwell, as a result of its tilted ceilings, projects the street-level light down into the station. From the first step to the staircase, one can already experience aboveground New York City. And one will see themselves overlaid with New York City when facing the glass wall.

How can design engage and exceed the limitations of memory for those with advanced states of dementia?

Alicia Valencia (MDes ADPD)
Design Studies Thesis
Advisor: Krzysztof Wodiczko

Dementia is a debilitating experience that challenges the recollection of normative behaviors and interpersonal relationships, causing intrapersonal strife from constantly confronting an unrecognizable world. People with dementia come to rely on instinct and environmental sensory triggers to confirm where and who they are, yet these ties are disrupted when an afflicted individual must move from home to a residential memory-care community. Often missing from these unfamiliar settings are opportunities for residents to extend beyond a search for solid ground and explore flashes of creativity that occur when materials aesthetically "appear," or, become noticeable for reasons beyond the sensuous or rational.

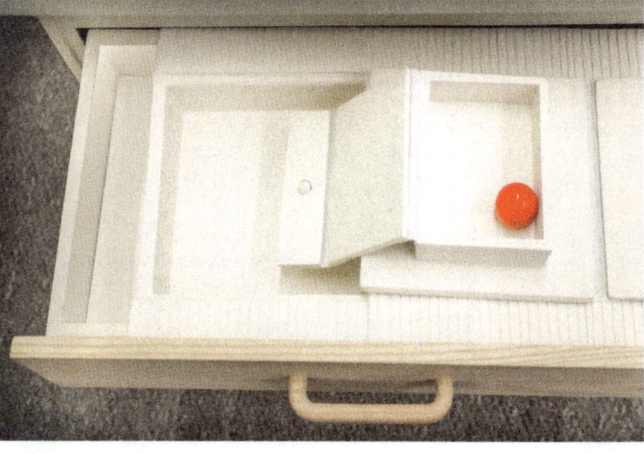

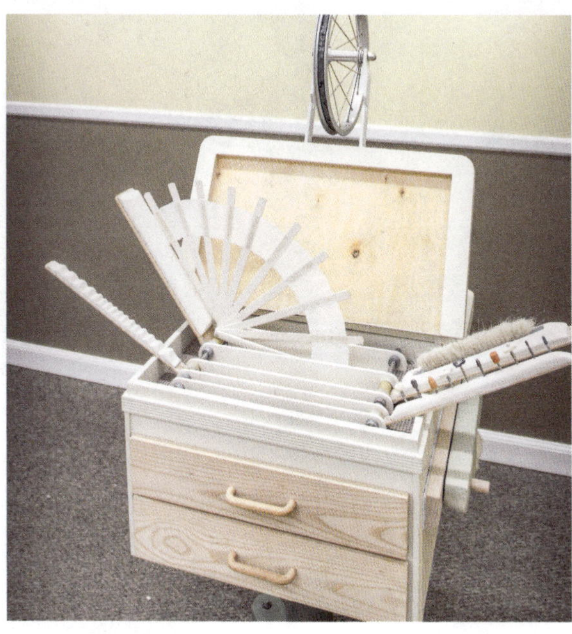

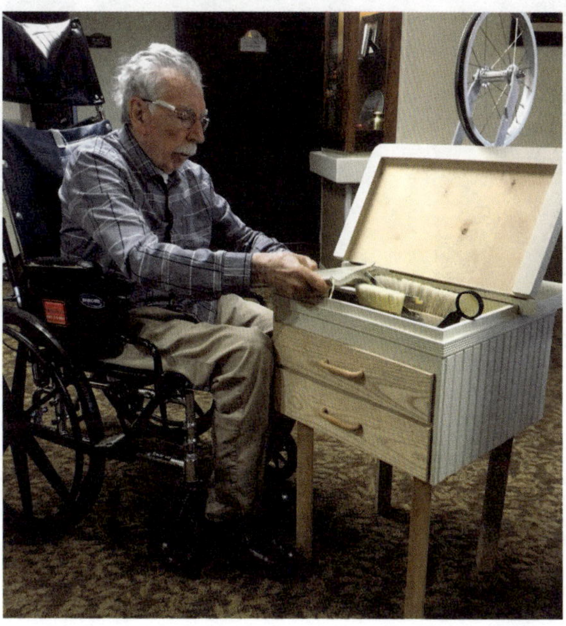

This project examines current and prospective avenues of behavioral engagement within residential memory care. Its site is Silverado Memory Care Community, an inpatient memory care facility in Escondido, California, where my 81-year-old father currently lives. Over the course of this design research, I respond to the state of engagement at my father's present home and construct playful furniture objects that seek to inspire self-motivated aesthetic engagement. I see this project as a blueprint for conceptualizing new therapeutic directions for designing an open dialogue about the nuanced behaviors and untapped creative capacities that are still retained by those with advanced stages of dementia. Outside of this goal, at its most intimate level, I see this project as a series of love letters, in the form of objects, addressed to my father.

How can the emotional power of the desert be made available when an in situ experience is out of reach?

Fletcher Phillips (MLA II)
SUPERBLOOM: Shelter, Drought, and Sculpture in the California Desert
Instructors: James Lord and Roderick Wyllie

Six courtyards in the new Community and Arts Center of Twentynine Palms, California, bring light and fresh air into a space that was formerly a big-box retail store. By analyzing the layered cultural imaginations of the desert Southwest, the project explores the capacity of gardens to evoke the myths embedded in a territory. Each garden room is designed to isolate and amplify an individual quality of the desert—hostility, infiniteness, detachment, disorientation, latency, and timelessness. This process results in spatial configurations that aim at evocation rather than imitation, with a focus on the relationship between an individual and the environment they are immersed within, thus capturing the emotional power of the desert when recreating its physical qualities is out of reach.

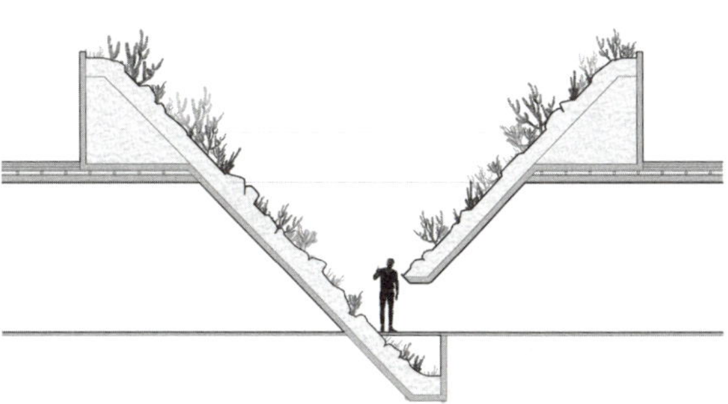

Hostility.

Detachment.

Infiniteness.

Timelessness.

How do we mourn in the digital age when memory prosthetics like the smartphone have rendered our memories accessible at all times?

Martin Ignacio Fernandez (MArch I)
Architecture Thesis
Advisors: Andrew Witt and Jeffrey Schnapp

How can the contemporary collection of digital memories, which our smartphones and social media store, become the major medium for collecting? How does this become part of our evolving notions of death?

This thesis grapples with the current phenomenon of digital memory prosthetics, questioning the detachment, representation, and storage of memories that the necropolis provides. Ultimately, this project seeks to place digital memories in the dominion of the dead. As a case study, the coupling of a columbarium and a data center in Miami Beach will serve as a lens to open the conversation.

Death
Memory
Monument
Technology
Thesis

What is the contemporary sublime? How can the invisible terrain of mass surveillance be grounded and illuminated?

Mark Heller (MLA I, MUP)
Landscape Architecture Thesis
Advisor: Robert Pietrusko

"NO SERVICE" introduces the latest addition to the National Park System: Timberline National Park. Whereas Congress has historically established national parks to preserve and make accessible the sublime—that is, the transcendent quality of the American landscape that overwhelms, defies comprehension, and induces awe—Timberline National Park is devoted to illuminating those same qualities of the information age: the sublime of the United States surveillance state.

Timberline sits within the heart of the U.S. National Radio Quiet Zone, a unique geography where electromagnetic signals are strictly banned. Through the design of a trail network and viewing platforms, this thesis revels in the sublime

juxtaposition of a covert intelligence apparatus intercepting all radio transmissions in a landscape devoid of electromagnetic communication channels, and more broadly tackles the urgent issue of grounding and illuminating the deliberately invisible terrain of mass surveillance.

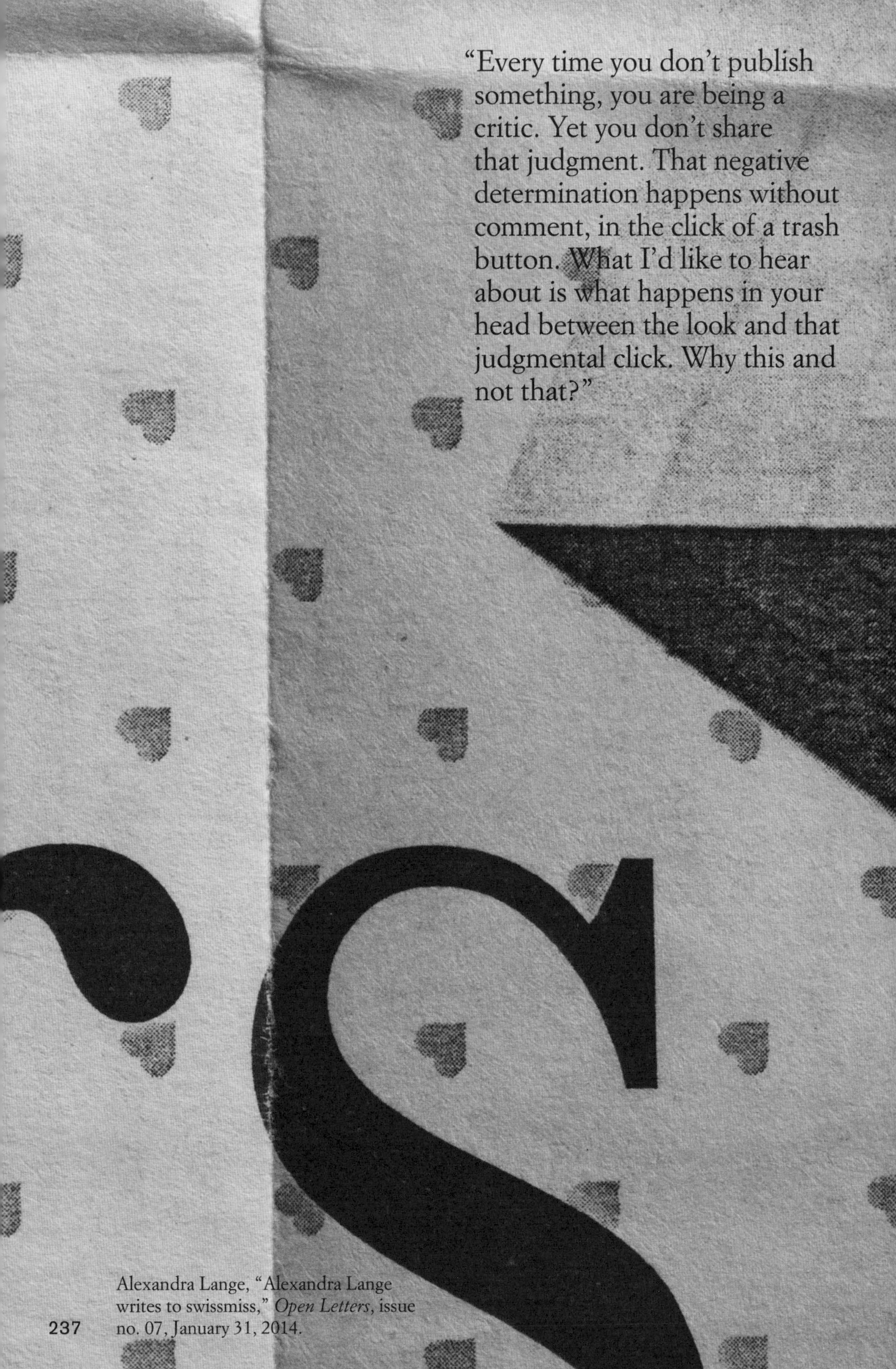

"Every time you don't publish something, you are being a critic. Yet you don't share that judgment. That negative determination happens without comment, in the click of a trash button. What I'd like to hear about is what happens in your head between the look and that judgmental click. Why this and not that?"

Alexandra Lange, "Alexandra Lange writes to swissmiss," *Open Letters*, issue no. 07, January 31, 2014.

CONCLUSION

Dean Hudnut:

Our purpose is to change the mild course of modern fashion architecture into a struggle for a revolution in the architectural world. Because of you, Harvard University has one of the best architectural schools in the world. Students from five continents testify to this fact.

We ask you to establish a review with DEFINITE PRINCIPLES OF CRITICISM. The commercial reviews based on a Gallup system of architectural criticism lead nowhere but to the confusion of public opinion. We want a small review of the "Focus" type, of perhaps no more than four issues a year, but with clarity of leadership. This review should be the center of a movement in architecture with the purpose of making the people of the United States aware of modern architecture, which is now known and understood only by a small group. Together with this review, this movement, through conferences and propaganda, should state the principles on which modern design is conceived, and, through a cold criticism of their work, should stimulate architects in the United States.

The main aim of this movement and of this review should be COLLABORATION: its possibility, its experiments.

COLLABORATION IS THE CREDO AND THE FAITH OF ARCHITECTURE TODAY.

John B. Bayley	Frank C. Treseder
Robert Hays Rosenberg	Arthur Koon Hing Cheang
Bruno Zevi	Wm. Joseph
John Taylor Moore, Jr.	Dahong Wang
Warren H. Radford	T. J. Willo

[16]

An Opinion on Architecture (1941).

Conclusion

In the first issue of *TASK* (1941), student editors proposed five initiatives they believed could ensure architectural education produced "good architects." Inspired by these students and others who came before us, we propose a vision, in the form of a photo essay, that calls for critical engagement with questions and conversations initiated and carried forward by our predecessors.

Understanding our intellectual and institutional history gives us the opportunity to reflect on a larger narrative and situate ourselves within it. Fluency in social, political, formal, and pedagogical conversations is essential to design education, and the subsequent role that we play in understanding our power and agency as designers to build a better future.

We call for the GSD community and designers at large to:

1 Engage deeply with our institutional history.

2 Reflect on our role in producing a design agenda that engages and challenges social, cultural, and political issues.

3 Participate in and hold conversations that invite, listen and respond to all voices and positions in order to evolve design culture, practice, and pedagogy.

4 Recognize the process of constructing history and our agency to engage with it through documentation.

5 Acknowledge and grapple with omissions in institutional archives and collections, and support the efforts to continue bringing in new and underrepresented voices, ideas, and perspectives to the Loeb Library.

6 Consider what values and agendas we are building on and around as we work together to build the future.

Harvard GSD
Platform 11

THE HARVARD ARCHITECTURE REVIEW
GSD Platform 3
GSD PLATFORM 4
Still Life
GSD PLATFORM 5

"Isn't it then a fallacy to expect that both historical and analytical approach alone produces creative ability? Can we afford to disregard the great potential source of promoting creative ability through direct participation in the making of our visible surroundings? Making is certainly not a mere auxiliary to thinking. It is a basic experience indispensible for the unity of purpose within the creative act. It is the only educational means which interrelates our perceptive and inventive faculties."
Walter Gropius, 1948
"A continuous training of basic manual skill in experimental workshops combined with disciplines in the fundamentals of surface, volume and space, and of composition-derived from objective findings-should therefore be developed on all levels of general education. Both the reinstatement of shop practice and the introduction of scientific courses leading to a common language of visual communication are basic requirements, I believe, for successfully teaching the arts of design."
Walter Gropius, 1948
"For no designer can fully grasp the many inter-relationships of form, construction and economy from intelectual classroom courses only, nor from paper design. In shop and field, however, he experiences their synthesis in close relation to the needs of the people he serves. It is then that he will realize that his knowledge of the language of vision, his skill in construction, in draftsmanship, and presentation, are all indispensable implements for expressing the all-important social end of his creative effort."
Walter Gropius, 1948
CLIP STAMP FOLD
METROPOLITAN
NEW STATE SPACES
INSTIGATIONS

"If the world of scholarship can at last accept Nelson Goodman's contention that "the arts must be taken no less seriously than the sciences as modes of discovery, creation and enlargement of knowledge," then the university may yet draw benefit from the peculiar capacity of architecture both to define and to question the relationships between human beings, their institutions, and the natural world. Architecture can indeed be practiced as a radical critique of the culture—a critique carried out in the language of forms rather than the language of words. Surely architecture so conceived and so practiced has something useful to bring to an ongoing discourse within the university; and should this hypothesis prove correct, architecture may yet find a place not merely at but unequivocally in and of the university."

Henry Cobb, 1985

"An ideologically driven modernist pedagogy, through its erasure of history as much as through the methodology of its design studios, profoundly shaped the practice of architecture in the decades following World War II. Unlike earlier pedagogies, which typically privileged one historical period over others, the pedagogy of the modern movement, as practiced by Gropius, sought to protect the student from contamination by all of history, so as to clear the way for an entirely New Architecture, liberated from the tyranny of dead styles, in which art, technology, and social purpose would be powerfully joined for the benefit of humanity. This attitude was elegantly summed up by Franz Kafka: "The decisive moment in human history is perpetually at hand. Hence those revolutionary movements that declare everything preceding them to be null and void are in the right, for nothing has yet happened."

Henry Cobb, 1985

"Zero. I'm 100 percent certain."
Heat, d
brush f
Then He Said. Now What Will Senators Say?
HIGH-STAKES DUE
San Francisco Chronicle
Major Climate Repor
Strong Risk of Crisis
CALAMITY
IS WIDENING
EL PAÍS
Las llamas devas
símbolo de la cul
GOD BLESS!
Herald
Ripped
Apart
THE COST OF
AMERICA'S
IMMIGRATION
CRACKDOWN
Migrant Children Drugged Without Consent
Government Centers, Court Documents Show
Domesticity at War
STREETFIGHT
OVERGROWN
S,M,L,XL
INSTIGATIONS

drought-parched
fuel ferocious fire
Music festival deaths rekindle drug concerns
'Fighting for our freedom' / Protesters flood on to Hong Kong's streets
'National disgrace' / Donald Trump attacks Sadiq Khan in tweets over deaths in London
China says the US has started 'the biggest trade war' in history
NOW HIRING
ARIZONA REPUBLIC
WORLD CHAMPIONS
The Guardian
arnage in New Zealand as
unman kills 49 in mosques
SHUTDOWN
gress stuck in funding stalemate
NEW STATE SPACES
METROPOLITAN
MIAMI
CLIP STAMP FOLD

Profoto
INSTIGATIONS
conversations

MANIFESTO
WE DEMAND
WE DEMAND A FUTURE

OFF
MENU
INFO.
START
STOP
LOCK
Spray Adhesive

ARTHUR M. SACKLER
PHARMACEUTICAL ENTREPRENEUR
ARTHUR M. SACKLER (1913-1987)
PIONEERED AGGRESSIVE MARKETING TECHNIQUES
USED TO SELL ADDICTIVE PAINKILLERS
AND DONATED WIDELY TO
CULTURAL INSTITUTIONS
we are your library.
and libraries are not neutral.
we welcome.
we listen.
we speak up.
we support.
we challenge.
we question.
we try,
and sometimes we fail.
we hope.
we lift our lamp inside this
golden door."

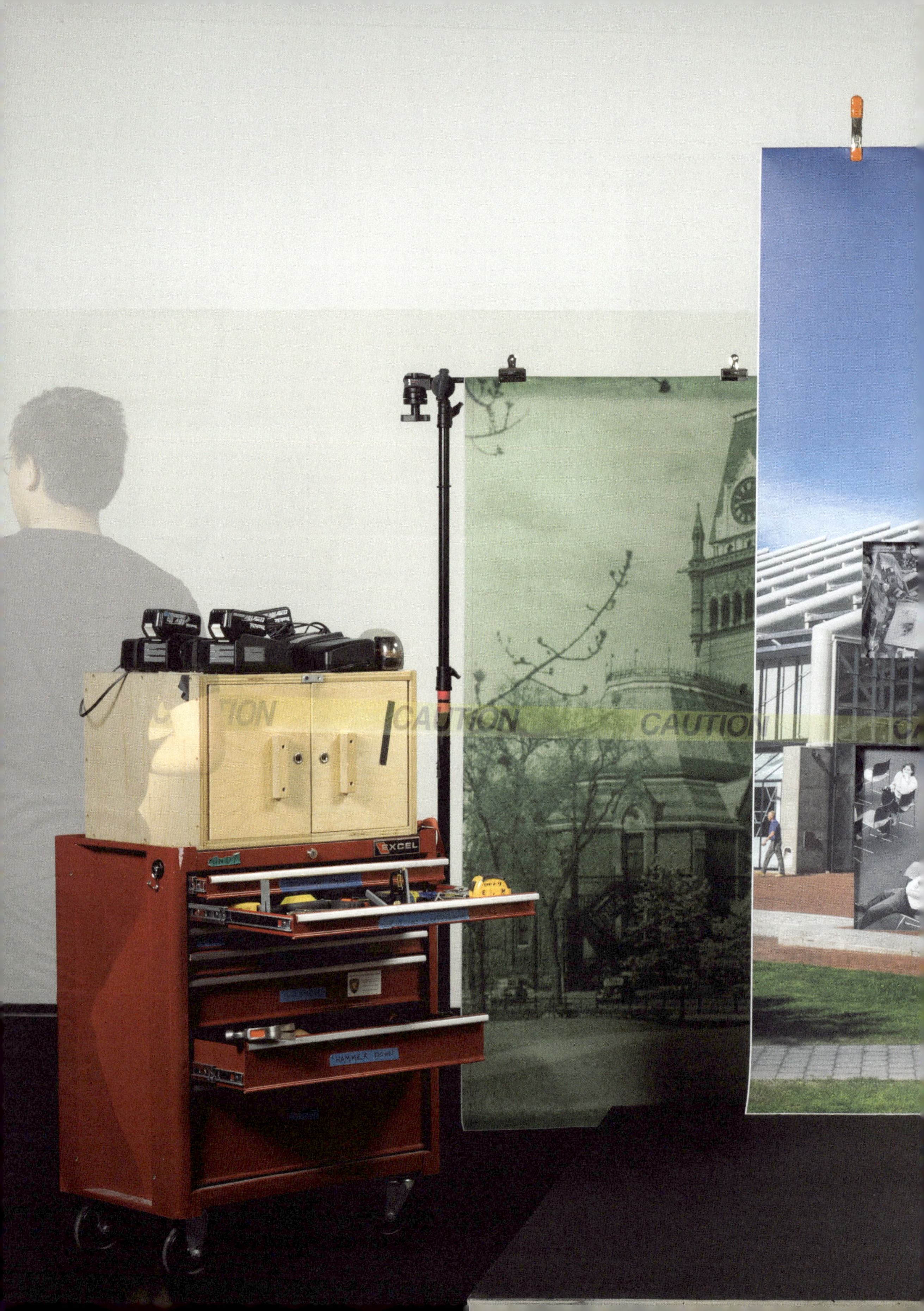
CAUTION
CAUTION
EXCEL
HAMMER DOWN

CAUTION

1

DISH OF THE DAY
The Herald
Brits among 207 killed
Easter Sunday massacre

I pledge to invite everyone to the table
LET'S ACT NOW
JUST CITY
GSD

queersindesign
Harvard Graduate School of Design

2

3

4

5

6

Appendix

Harvard GSD Leadership 2018–2019

Lawrence S. Bacow
President of Harvard University

Mohsen Mostafavi
Dean and Alexander and Victoria Wiley Professor of Design

Patricia J. Roberts
Executive Dean

HARVARD GSD EXECUTIVE COMMITTEE

Martin Bechthold
Kumagai Professor of Architectural Technology; Director of the Doctor of Design Studies Program; Codirector of the Master in Design Engineering Program

Anita Berrizbeitia
Professor of Landscape Architecture; Chair of the Department of Landscape Architecture

Diane E. Davis
Charles Dyer Norton Professor of Regional Planning and Urbanism; Chair of the Department of Urban Planning and Design

Mark Goble
Associate Dean for Operations and Finance

K. Michael Hays
Eliot Noyes Professor of Architectural Theory; Associate Dean for Academic Affairs

Mark Lee
Professor in Practice of Architecture; Chair of the Department of Architecture

Mohsen Mostafavi
Dean and Alexander and Victoria Wiley Professor of Design

Erika Naginski
Robert P. Hubbard Professor of Architectural History; Director of Doctoral Programs and the Doctor of Philosophy Program

Jackie Piracini
Associate Dean for Administration

Antoine Picon
G. Ware Travelstead Professor of the History of Architecture and Technology; Director of Research

Patricia J. Roberts
Executive Dean

ARCHITECTURE

Mark Lee
Professor in Practice of Architecture; Chair of the Department of Architecture

Jon Lott
Assistant Professor of Architecture; Director of the Master in Architecture I Program

Jennifer Bonner
Assistant Professor of Architecture; Director of the Master in Architecture II Program

LANDSCAPE ARCHITECTURE

Anita Berrizbeitia
Professor of Landscape Architecture; Chair of the Department of Landscape Architecture

Gareth Doherty
Assistant Professor of Landscape Architecture; Director of the Master in Landscape Architecture Programs

Chris Reed
Professor in Practice of Landscape Architecture; Codirector of the Master of Landscape Architecture in Urban Design Program

URBAN PLANNING AND DESIGN

Diane E. Davis
Charles Dyer Norton Professor of Regional Planning and Urbanism; Chair of the Department of Urban Planning and Design

Ann Forsyth
Ruth and Frank Stanton Professor of Urban Planning; Codirector of the Master in Urban Planning Program

Richard Peiser
Michael D. Spear Professor of Real Estate Development; Codirector of the Master in Urban Planning Program

Rahul Mehrotra
Professor of Urban Design and Planning; Director of the Master of Architecture in Urban Design Program; Codirector of the Master of Landscape Architecture in Urban Design Program

DESIGN STUDIES

John May
Assistant Professor of Architecture; Director of the Master in Design Studies Program

DESIGN ENGINEERING

Martin Bechthold
Kumagai Professor of Architectural Technology; Director of the Doctor of Design Studies Program; Codirector of the Master in Design Engineering Program

Fawwaz Habbal
Executive Dean for Education and Research at the Harvard University John A. Paulson School of Engineering and Applied Sciences; Codirector of the Master in Design Engineering Program

DOCTORAL PROGRAMS

Erika Naginski
Robert P. Hubbard Professor of Architectural History; Director of Doctoral Programs and the Doctor of Philosophy Program

Martin Bechthold
Kumagai Professor of Architectural Technology; Director of the Doctor of Design Studies Program; Codirector of the Master in Design Engineering Program

RESEARCH

Antoine Picon
G. Ware Travelstead Professor of the History of Architecture and Technology; Director of Research

Academic Programs 2018–2019

ARCHITECTURE

Master in Architecture I (MArch I)
MArch I students come from a mix of backgrounds: some enter the GSD with a bachelor of arts in architecture, while others have majored in the sciences, liberal arts, or fine arts. The core program involves two years of required courses, followed by one year of option studios, elective classes, and a final thesis semester. Each semester, students take one studio course (or thesis) and typically three additional courses (or the equivalent of half-semester modular courses).

Master in Architecture I Advanced Placement (MArch I AP)
MArch I AP candidates typically hold a four-year bachelor of science in architecture from an intensive undergraduate program. AP students place out of the first year of the MArch I program and join the class in its third semester. While enrolled in second-year core studios, some AP students may be able to place out of one or more required courses and take electives instead. Students may be able to waive required courses if they can provide supporting evidence of successful completion of an equivalent course at another institution.

Master in Architecture II (MArch II)
MArch II candidates come to the GSD with a prior professional degree in architecture—at minimum, a five-year bachelor in architecture—and many have gained professional experience before returning to school. The MArch II is a two-year program, with students beginning at the option-studio level. In their first semester, MArch II students take a required proseminar. Afforded a high degree of flexibility, MArch II candidates are in the enviable position of designing a large portion of their own curriculum.

LANDSCAPE ARCHITECTURE

Master in Landscape Architecture I (MLA I)
The MLA I is a first professional degree for students with a four-year bachelor's degree in any field of study. MLA I students follow a core curriculum for their first four semesters, after which they are eligible to pursue option studios, thesis, and/or electives during their final year.

Master in Landscape Architecture I Advanced Placement (MLA I AP)
Those who hold an accredited professional degree in architecture, a preprofessional undergraduate degree in landscape architecture, or a preprofessional undergraduate degree in architecture with an exceptionally strong design portfolio qualify for advanced standing. These students place out of the first year of the program and join the class in its third semester. AP students take their required history courses in the second year.

Master in Landscape Architecture II (MLA II)
MLA II students enter the landscape architecture program holding an accredited four- or five-year bachelor in landscape architecture. Because many enter the program with professional experience, MLA II students can provide valuable insight into both academic and professional pursuits in landscape architecture. The MLA II program lasts four semesters, with one core studio and the option of enrolling in thesis instead of studio during the final semester.

URBAN DESIGN

Urban design is offered at the GSD as a four-semester, post-professional, studio-based program that combines intense design instruction, extensive applied research, and knowledge of urban history and theory. Master of Architecture in Urban Design (MAUD) and Master of Landscape Architecture in Urban Design (MLAUD) candidates share a strong core curriculum in their first semester, which includes the "Elements of Urban Design Core Studio," the "Urban Design Proseminar," and the "Cities by Design" lecture course. The remaining three semesters offer a more flexible academic path that allows students to take advanced studios and elective courses across all three GSD departments. The curricular structure encourages advanced individual and collective research and the possibility to develop an elective thesis.

Master of Architecture in Urban Design (MAUD)

The program leading to the MAUD is intended for individuals who have completed a five-year undergraduate professional program in architecture, an MArch, or equivalent. After a one-semester core studio, students may opt to pursue option studios, thesis, or coursework (with approval) during their remaining semesters.

Master of Landscape Architecture in Urban Design (MLAUD)

Jointly administered with the Department of Landscape Architecture, the program leading to the MLAUD is intended for individuals who have completed a five-year undergraduate professional degree in landscape architecture, an MLA, or equivalent. Students begin with the same one-semester core studio as MAUD candidates and may opt to pursue option studios, thesis, or coursework (with approval) during their remaining semesters.

URBAN PLANNING

The Master in Urban Planning (MUP) professional degree program is focused on the understanding, analysis, and influence of the variety of forces that shape the built environment and affect the quality of human experience. The program is rooted in four fundamental themes: sustainable development, international planning, social and critical concerns, and urban design. In the first year, students enroll in a two-semester core studio. During the second year, students may pursue option studios, thesis, or coursework (with approval). Students must choose at least one concentration area or design their own concentration in consultation with the program director.

Concentration Areas:

Environmental Planning
History and Theory
Housing and Neighborhood Development
International Planning
Real Estate and Urban Development
Transportation and Infrastructure
Urban Analytics
Urban Design

DESIGN STUDIES

Master in Design Studies (MDes)

The MDes is a post-professional, project- and research-based program that uses novel and alternative methodologies in a collaborative, immersive, and multimedia environment of students, researchers, scholars, and practitioners. Students customize a cross-disciplinary course of study with a high level of specialization in addressing contemporary practices of design and modes of production that transcend disciplinary boundaries. Students often contribute to work performed in GSD research labs and initiatives. MDes is a three-semester program with an option to split the final semester. Advanced-placement status may be granted on rare occasions.

Concentration Areas:

Art, Design, and the Public Domain (ADPD) seeks creative and ambitious individuals from all backgrounds and academic disciplines with a keen interest in contemporary issues of urban, historical, aesthetic, and technological culture, and with a predilection for intervention, exhibition, and public work. Of particular importance are the practices that seek to engage with the public and social realm with a view to shaping and transforming human action and historical experience. ADPD engages in forms of spatial practice that are defining the new and moving boundaries of the design disciplines.

Critical Conservation (CC) applies issues of culture, history, and identity to design and development, transcending such outdated dialectics as past-future, traditional-modern, and us-them. Unlike preservation programs that presume the permanence of architecture and use top-down regulation to reinforce existing power structures, CC extends beyond issues of age, history, and aesthetics to offer a framework of theory and research tools encompassing social, political, and cultural meaning to offer students an understanding of the tensions between progress and tradition, the issues of permanence and obsolescence, and underlying forces often masked by the union of ideologies, preservation, and politics.

Energy and Environments (EE) allows students to examine material and energy issues—broadly defined, from the molecular to the territorial—across disciplines and scales, expanding the discourse on sustainable design to a more ambitious and totalizing praxis of energy and environments. How designers might better characterize the exchanges and coupling of matter and energy across multiple spatial and temporal scales is central to the pedagogy necessary for a more thermodynamically cogent design practice in the 21st century.

History and Philosophy of Design and Media (HPDM) is a platform for inquiry into the disciplines of architecture, urbanism, and landscape architecture, and their aligned aesthetic, technological, and spatial practices. The program provides students the opportunity for historical and philosophical explorations into the social, cultural, technical, and political contexts of design, and is directed toward individuals for whom advanced study can serve as preparation for future work in pursuit of a PhD degree, practice, and design pedagogy, as well as careers in journalism, film and digital media, or design curation related to the built environment.

Real Estate and the Built Environment (REBE) places design within the crucible of finance, examining the ways each can add value to the other. As part of a design discourse, financial analyses—feasibility studies, economic models, and investment strategies—acquire added social, cultural, and aesthetic dimensions. Mirroring the experience many graduates encounter in practice, students explore how form can have an impact on investment and value.

Risk and Resilience (RR) sets out to support novel approaches to sociospatial planning through design. Design as a discipline provides cities, communities, and individuals with tools to effectively prepare for, cope with, and anticipate rapid change within the spatial, social, and economic vulnerabilities it produces. The program prepares students to identify, articulate, and propose preemptive forms of practice.

Technology (Tech) advances innovative methods for making and understanding form and technologically driven design through technological experimentation. Students pursue a broad spectrum of inquiries, including design computation, digital fabrication, robotics, and the exploration of responsive environments. Cutting across scales, students engage subjects from the level of a single artifact or building to landscapes and urban systems.

Urbanism, Landscape, Ecology (ULE) invites an examination of contemporary practices of design and modes of production as they inform and manifest urbanism. Students pursue topics related to contemporary urbanism, landscape, geography, or territory within the broader contexts of the global, social, and natural environment, where longstanding disciplinary divides between the urban and the ecological have given way to more fluid, polyvalent, and potentially more productive relations.

DESIGN ENGINEERING

Master in Design Engineering (MDE)

The MDE is a unique collaborative program between the GSD and the John A. Paulson School of Engineering and Applied Sciences (SEAS). As our world faces increasingly complex, often unpredictable dilemmas of consequence to human lives and environments—including rapid urbanization, ecological changes, and resource scarcity, and their negative impact on sociocultural dynamics—these and other problems demand innovative, multifaceted solutions that transcend disciplines and scales. By training a new generation of innovators who operate both creatively and analytically, think strategically, and collaborate broadly, the MDE program develops graduates capable of leading change and advancing novel, real-world solutions. The integrated fields of design and engineering are uniquely positioned to address the world's toughest challenges and this two-year program prepares the next generation of leaders to create transformative solutions that positively impact society.

In the first year, students take a year-long interdisciplinary design studio along with elective courses complemented by a series of public lectures and intimate discussions with prominent innovators, designers, and thought leaders. During the second year, students complete an independent design engineering project on a topic of their choice. The MDE pedagogical model is geared toward enabling synergies that emerge through the collaboration of the interdisciplinary cohort. The instruction further emphasizes collaborative problem solving by bridging the gaps between academic fields and practical, real-world stakeholders, and fosters a design intelligence that engages quantitative and qualitative thinking, combining computational, visual, experimental, strategic, and aesthetic methods.

DOCTORAL STUDIES

Doctor of Philosophy (PhD)

The PhD program in architecture, landscape architecture, and urban planning is cogoverened by the GSD and the Graduate School of Arts and Sciences (GSAS). It is intended for those who wish to enter teaching and advanced research careers in the history and theory of architecture, architectural technology, landscape architecture, and urban form from antiquity to the present; or the analysis and development of buildings, cities, landscapes, and regions with an emphasis on social, economic, technological, ecological, and infrastructural systems.

The additional track in architectural technology aims to advance the state of knowledge in green building, and typically includes issues related to computation and simulation, environmental concerns, energy performance, and the history and philosophy of technology. Students will be associated with the Harvard Center for Green Buildings and Cities, which will provide the intellectual context for this research.

Doctor of Design (DDes)

The DDes program is geared toward applied research that advances design-related knowledge in a broad range of scales, from product design to buildings and landscapes to urban design and regional planning. It is an accelerated doctoral degree for students who already hold a masters degree. DDes research investigations express how design research makes essential contributions to understanding, analyzing, and ultimately improving the built environment in our increasingly complex world. Students are linked to the GSD's research labs and programs both intellectually and operationally as investigators in ongoing research projects.

Faculty 2018–2019

Iñaki Ábalos
Design Critic in Architecture

Nadir Abdessemed
Lecturer in Landscape Architecture

Viola Ago
Lecturer in Architecture

Pablo Allard Serrano
Robert F. Kennedy Visiting Professor of Latin American Studies

Stefano Andreani
Research Associate and Lecturer in Architecture

Frank Apeseche
Lecturer in Urban Planning and Design

Iwan Baan
Rouse Design Critic in Architecture

Sai Balakrishnan
Assistant Professor of Urban Planning

Katarzyna Balug
Instructor in Landscape Architecture

Martin Bechthold
Kumagai Professor of Architectural Technology

Francesca Benedetto
Design Critic in Landscape Architecture

Silvia Benedito
Associate Professor of Landscape Architecture

Anita Berrizbeitia
Professor of Landscape Architecture

Tatiana Bilbao
Design Critic in Architecture

Eve Blau
Adjunct Professor of the History and Theory of Urban Form and Design

Jennifer Bonner
Assistant Professor of Architecture

Ruth Bonsignore
Lecturer in Urban Planning and Design

Montserrat Bonvehi Rosich
Lecturer in Landscape Architecture

Dan Borelli
Lecturer in Architecture

Neil Brenner
Professor of Urban Theory

Barbara Brooks
John T. Dunlop Design Critic in Architecture

Jeffry Burchard
Assistant Professor in Practice of Architecture

Howard Burns
Lecturer in Architecture

Joan Busquets
Martin Bucksbaum Professor in Practice of Urban Planning and Design

Claire Cahan
Instructor in Architecture

Sean Canty
Design Critic in Architecture

Ignacio Cardona
Instructor in Urban Planning and Design

Michelle Chang
Assistant Professor of Architecture

Danielle Choi
Assistant Professor of Landscape Architecture

Preston Scott Cohen
Gerald M. McCue Professor in Architecture

Daniel D'Oca
Associate Professor in Practice of Urban Planning

Dilip da Cunha
Lecturer in Urban Planning and Design

James Dallman
Design Critic in Architecture

Diane E. Davis
Charles Dyer Norton Professor of Regional Planning and Urbanism

Eric de Broche des Combes
Lecturer in Landscape Architecture

Timothy Dekker
Lecturer in Landscape Architecture

Tomás dePaor
Design Critic in Architecture

Jill Desimini
Associate Professor of Landscape Architecture

Gareth Doherty
Assistant Professor of Landscape Architecture

Shaun Donovan
Design Critic in Urban Planning and Design

Craig Douglas
Lecturer in Landscape Architecture

Stylianos Dritsas
Lecturer in Architecture

Sonja Dümpelmann
Associate Professor of Landscape Architecture

Edward Eigen
Senior Lecturer in the History of Landscape and Architecture

Rosetta S. Elkin
Associate Professor of Landscape Architecture

Stephen Ervin
Lecturer in Landscape Architecture and Urban Planning and Design

Hossein Estiri
Lecturer in Urban Planning and Design

Teman Evans
Lecturer in Architecture

Teran Evans
Lecturer in Architecture

Iman Fayyad
Lecturer in Architecture

Kathryn Firth
Design Critic in Urban Planning and Design

David Fixler
Lecturer in Architecture

Ann Forsyth
Ruth and Frank Stanton Professor of Urban Planning

Jenny French
Design Critic in Architecture

Alice Friedman
Visiting Professor in Architecture

Simon Frommenwiler
Design Critic in Architecture

Yun Fu
Instructor in Urban Planning and Design

Sosuke Fujimoto
Design Critic in Architecture

Stanislaus Fung
Lecturer in Landscape Architecture

Teresa Galí-Izard
Associate Professor of Landscape Architecture

David Gamble
Lecturer in Urban Planning and Design

Jeanne Gang
Professor in Practice of Architecture

Kersten Geers
Design Critic in Architecture

Elle Gerdeman
Design Critic in Architecture

Carlisle Gill
Design Critic in Architecture

José Gómez-Ibáñez
Derek Bok Professor of Urban Planning and Public Policy

Stephen Gray
Assistant Professor of Urban Design

Toni L. Griffin
Professor in Practice of Urban Planning

Jonathan Grinham
Lecturer in Architecture and Research Associate

Lisa Haber-Thomson
Design Critic in Architecture

Allan Hamilton
Lecturer in Urban Planning and Design

Helen Han
Instructor in Architecture

Ewa Harabasz
Lecturer in Architecture, Landscape Architecture, and Urban Planning and Design

Michael Haroz
Lecturer in Urban Planning and Design

Simon Hartmann
Design Critic in Architecture

K. Michael Hays
Eliot Noyes Professor of Architectural Theory

Briana Hensold
Design Critic in Urban Planning and Design

Christopher Herbert
Lecturer in Urban Planning and Design

Anna Heringer
Aga Khan Design Critic in Architecture

Tilo Herlach
Design Critic in Architecture

Jock Herron
Design Critic in Architecture

Gary Hilderbrand
Peter Louis Hornbeck Professor in Practice of Landscape Architecture

Chuck Hoberman
Pierce Anderson Lecturer in Design Engineering

Andrew Holder
Assistant Professor of Architecture

Michael Hooper
Associate Professor of Urban Planning

Eric Höweler
Associate Professor of Architecture

Catherine Ingraham
Lecturer in Architecture

Karen Janosky
Lecturer in Landscape Architecture

Mark R. Johnson
Lecturer in Architecture

Sharon Johnston
Professor in Practice of Architecture

Sawako Kaijima
Assistant Professor of Architecture

Mits Kanada
Lecturer in Architecture

Hanif Kara
Professor in Practice of Architectural Technology

Paul Kassabian
Design Critic in Architecture

Jerold S. Kayden
Frank Backus Williams Professor of Urban Planning and Design

Zhang Ke
Design Critic in Architecture

Jesse M. Keenan
Lecturer in Architecture

Matthew Kiefer
Lecturer in Architecture

Jungyoon Kim
Design Critic in Landscape Architecture

Jonathan King
Lecturer in Architecture

Niall Kirkwood
Professor of Landscape Architecture and Technology

Rem Koolhaas
John Portman Professor in Practice of Architecture

Zeina Koreitem
Design Critic in Architecture

Alex Krieger
Professor in Practice of Urban Design

Seng Kuan
Lecturer in Architecture

Detlef Kuehn
Design Critic in Architecture

Wilfried Kuehn
Design Critic in Architecture

Jeannette Kuo
Assistant Professor In Practice of Architecture

Max Kuo
Lecturer in Architecture

Grace La
Professor of Architecture

Vittorio Lampugnani
Lecturer in Architecture

Amanda Reeser Lawrence
Visiting Associate Professor of Architecture

Christopher Lee
Associate Professor in Practice of Urban Design

Mark Lee
Professor in Practice of Architecture

George L. Legendre
Associate Professor in Practice of Architecture

Ani Liu
Lecturer in Architecture

Sergio Lopez-Pineiro
Lecturer in Landscape Architecture

James Lord
Design Critic in Landscape Architecture

Jon Lott
Assistant Professor of Architecture

Jaron Lubin
Design Critic in Architecture and Urban Planning and Design Ali Malkawi
Professor of Architectural Technology and Founding Director of the Harvard Center for Green Buildings and Cities

Simona Malvezzi
Design Critic in Architecture

Michael Manfredi
Design Critic in Urban Planning and Design and Expert-in-Residence

Edward Marchant
Lecturer in Urban Planning and Design

Ben Markham
Lecturer in Architecture

Sebastien Marot
Lecturer in Architecture

Sofia Martinez
Design Critic in Architecture

Christopher Matthews
Lecturer in Landscape Architecture

John May
Assistant Professor of Architecture

Patrick McCafferty
Lecturer in Architecture

Alistair McIntosh
Lecturer in Landscape Architecture

John McMorrough
Visiting Associate Professor in Architecture

Rahul Mehrotra
Professor of Urban Design and Planning

Panagiotis Michalatos
Lecturer in Architecture

Jennifer Molinsky
Lecturer in Urban Planning and Design

Rosalea Monacella
Design Critic in Landscape Architecture

Toshiko Mori
Robert P. Hubbard Professor in the Practice of Architecture

Catherine Mosbach
Aga Khan Design Critic in Landscape Architecture

Farshid Moussavi
Professor in Practice of Architecture

Sara Myerson
Lecturer in Architecture and Urban Planning and Design

Erika Naginski
Robert P. Hubbard Professor of Architectural History

Paul Nakazawa
Associate Professor in Practice of Architecture

Nicholas Nelson
Lecturer in Landscape Architecture

Caroline O'Donnell
Visiting Associate Professor in Architecture

Yusuke Obuchi
Lecturer

Chelina Odbert
Design Critic in Urban Planning and Design

Kayoko Ota
Lecturer in Architecture

Megan Panzano
Assistant Professor of Architecture

Yoon-Jin Park
Design Critic in Landscape Architecture

Richard Peiser
Michael D. Spear Professor of Real Estate Development

Pablo Pérez-Ramos
Assistant Professor of Landscape Architecture

John Peterson
Lecturer in Architecture

Mauricio Pezo
Design Critic in Architecture

Antoine Picon
G. Ware Travelstead Professor of the History of Architecture and Technology

Dennis Pieprz
Design Critic in Urban Planning and Design

Robert Pietrusko
Associate Professor of Landscape Architecture

Andrew Plumb
Lecturer in Architecture

Marty Poirier
Design Critic in Landscape Architecture

Linda Pollak
Design Critic in Urban Planning and Design

Marianne Potvin
Instructor in Urban Planning and Design

George Proakis
Lecturer in Urban Planning and Design

Chris Reed
Professor in Practice of Landscape Architecture

Doug Reed
Lecturer in Landscape Architecture

Jing Ren
Lecturer in Urban Planning and Design

Kirt Rieder
Lecturer in Landscape Architecture

Benjamin Rosenberg
Instructor in Architecture

Peter Rowe
Raymond Garbe Professor of Architecture and Urban Design and Harvard University Distinguished Service Professor

Thomas Ryan
Lecturer in Landscape Architecture

Moshe Safdie
Design Critic in Architecture and Urban Planning and Design

Frederick Salvucci
Lecturer in Urban Planning and Design

Holly Samuelson
Assistant Professor of Architecture

Allen Sayegh
Associate Professor in Practice of Architectural Technology

Ashley Schafer
Lecturer and Research Associate

Martha Schwartz
Professor in Practice of Landscape Architecture

Mack Scogin
Kajima Professor in Practice of Architecture

Annabelle Selldorf
Design Critic in Architecture

Andres Sevtsuk
Assistant Professor of Urban Planning

Malkit Shoshan
Lecturer in Urban Planning and Design

Jay Siebenmorgen
Design Critic in Architecture

Elisa Silva
Design Critic in Landscape Architecture

Jorge Silvetti
Nelson Robinson Jr. Professor of Architecture

Christine Smith
Robert C. and Marian K. Weinberg Professor of Architectural History

Susan Snyder
Lecturer in Architecture

Carl Solander
Lecturer in Architecture

Laura Solano
Associate Professor in Practice of Landscape Architecture

Lily Song
Lecturer in Urban Planning and Design and Research Associate

Kathy Spiegelman
Design Critic in Urban Planning and Design

Abby Spinak
Lecturer in Urban Planning and Design

Oana Stanescu
Design Critic in Architecture

John R. Stilgoe
Robert and Lois Orchard Professor in the History of Landscape Development

James Stockard
Lecturer in Urban Planning and Design

Paola Sturla
2018–2019 Daniel Urban Kiley Fellow and Lecturer in Landscape Architecture

Lea-Catherine Szacka-Marier
Lecturer in Architecture

Pier Paolo Tamburelli
Design Critic in Architecture

Maria Belinda Tato Serrano
Design Critic in Architecture

George Thomas
Lecturer in Architecture

Mary Tolikas
Instructor in Design Engineering

Raymond Torto
Lecturer in Urban Planning and Design

Rebecca Uchill
Lecturer in Architecture

José Luis Vallejo
Design Critic in Urban Planning and Design

Ben van Berkel
Kenzo Tange Design Critic in Architecture

David van Severen
Design Critic in Architecture

Christian Veddeler
Design Critic in Architecture

Alexander von Hoffman
Lecturer in Urban Planning and Design

Charles Waldheim
John E. Irving Professor of Landscape Architecture

Alexander Wall
Design Critic in Landscape Architecture

Bing Wang
Associate Professor in Practice of Real Estate and the Built Environment

Emily Waugh
Lecturer in Landscape Architecture

Daniel Weissman
Lecturer in Architecture

Emily Wettstein
Design Critic in Landscape Architecture

Amy Whitesides
Design Critic in Landscape Architecture

Elizabeth Whittaker
Associate Professor in Practice of Architecture

Andrew Witt
Assistant Professor in Practice of Architecture

Krzysztof Wodiczko
Professor in Residence of Art, Design, and the Public Domain

Roderick Wyllie
Design Critic in Landscape Architecture

Dingliang Yang
Instructor in Urban Planning and Design

Students 2018–2019

MASTER IN ARCHITECTURE I (MARCH I)

Mena Wasti Ahmed
Kofi Akakpo
Chantine Akiyama
Rana Aksoy
Miriam Alexandroff
Sheldon Alfred
Ahmad Altahhan
Emily Ashby
Peiying Ban
Ian Bankhead
Angela Blume
Willem Bogardus
Alexis Boivin
Sandra Bonito
Calvin Boyd
Benjamin Bromberg Gaber
Charles Burke
Biru Cao
Gustavo Antonio Casalduc-Rivera
Stanislas Chaillou
Caroline Chao
Ching Him Chee
Amy Chen
Peitong Chen
Sihui (Iris) Chen
Sum In Sarah Cheung
Jeremy Chevis-Benson
Jocelyn Chiou
Seo Won Choi
Kevin Chong
Kai-hong Chu
Isabel Chun
Graham Coffman
Taylor Cook
Rachel Coulomb
Amanda Darmosaputro
Elizabeth De Angelis
Cynthia Deng
Zixuan Deng
Marc Dessauvage
Claire Djang
Stella Dwifaradewi
Panharith Ean
Elif Erez
Zhixing Fei
Martin Fernandez
Ariel Flotte
Allison Frost
Danmo Fu
Cherry Fung
Christopher Gallegos
Dania Ghuneim
Angeliki Giannisi
Vladimir Gintoff
Cassie Gomes
Marianna González-Cervantes
Brayton Gregory
Jonathan Gregurick
Chris Grenga
Aria Griffin
Ian Grohsgal
Xiangyu Guo
Yuqiao Guo
Daniel Haidermota
Taylor Halamka
Myo Han
Rebecca Han
Won Jeong Han
Adrian Harrison
Kenneth Hasegawa
Benjamin Hayes
Matthew Hayes
Chen He
Isa He
Christina Hefferan
Ashley Hickman
An Hoang
Konrad Holtsmark
Kira Horie
Olivia Howard
Hannah Hoyt
Jingyuan Huang
Shihao Huang
Jihoon Hyun
Golnoush Jalali
Hangsoo Jeong
Suthata Jiranuntarat
Young Eun Ju
Jia Jung
Anna Kaertner
Nyeonggeun Kang
Lina Karain Silwani
Evan Kettler
Aryan Khalighy
Minyong Kim
Su In Kim
Yuna Kim
Lindsey Krug
Karen Kuo
Ho In Kuong
Jan Kwan
Daniel Kwon
Hoi Ying Lam
Shun Yin Gabriel Lam
Peteris Lazovskis
Alice Lee
Brian Bo Ying Lee
Dohyun Lee
Ezra Lee
Jungwoo Lee
Seoyoung Lee
Naomi Levine
Keira Li
Loren Li
Ruize Li
Jessica Lim
Keunyoung Lim
David Ling
Qinrong Liu
Yaxuan Liu
Stephanie Lloyd
Anna Kalliopi Louloudis
Kaoru Lovett
Fan Lu
Kun Luo
Radu-Remus Macovei
Caleb Marhoover
Glen Marquardt
Adam Maserow
Grace McEniry
Milos Mladenovic
Matthew Moffitt
Yina Moore
Adam Moqrane
Khorshid Naderi-Azad
Caleb Negash
Paris Nelson
Jonathan Ng
Andrew Ngure
Donald O'Keefe
Tara Oluwafemi
Evan Orf
Bryan Ortega-Welch
Mark Pantano
Andy Park
Sujie Park
Francesca Perone
Luisa Pineros Sanchez
Ethan Poh
Isaac Henry Pollan
Diandra Rendradjaja
Luisa Respondek
Fiona Riley
Jihyun Ro
Cara Roberts
Julia Roberts
Jack Rodat
Tyler Rodgers
Matthew Rosen
Lane Raffaldini Rubin
Thomas Schaperkotter
Julia Schubach
Nima Shariat
Sam Sheffer
Adam Sherman
Gio Shin
Veronica Smith
David Solomon
Humbi Song
Anne Stack
Marie Stargala
Morgan Starkey
Edda Steingrimsdottir
Isabel Strauss
Adam Strobel
Mahfuz Sultan
Tracy Tang
Xiaotang Tang
Noelle Tay
Breanne Taylor
Lee Teng
Bijan Thornycroft
Y-Nhi Tran
Hidekatsu Uchida
Omar Valentin
Samantha Vasseur
Khoa Vu
Son Vu
John Yau Chung Wang
Tiange Wang
Yiou Wang
Luke Warren
Taylor Wasson
Kyle Winston
Jacqueline Wong
Paul Wood
Bella Wu
Dixi Wu
Vanessa Wu
Siyuan Xi
Jialiang Xiang
Shaina Yang
Yuhou Yang
Jung Chan Yee
Tsun Hong Jonathan Yeung
Carolyn Yi
Euipoom Yoon
Jae Ho Yoon
Steven Young
Jessica Yuan
Renee Yuen
Hyunsuk Yun
Ailing Zhang
George Zhang
Huopu Zhang
Yiran Zhang
Sheng Zhao
Sylvia Zhao
Pengpeng Zheng
Brian Zug

MASTER IN ARCHITECTURE I AP (MARCH I AP)

Andrew Bako
Zoey Cai
Andres Camacho
Jing Chang
Beining Chen
Katy Cheng
Julian Daly
Benjamin William Dinapoli
Karen Duan
Alejandro Fernandez Grande
Christina Graydon
Jun Ho Han
Wilson Harkhono
Tsz Hung Hu
I-Yang Huang
Meng Jiang
Han Jin
Yungi Jung
Charles Kim
Yeonmoon Kim
Joshua Kuhr
Yueyan Li
Zhixin Lin
Benoit Maranda
Jiangpu Meng
Chun Hin Pun
Yue Shao
Bradley Silling
Igsung So
Alexandru Vilcu
Edward Wang
Mark Wang
Zai Xi Jeffrey Wong
Han Cheol Yi

MASTER IN ARCHITECTURE II (MARCH II)

George Abraham
Meric Arslanoglu
Danielle Aspitz
Dylan Bachar
Yotam Ben Hur
Jingyi Bi
Astrid Cam Aguinaga
James Carrico
Gloria Chang
Giorgos Chatzopoulos
Sichuan Chen

Ningxin Cheng
Aimilios Davlantis Lo
Nicolás Delgado Álcega
Fang Fan
Yang Fei
Evangelos Fokialis
Trent Fredrickson
Daniel Garcia
Matthew Gehm
Anastasios Giannakopoulos
Anna Goga
Jin Guo
Benjamin Hait
Xiao Han
Minyoung Hong
Henrik Ilvesmaki
Samantha Ingallina
Hiroshi Kaneko
Danielle Kemble
Sami Khoury
David Kim
Jinwoo Kim
Sean Kim
Jonathan Lee
Xinyun Li
Yalun Li
Proey Liao
Diastika Lokesworo
Nabila Mahdi
Eduardo Mediero
Hanh Nguyen
Jack Oliva-Rendler
Sampath Pediredla
Benjamin Pennell
Benjamin Pollak
Alkiviadis Pyliotis
Hee Young Pyun
Francisco Ramos
Courtney Richeson
Edgar Rodriguez
Dylan Rupar
Daniel Saenz
Huma Sahin
Melodie Sanchez
Poyao Shih
Aticha Siriphand
William Smith
Sejung Song
Alexandros Spentzaris
Jacob Stinson
Yang Chun Su
Shining Sun
Peeraya Suphasidh
Justin Tan
Hua Tian
Sevki Topcu
Julio Torres Santana
Aime Vailes-Macarie
Ever Vargas
Cassidy Viser
John Wagner
Chi-Hsuan Wang
Claire Watson
Zachary Weimer
Adrian Wong
Wei Wu
Hong Xi
Wei Xiao
Sol Yoon
Xin Zheng

MASTER IN LANDSCAPE ARCHITECTURE I (MLA I)

Michael Ahn
Ayami Akagawa
Dylan Anslow
Naoko Asano
Xiao He Bi
Carson Booth
Yoni Angelo Carnice
Colin Chadderton
Hannah Chako
Joan Chen
Xi Chen
Su-Yeon Choi
Nora Chuff
Kira Clingen
Helena Cohen
Sydney Conaway
Caroline Craddock
Jingzi Cui
Anna Curtis-Heald
Qiaoqi Dai
Warwin Davis
Sarah Diamond
Yuru Ding
Alexandra Distefano
Chelsea Dombroskie
Sarah Doonan
Sophie Elias
Yvonne Fang
Carson Fisk-Vittori
Isabella Caterina Frontado
Samuel Gilbert
Brittany Giunchigliani
Alana Godner-Abravanel
Melissa Green
Diana Guo
Benjamin Hackenberger
Annie Hayner
Kongyun He
Mark Heller
Caroline Hickey
Emily Hicks
Dana Hills
Zoe Holland
Jenjira Holmes
Xingyue Huang
Cecilia Huber
Jiyun Jeong
Edyth Jostol
Esther Kim
Jonathan Kuhr
Jan Kwan
Sirinya Laochinda
Tian Wei Li
Zhenheng Li
Charlotte Leib
Matthew Liebel
Danica Liongson
Jiacheng Liu
Siyu Liu
Zeqi Liu
Ann Lynch
Hannah Lyons-Galante
Tiangang Lyu
Malone Matson
Jaline McPherson
McKenna Mitchell
Angela Moreno-Long
Isabel Preciado
Andres Quinche
Estello Raganit
Scarlet Rendleman
Dominic Riolo
Eleanor Rochman
David Schoen
Joel Seidner
Sophia Sennett
Evangeline Sheridan
Polly Sinclair
Maxwell Smith-Holmes
Olivia So
Chloe Soltis
Ciara Stein
Melody Stein
Jena Tegeler
Ada Thomas
Runjia Tian
Connie Trinh
Hannah Van der Eb
Eric Van Dreason
Andreea Vasile
Gracie Villa
Parawee Wachirabuntoon
Kanchan Wali-Richardson
Amanda Walker
Guanyi Wang
Yifan Wang
Yujue Wang
Zhaodi Wang
Timothy Webster
Yue Wu
Siwen Xie
Nan Yang
Jiani Zhang
Jinying Zhang
Ying Zhang
Yuning Zhang
Haoyu Zhao
Xin Zhong
Xinyi Zhou

MASTER IN LANDSCAPE ARCHITECTURE I AP (MLA I AP)

Mena Wasti Ahmed
Lamia Almuhanna
Aiysha Alsane
Isabel Brostella
Laura Cabral
Michael Cafiero
Karissa Lyla Campos
Meredith Chavez
Kuzina Cheng
Nai Tzu Cheng
Oi Wai Charity Cheung
Mariel Collard
Lu Dai
Wei Dou
Simon Escabi
Luis Flores
Juan Grisales
Shira Grosman
Kevin Jin He
Christin Hu
Camila Huber Horta Barbosa
Kimberley Huggins
Chelsea Kilburn
Eunsu Kim
Nam Jung Kim
Jonathon Koewler
Andy Lee
Juhyuk Lee
Sang Yoon Lee
Sunmee Lee
Wan Fung Lee
Hanying Li
Jingyun Li
Mengfei Li
Xiuzheng Li
Ting Liang
Varat Limwibul
Maria De La Luz Lobos Martinez
Haey Ma
Yanni Ma
Chenxiang Meng
Monica Miyagusuku
Koby Moreno
Melissa Naranjo
Alykhan Neky
Kai Chi Ng
Hanh Nguyen
Nadyeli Quiroz
Roberto Ransom Ruiz
Stefano Romagnoli
Kari Roynesdal
Lane Raffaldini Rubin
Hye Rim Shin
Ui Jun Song
Joshua Stevens
An Sun
Amanda Ton
Yun-Ting Tsai
Zishen Wen
Ting Fung Wong
Shing Hin Bryan Woo
Alysoun Wright
Cho-Hao Wu
Leilei Wu
Qiao Xu
Zhenyu Yang
Chengzhang Zhang
Tongtong Zhang
Xiaowei Zhang
Xiaoyuan Zhang
Xijia Zhang
Chuanying Zheng

MASTER IN LANDSCAPE ARCHITECTURE II (MLA II)

Zheng Cong
Zilin Gui
Peilin Li
Yinan Liu
Matthew Macchietto
Paul Phillips
Chavapong Phipatseritham
Xiwei Shen
Isaac Stein
Boxiang Yu
Wei Zeng
Chengzhe Zhang
Bailun Zhang

MASTER OF ARCHITECTURE IN URBAN DESIGN (MAUD)

Samuel Adkisson
Aranzazu de Arino Bello
Maria Veronica Cardenas Vignes
Justin Cawley
Firas Chamas
Weihsiang Chao
Meredith Chavez
Yamei Chen
Yoeun Chung
John Crowley
Haoyu Dong
Yuebin Dong
Jiawei Dou
Jose De La Luz Esparza Murillo
Chang Gao
Sebastian Gaviria Gomez
Zehui Gong
Jungeun Goo
Laura Greenberg
Yao Gu
Jing Hai
Olivia Hansberg
Yunyan Hu
Camila Huber Horta Barbosa
Xingjian Jiang
Hiroki Kawashima
Saeb Ali Khan
Tatum Lau
Chen Li
Zhiyu Li
Ting Liang
Lizbeth Lopez Lopez
Minzi Long
Yueheng Lu
Young Lv
Chenhao Ma
Ambika Malhotra
Rafael Marengoni
Christopher Nelson
Mengying Ouyang
Zirui Pang
Bomin Park
Soledad Patino
Yuzhou Peng
Maria Peroni
Loyiso Qaqane
Xin Qian
Ming Qin
Sudeshna Sen
Shovan Shah
Evan Shieh
Ye Chan Shin
Ashutosh Singhal
Jichao Sun
Maoran Sun
Pengcheng Sun
Shining Sun
Luke Tan
William Toohey III
Han Ning Tsai
Jiayi Wang
Shenting Wang
Wen Wang
Steven Ward
Xin Wen
Cindy Xiao
Eileen Xie
Zhile Xie
Zhou Xu
Zeming Yang
Xiaoyan Yin
Lanchun Zeng
Jie Zhang
Nigel (Haoyang) Zhang
Renyi Zhang
Shunfan Zheng
Yuchen Zheng
Zhi Zheng
Keting Zhou
Yasong Zhou
Eduardo Zizumbo Colunga

MASTER OF LANDSCAPE ARCHITECTURE IN URBAN DESIGN (MLAUD)

Ruanlanming Du
Sarah Fayad
Ruocan Fu
Linyu Liu
Charles Smith
Abbey Wallace
Boxiang Yu
Pu Yu
Chengzhe Zhang
Tongtong Zhou

MASTER IN URBAN PLANNING (MUP)

Muniba Ahmad
Syed Ali
Carolyn Angius
Mariah Barber
Maura Barry-Garland
Jesus Becerra Sinuco
Mark Bennett
Kimberly Bernardin
Roody Botros
Patrick Braga
Amaya Bravo-France
Juan Caicedo (HKS)
Astrid Cam Aguinaga
Paul Caporaso
Anna Carlsson (HLS)
James Carrico
Antonio Castaneda
Evita Chavez
Gina Ciancone
Matthew Coogan (HLS)
Jimena David Garza
Cynthia Deng
Sury Dewa Ayu
Erick Diaz (HKS)
Emily Duma
McKayla Dunfey
Isabelle Dupraz
Ross Eisenberg (HKS)
Sidra Fatima
José Carlos Fernández Salas
Amy Friedlander
Angela Gile
Vladimir Gintoff
Katie Gourley
Solomon Green-Eames
Margaret Haltom
Evan Hazelett
Mark Heller
Natasha Hicks
Abby Jamiel
Asad Jan
Jia Jung
Jennifer Kaplan
Benjamin Keller
Emily Klein
Gal Kramer
Willow Latham (HKS)
Andy Lee
Chelsea Lee
Malika Leiper
Saul Levin
Yinan Li (HKS)
Laura Lopez Cardenas
Kimberly Lum
Radu-Remus Macovei
Eleni Macrakis
Henna Mahmood
Daisha Martin
Catherine McCandless
Moira McCrave-Carragee
Ayesha Tara Mehrotra
Brett Merriam
Amelia Muller
Amirah Ndam Njoya
Jonathan Ngige
Benjamin Notkin
Eamon O'Connor (HKS)
Emma Ogiemwanye
Sarai Osorio
Daniel Padilla
Sydney Pedigo
Yakima Pena Perez
Mariana Pereira Guimaraes (HSPH)
Yuki Perry
Emma Phillips
Joshua Pi
Nevena Pilipovic-Wengler
Andres Quinche
Gabriel Ramos
Timothy Ravis
Alexander Rogala
Rian Rooney
Chandra Rouse
Benjamin Sadkowski
Tiera Satchebell
David Schoen
Sanjay Seth (HKS)
Safeer Shersad
Megan Slavish
Laier-Rayshon Smith
Ciara Stein
Rui Su
Firas Suqi
Malia Teske
Stefan Trevisan
Sydney Upchurch
Finn Vigeland
Hung Vo
Robert Wang
Alysoun Wright
Sarah Zou

MASTER IN DESIGN STUDIES, ART, DESIGN, AND THE PUBLIC DOMAIN (MDES ADPD)

Kathryn Abarbanel
Nadia Asfour
Inés Benítez
Aránzazu de Ariño
Aleiya Evison
Isabella Caterina Frontado
David Gil
Qian Guo
Jungmoon Ham
Wenwen He
Yutong Jiang
Hanna Kim
Sean Kim
Stella Kim
Je Sung Lee
Angela Mayrina
Eric Moed
Mallory Nezam
Sunyoung Park
Penelope Phylactopoulos
Delaram Rahim
Andrew Scheinman
Carolina Sepulveda
Mindy Seu
Daniel Shieh
Sujie Park
Runjia Tian
Daniel Tompkins
Alicia Valencia
Mengfei Wang
Natthida Wiwatwicha
Iris Xia
Shikun Zhu

MASTER IN DESIGN STUDIES, CRITICAL CONSERVATION (MDES CC)

Francisco Brown-Ortega
Weiyi Cao
Elena Clarke
Francisco Colom Jover
Haoming Fu
Carrie Gammell
Yanan He
Mingya Hsu
Linda Just
Izzy Kornblatt-Stier
Yiyi Liang
Xiaoxiao Liu
Jennifer Elizabeth Matchett
Corine Morain
Longyun Ren
Karan Saharya
Alexandra Sanyal
Lei Song
Betzabe Valdes Lopez
Zhoutong Wang
Zhongnan Yang
Jingxuan Zhang

MASTER IN DESIGN STUDIES, ENERGY AND ENVIRONMENTS (MDES EE)

Aditi Agarwal
Pamela Cabrera
Kenner Carmody
Xinzhu Chen
Margaret George
Iain Gordon
Aurora Jensen
Ao Li
Wenting Li
Victoria Lopez Cabeza
Santiago Mota
Peter Osborne
Zlatan Sehovic
Bohan Zhang

MASTER IN DESIGN STUDIES, HISTORY AND PHILOSOPHY OF DESIGN (MDES HPDM)

Ryan Beitz
Carrie Bly
Charles Burke
Elif Erez
Wilfred Guerron
Anirudh Gurumoorthy
Savinia Hawkins
Henrik Ilvesmaki
Bobby K. Anthony Jones
Fiona Kenney
Proey Liao
Charlotte Leib
Cody Pan
Vaissnavi Shukl
Yashada Wagle
Samantha Vasseur

MASTER IN DESIGN STUDIES, REAL ESTATE AND THE BUILT ENVIRONMENT (MDES REBE)

Dalia Al Derzi
Jonathan Andrews
Zarina Ateig
Hannah Bao
Adriel Beitsch-Deller
Andrey Drozdov
Ruanlanming Du
Mohamad El Bakri
Jordan Girard
Bingzhang Huang
Augustinas Indrasius
Ankita Jain
Young Jee Jang
Christel Jarrouj
Maya Kazamel
Ben Hanan Kessler
Jung Joon Kim
Siyu Long
Ziyu Lu
Edward Madigan Ii
Risa Meyers
Rishad Netarwala
Varzan Patel
Pond Punyanaramitdee
Huan Wang
Yifan Wang
Dixi Wu
Wei Xiao
Hong Yang
Jisoo Yang
Boxuan Zhang
Hao Zhang
Mamun Uz Zoha

MASTER IN DESIGN STUDIES, RISK AND RESILIENCE (MDES RR)

Gloria Chang
Kira Clingen
Mariel Collard
Tessa Crespo
Armida Fernandez
Pablo Izaga Gonzalez
Natasha Hicks
Lizbeth Lopez Lopez
Jimmy Pan
Susanna Pho
Maclean Sarbah
Fernando Schrupp Rivero
Isaac Stein
Amy Thornton
Natalie Wang
Viviana Wei
Naomi Woods

MASTER IN DESIGN STUDIES, TECHNOLOGY (MDES TECH)

Sulaiman Alothman
Shirin Amouei
Nicolas Ayoub
Maharshi Bhattacharya
Peitong Chen
Lins Derry
Guangyu Du
Romy El Sayah
Christina Glover
Sinan Goral
Ming Guo
Jackson Howell
Hyeon Ji Im
Mari Jo
Francisco Jung
Eunsu Kim
Yonghwan Kim
Karen Kuo
Peilin Li
Phoebe Lin
Lubin Liu
Minzi Long
Vaishnavi Magar
Nicolas Oueijan
Xiaobi Pan
Shiyi Peng
Styliani Rossikopoulou Pappa
Sejung Song
Maoran Sun
Robert Wang
Lucy Yip
Huopu Zhang
Yiqi Zhao

MASTER IN DESIGN STUDIES, URBANISM, LANDSCAPE, AND ECOLOGY (MDES ULE)

Rajji Desai
Juan Grisales
Shira Grosman
Fangyuan Hu
Danica Liongson
Samuel Maddox
Benjamin Notkin
Eduardo Pelaez
Nadyeli Quiroz
Beilei Ren
Samantha Saona
Ryan Thomas
Maggie Tsang
Yujue Wang
Sofia Xanthakou
Kuangyu Xiong
Ankang Xu
Frank Yao
Erin Yook
Adelle York
Ziwei Zhang

MASTER IN DESIGN ENGINEERING (MDE)

Nicole Adler
Berlynn Bai
Jeronimo Beccar Varela
Yash Bhutada
Humberto Ceballos
Sam Clay
Jenny Fan
David Gomez Gil
Taylor Greenberg Goldy
Mitsue Guerrero Monsalve
Vivek Haligeri Veerana
Saif Haobsh
Audrey Haque
Anesta Iwan
Togo Kida
Oliver Luo
Erin McLean
Arjun Menon
Terra Moran
Anahide Nahhal
Elisa Ngan
Saad Rajan
Hane Roh
Carla Saad
Jacob Schonberger
Julian Siegelmann
Kenneth So
Katherine Spies
Vish Srivastava
Zongheng Sun
Janet Sung
Mengxi Tan
Daniela Teran
Kiran Wattamwar
Hanif Wicaksono
Emily Yang
Mia Zaidan

DOCTOR OF DESIGN (DDES)

Suleiman Alhadidi
Spyridon Ampanavos
Aleksandar Bauranov
Ignacio Cardona
Yonghui Chen
Yujiao Chen
Michael Chieffalo
Somayeh Chitchian
Sang-Yong Cho
Daniel Daou
Yun Fu
Jose Garcia del Castillo Lopez
Mariano Gomez Luque
Boya Guo
Ellie Han
Yujie Hong
Vaughn Horn
Xiaokai Huang
Kristen Hunter
Daniel Ibañez
Esesua Ikpefan
Seung Kyum Kim
Elitza Koeva
Jingping Liu
Miguel Lopez Melendez
Yingying Lu
Mojdeh Sadat Mahdavi Moghaddam
Jeffrey Nesbit
Xuanyi Nie
Sarah Norman
Carolina San Miguel
Andreina Seijas
Julia Smachylo
Jihoon Song
Ashley E. Tannebaum
Daniel Tish
Lara Tomholt
Guy Trangos
Juan Ugarte
Hubertina van den Berg
Liang Wang
Jung Hyun Woo
Longfeng Wu
Dingliang Yang
Nari Yoon
Jeongmin Yu
Jingyi Zhang

DOCTOR OF PHILOSOPHY (PHD)

Salma Abouelhossein
Matthew Allen
Maria Atuesta
Katarzyna Balug
Aleksandr Bierig
Yazmin Crespo
Brett Michael Culbert
Taylor Davey
Phillip Denny
Igor Ekstajn
Samaa Elimam
Tamer Elshayal
Natalia Escobar Castrillón
Caroline Filice Smith
Brandon Finn
Swarnabh Ghosh

Matthew Gin
Lisa Haber-Thomson
Thomas Hill
Jacobe Huet
Sarah Hutcheson
Hannah Kaemmer
Hanan Kataw
Diana Louise Lempel
Manuel Lopez Segura
Bryan Norwood
Sabrina Osmany
Sun Min (Melany) Park
Marianne Potvin
Etien Santiago
Christina Shivers
Justin Stern
Gideon Unkeless
Rodanthi Vardouli
Dimitra Vogiatzaki
Eldra D. Walker
Xiaoshi Wang
Angela Wheeler
Wei Zhang

Staff

Whitney Airgood-Obrycki
Senior Research Analyst; Joint Center for Housing Studies

Dalya Al Mharib
Facilities Operations Coordinator; Building Services

Afshaan Alter Burtram
Program Coordinator; Architecture

Joseph Amato
Facilities Operations Assistant; Building Services

Kathleen Anderson
Staff Assistant; Executive Education

Corinna Anderson
Publications Coordinator; Joint Center for Housing Studies

Alla Armstrong
Director of Finance for Academic Affairs; Academic Finance

John Aslanian
Director of Recruitment, Student Affairs, and Career Development; Student Services

Iris Ayala
Staff Assistant; Computer Resources

Lauren Baccus
Assistant Dean of Human Resources; Human Resources

Kermit Baker
Program Director for Remodeling Studies; Joint Center for Housing Studies

Pamela Baldwin
Assistant Dean for Faculty Affairs; Faculty Affairs

Lauren Beath
Payroll Coordinator; Finance Office

Tessalina Beljean
Staff Assistant; Student Services

Todd Belton
Web Developer; Computer Resources

Sue Boland
Web Developer; Computer Resources

Dan Borelli
Director of Exhibitions; Exhibitions

Naisha Bradley
Assistant Dean for Diversity, Inclusion, and Belonging; Executive Dean's Office

Francesco Buccella
Executive Coordinator; Urban Planning and Design

Christina Burkot
Research Programs Administrator; Research Administration

Kevin Cahill
Director of Facilities Management; Building Services

Bonnie Campbell
Executive Assistant; Development

James Chaknis
Communications and Outreach Coordinator; Joint Center for Housing Studies

Maggie Chang
Executive Coordinator; Architecture

Joseph Chart
Senior Major Gift Officer; Development

Lindsey Cimochowski
Associate Director of Operations and Administration; Development

Julie Cirelli
Design News Editor and Assistant Director; Communications

Carra Clisby
Assistant Director of Donor Relations; Development

Sean Conlon
Registrar

Anne Cowie
Senior Major Gift Officer; Development

Kathryn Cox
Controller; Finance Office

Anne Creamer
Coordinator; Career Services

Travis Dagenais
Assistant Director of Communications; Communications

Anna Devine
Communications Manager, Digital Media; Communications

Sarah Dickinson
Research Support Services Librarian; Collections

Kerry Donahue
Associate Director of Communications and External Relations; Joint Center for Housing Studies

Stephen Ervin
Assistant Dean for Information Technology; Computer Resources

Alaina Fernandes
Executive Coordinator; Landscape Architecture

Ernesto Fernandez
Business Analyst, Development Data Strategy; Development

Jeffrey Fitton
Outreach and Events Manager; Harvard Center for Green Buildings and Cities

Angela Flynn
Center and Finance Coordinator; Joint Center for Housing Studies

Rena Fonseca
Director of Executive Education and International Programs; Executive Education

Nicole Freeman
Senior Major Gift Officer; Development

Riordan Frost
Associate Research Analyst; Joint Center for Housing Studies

Charles Gaillard
Research Assistant; Research Administration

Heather Gallagher
Financial Associate; Finance Office

Erica George
Coordinator of Student Activities and Outreach; Student Services

Keith Gnoza
Director of Financial Assistance/Assistant Director of Student Services; Financial Assistance

Mark Goble
Associate Dean for Operations and Finance; Finance Office

Michelle Goldberg
Staff Assistant; Human Resources

Meryl Golden
Director of Career and Community Service; Career Services

Santiago Gomez
Admissions and Data Coordinator; Admissions

Hal Gould
Manager of User Services; Computer Resources

Arin Gregorian
Financial Associate; Academic Finance

Linda Gregory
Staff Assistant; Frances Loeb Library

Gail Gustafson
Director of Admissions and Student Learning Resources Manager; Admissions

Mark Hagen
Windows System Administrator; Computer Resources

Ryanne Hammerl
Staff Assistant; Student Services

Christopher Hansen
Digital Fabrication Technical Analyst; Computer Resources

Barry Harper
Staff Assistant; Building Services

Christopher Herbert
Managing Director of the Joint Center for Housing Studies; Joint Center for Housing Studies

Alexander Hermann
Research Analyst; Joint Center for Housing Studies

Johann Hinds
Help Desk Technician; Computer Resources

Timothy Hoffman
Faculty Planning Administrator; Faculty Affairs

Taylor Horner
Department Manager, Architecture and Academic Programs; Architecture

Clare Jan-Ru Huang
Assistant Director of Executive Education for Marketing, Technology, and Global Programs; Executive Education

Sarah Hutchinson
Program Coordinator; Urban Planning and Design

Estefania Ibáñez Moreno
Coordinator, Academic Affairs; Academic Services

Ryan Jacob
Department Manager of Landscape Architecture and Urban Planning and Design; Academic Services

Maggie Janik
Multimedia Producer; Communications

William Jenkins
Facilities Operations Supervisor; Building Services

Paige Johnston
Public Programs Manager; Communications

Beth Kass
Associate Director, Development and Alumni Communications; Development

Johanna Kasubowski Abe
Materials and Media Collections Librarian; Visual Resources

Thomas Kitchen
Web/UX Developer; Computer Resources

Jeffrey Klug
Director of Design Discovery; Design Discovery

Elizabeth La Jeunesse
Senior Research Analyst; Joint Center for Housing Studies

Lindsey Lagrasse
Assistant Director of Events and Special Projects; Development

Mary Lancaster
Associate Director for Finance and Administration; Joint Center for Housing Studies

Ashley Lang
Director of Administration for Academic Affairs; Academic Services

Amy Langridge
Finance Manager; Executive Education

Pamela Larsen
Events Coordinator; Development

Kevin Lau
Head of Instructional Technology Group and Library; Frances Loeb Library

Seah Lee
Recruitment Assistant; Student Services

Burton LeGeyt
Fabrication Technical Specialist and Shop Supervisor; Computer Resources

Donna Lewis
Executive Assistant, Academic Affairs; Academic Services

David Luberoff
Deputy Director of the Joint Center for Housing Studies; Joint Center for Housing Studies

Laura Lubin
Alumni Relations and Annual Giving Manager; Development

Anna Lyman
Director of External Administration; Dean's Office

Robert Marino
Finance and Grants Manager; Harvard Center for Green Buildings and Cities

Edwin Martinez
Help Desk Technician; Computer Resources

Anne Mathew
Assistant Dean of Research Administration; Research Administration

Daniel McCue
Senior Research Associate; Joint Center for Housing Studies

Amanda McMahan
Senior Administrative Coordinator; Dean's Office

Daniela Miclea
Accounting Assistant; Academic Finance

Jennifer Molinsky
Senior Research Associate; Joint Center for Housing Studies

Margaret Moore De Chicojay
Programs Administrator; Advanced Studies Program

Janina Mueller
GIS and Data Librarian, Frances Loeb Library

Janessa Mulepati
Program Coordinator for Design Engineering; Advanced Studies Program

Michelle Muliro
Human Resources and Payroll Coordinator; Human Resources

Gerilyn Nederhoff
Director of Admissions and Diversity Recruitment Manager; Admissions

Caroline Newton
Director of Internal Administration; Dean's Office

Ketevan Ninua
Staff Assistant; Development

Trevor O'Brien
Manager of Building Services; Building Services

Christine O'Brien
Administrative and Financial Coordinator; Communications

Lauren O'Brien
Faculty Affairs Coordinator; Faculty Affairs

Barbara Perlo
Program Manager; Executive Education

John Peterson
Curator of the Loeb Fellowship

Jackie Piracini
Associate Dean for Administration; Executive Dean's Office

Lisa Plosker
Associate Director of Human Resources; Human Resources

Brad Quigley
Interim Codirector of Development and Alumni Relations; Development

Christopher Raichle
Program Manager; Executive Education

Pilar Raynor Jordan
Financial Associate; Academic Finance

Alix Reiskind
Research and Teaching Support Team Lead Librarian; Visual Resources

Patricia J. Roberts
Executive Dean; Executive Dean's Office

Meghan Sandberg
Publications Manager; *Harvard Design Magazine* and Communications

Jocelyn Sanders
Senior Major Gift Officer; Development

Madelin Santana
Assistant Director for Global Programs; Executive Education

Ronee Saroff
Assistant Director of Web Administration and Innovation; Communications

Venecia Siders
Coordinator; Research Administration

Jennifer Sigler
Editor in Chief; *Harvard Design Magazine* and Communications

James Skypeck
Development Coordinator; Development

Robin Slavin
Career Services Counselor; Student Services

Randa-Gae Smith
Academic Appointments and Payroll Coordinator; Faculty Affairs

Matthew Smith
Media Services Manager; User Services

Laura Snowdon
Dean of Students/Assistant Dean for Enrollment Services; Student Services

Shiona Sommerville
Associate Director; Executive Education

Jonathan Spader
Senior Research Associate; Joint Center for Housing Studies

Kelly Sprouse
Staff Assistant; Development

Ken Stewart
Assistant Dean and Director of Communications and Public Programs; Communications

Whitney Stone
Assistant Director of Leadership Gifts; Development

Amber Stout
Donor Relations Coordinator; Development

Rebeccah Stromberg
Executive Assistant to the Dean; Dean's Office

Marielle Suba
Associate Editor; Communications

Aimee Taberner
Senior Director of Curricular Affairs and Institutional Research; Academic Services

Charis Talcott
Administrative Coordinator; Academic Services

Ellen Tang
Assistant Director of Financial Aid; Financial Assistance

Elizabeth Thorstenson
Program Coordinator; Advanced Studies Program

Kathan Tracy
Interim Codirector of Development and Alumni Relations; Development

Jennifer Vallone
Accounting Assistant; Finance Office

Sean Veal
Research Assistant; Joint Center for Housing Studies

Patric Verrone
Public Programs Assistant; Communications

Michael Voligny
Assistant Dean; Development

Rachel Vroman
Manager of the Digital Fabrication Laboratory; Computer Resources

Elizabeth Walat
Assistant Dean, Finance; Finance Office

Courtney Ward
Associate Director of Leadership Gifts; Development

Ann Whiteside
Assistant Dean for Information Services; Frances Loeb Library

Sara Wilkinson
Director of Human Resources; Human Resources

Abbe Will
Research Associate; Joint Center for Housing Studies

Kelly Wisnaskas
Manager of Special Programs for Student Services; Student Services

Justin Wong
Building Services Coordinator; Building Services

Sally Young
Coordinator of Loeb Fellowship Program

Ines Zalduendo
Special Collections Archivist and Reference Librarian; Frances Loeb Library

David Zimmerman-Stuart
Exhibitions Coordinator; Exhibitions

Courses Fall 2018

CORE STUDIOS

First Semester Architecture Core: Project
Mark Lee (coordinator), Sean Canty, Jenny French, Elle Gerdeman, Lisa Haber-Thomson, Zeina Koreitem

Landscape Architecture I: First Semester Core Studio
Anita Berrizbeitia and Danielle Choi (coordinators), Francesca Benedetto, Jungyoon Kim, Pablo Perez-Ramos, with Emily Wettstein (workshop and consultant), Alistair McIntosh (workshop)

First Semester Core Urban Planning Studio
Toni L. Griffin (coordinator), Sai Balakrishnan, Kathryn Firth, Lily Song, with David Gamble (workshop)

Elements of Urban Design
Rahul Mehrotra (coordinator and consultant), Yun Fu, Stephen Gray, Dennis Pieprz, Linda Pollak, with Michael Manfredi (consultant)

Third Semester Architecture Core: Integrate
Jon Lott (coordinator), Grace La, John May, Jay Siebenmorgen, Oana Stanescu, Belinda Tato

Landscape Architecture III: Third Semester Core Studio
Rosetta S. Elkin and Robert Pietrusko (coordinators), Montserrat Bonhevi Rosich, Sergio Lopez-Pineiro, Rosalea Monacella, Paola Sturla

Collaborative Design Engineering Studio I (with SEAS)
Andrew Witt, Arianna Mazzeo, Jock Herron

OPTION STUDIOS

Utopia/Dystopia: Post-work (Place) in 2068
Annabelle Selldorf

Dwelling/Garden/Being, Suzhou
Zhang Ke

The House: The Waken Desire
Tatiana Bilbao, Iwan Baan

On Health II: Amsterdam Health Kitchen
Ben Van Berkel, Christian Veddeler

Natural Monument
Mauricio Pezo, Sofia von Ellrichshausen

An American Plan
Kersten Geers, David Van Severen

reCYCLO: Architectures of Waste
Caroline O'Donnell

Architecture as a Tool to Improve Lives: Development of a Day Care Center for Rohingya Children
Anna Heringer

Soft Spaces
Simon Frommenwiler, Simon Hartmann, Tilo Herlach

New Formations for the Social Metropolis
Alison Brooks

The Future Provincetown
Preston Scott Cohen

Rotterdam Study Abroad Option Studio: Countryside III
Rem Koolhaas

Central Art-Park for North Adams
Martha Schwartz

Now Arriving: A Manhattan Transit Landscape
Gary R. Hilderbrand

Alternative Futures for Al-'Ula, Saudi Arabia
Craig Douglas, Stephen Ervin

Rhizosphere
Teresa Gali-Izard

Arlington National Cemetery: Engaging Hallowed Ground
Marty Poirier

The New Selma
Daniel D'Oca

A Campus in a City—A City in a Campus: Harvard and Allston
Shaun Donovan, David Gamble

Gendering Urban Development: Making Room for Women in Urban Planning and Design in Argentina
Chelina Odbert

Multiple Miamis
Chris Reed, Sean Canty

The Agency of Mezcal in the Oaxaca Valley of Mexico
Elisa Silva

VISUAL STUDIES AND COMMUNICATION

Architectural Representation I
Megan Panzano

Architectural Representation II
Iman Fayyad

Spatial Analysis and the Built Environment
Andres Sevtsuk

Landscape Representation I
Emily Wettstein

Digital Media: Design Systems
Sawako Kaijima

Digital Media: Image
Zeina Koreitem

Landscape Representation III: Landform and Ecological Process
Craig Douglas, Rosalea Monacella

Communication for Designers
Emily Waugh

Constructing Visual Narratives of Place
Francesca Benedetto

Representation First (!!!), Then Architecture
Jennifer Bonner

MAKE/BELIEVE
Dan Borelli, Rebecca Uchill

Graphic/Volume Conflations
Viola Ago

Paper or Plastic: Reinventing Shelf-life in the Supermarket Landscape
Teman Evans, Teran Evans

Drawing for Designers: Techniques of Expression, Articulation, and Representation
Ewa Harabasz

Immersive Landscape: Representation through Gaming Technology
Eric de Broche des Combes

Public Projection: Projection as a Tool for Expression and Communication in Public Space
Krzysztof Wodiczko

Art, Design, and the Public Domain Proseminar
Krzysztof Wodiczko

DESIGN THEORY

Theories of Landscape as Urbanism
Charles Waldheim

Culture, Conservation, and Design
Susan Snyder, George Thomas

The Idea of Environment
Dilip da Cunha

Field Methods and Living Collections
Rosetta S. Elkin

An Unsentimental Look at Architecture and Social Craft
John Peterson

Spaces of Solidarity
Malkit Shoshan

New Cyclical City: Landscape and the Longview
Jill Desimini

Werewolf: Architectures of Change
Caroline O'Donnell

Selected Current (and Recurrent) Topics in Architecture Theory and Design Practice
Jorge Silvetti

Style Worry or #FOMO
Max Kuo

HISTORY AND THEORY

Studies of the Built North American Environment: 1580 to the Present
John R. Stilgoe

Buildings, Texts, and Contexts I
Erika Naginski, Andrew Holder

Histories of Landscape Architecture I: Textuality and the Practice of Landscape Architecture
Edward Eigen

North American Seacoasts and Landscapes: Discovery Period to the Present
John R. Stilgoe

Michelangelo Architect: Precedents, Innovation, Influence
Christine Smith

Structuring Urban Experience: From the Athenian Acropolis to the Boston Common
Christine Smith

Signal, Image, Architecture III: The Automatic Present
John May

Building Conservation and Renewal: Assessment, Analysis, Design
David Fixler

Mountains and the Rise of Landscape
Edward Eigen

Domesticity, Privacy, Transparency, Performance
Alice Friedman

Topology and Imagination: Between Chinese Landscapes and Architecture
Stanislaus Fung

Architecture in Early Modern England: Themes and Methods
Erika Naginski

Rotterdam Study Abroad Seminar: Exhibiting Architecture in the Agency of Display
Léa-Catherine Szacka

Rotterdam Study Abroad Seminar: Architecture, Urbanism, and Agriculture
Sébastien Marot

SOCIOECONOMIC STUDIES

Real Estate Finance and Development
Richard Peiser, David Hamilton

Cities by Design I
Rahul Mehrotra and Peter Rowe (course coordinators) with Eve Blau, Joan Busquets, Felipe Correa, Jerold S. Kayden, Alex Krieger

Field Studies in Real Estate, Planning, and Urban Design: Buenos Aires, Los Angeles, and Andover, MA
Richard Peiser

Policy Making in Urban Settings (at HKS)
James Carras

Analytic Methods of Urban Planning: Quantitative
Michael Hooper

Analytic Methods: Qualitative
Ann Forsyth

Transportation Policy and Planning (at HKS)
José Gómez-Ibáñez

Housing and Urbanization in the United States
James Stockard, Jennifer Molinsky

Healthy Places
Ann Forsyth

Sustainable Real Estate
Jesse M. Keenan

Critical Perspectives in Environmental Planning
Abby Spinak

Contemporary Developing Countries: Entrepreneurial Solutions to Intractable Problems (at FAS)
Tarun Khanna, Satchit Balsari

Metropolitics: Comparative Metropolitan Governance
Pablo Allard

Economic Development Planning
George Proakis

Experimental Infrastructures
Abby Spinak

Form and Finance: the Design of Real Estate
Bing Wang, David Gamble

The Spatial Politics of Land: A Comparative Perspective
Sai Balakrishnan

Public Space
Jerold S. Kayden

SCIENCE AND TECHNOLOGY

Environmental Systems 1
Ali Malkawi

Environmental Systems 2
Holly Samuelson

Construction Systems
Carl Solander

Ecologies, Techniques, Technologies I
Teresa Galí-Izard, Doug Reed

Structural Design II
Martin Bechthold

Ecologies, Techniques, Technologies III: Ecology and the Design World
Steven Handel, Chris Matthews

The Innovator's Practice: Finding, Building, and Leading Good Ideas with Others (at SEAS)
Beth Altringer

Innovation in Science and Engineering: Conference Course (at SEAS)
David Weitz

Material Systems: Digital Design and Fabrication
Nathan King

Mapping: Geographic Representation and Speculation
Robert Pietrusko

Brownfields: Remediation and Regeneration Practices
Niall Kirkwood

Water, Land-Water Linkages, and Aquatic Ecology
Timothy Dekker, Nicholas Nelson

Introduction to Computational Design
Panagiotis Michalatos

Applied Urban Analytics
Andres Sevtsuk

Digital Fabrication and Robotics
Stylianos Dritsas

Deployable Surfaces: Dynamic Performance through Multi-Material Architectures
Chuck Hoberman

Visualization (at SEAS)
Hanspeter Pfister

Architectural Acoustics
Ben Markham

Nano Micro Macro: Adaptive Material Laboratory (with SEAS)
Jonathan Grinham, Joanna Aizenberg

LIT: A Survey and Design Research Seminar of Architectural Lighting
Dan Weissman

PROFESSIONAL PRACTICE

Foundations of Practice
Jeffry Burchard, Jesse M. Keenan

Integrative Frameworks for Technology, Environment, and Society I
Nabil Harfoush with GSD faculty

Practices of Landscape Architecture
Karen Janosky, Paola Sturla

Frameworks of Practice
Paul Nakazawa

Innovation in Project Delivery
Mark R. Johnson

Elements of the Urban Stack
Paul Nakazawa

PROPAEDEUTIC AND ADVANCED RESEARCH

Thing Power in the Arles Region: Assemblages, Depositions, and Displacements
Anita Berrizbeitia, Katarzyna Balug

Real Estate and City Making in China
Bing Wang

Multiple Miamis Project-based Course: Infrastructure, Affordability, Identity, and the Public
Lily Song

Preparation for Independent Thesis Proposal for MUP, MAUD, or MLAUD
Michael Hooper

Preparation of MLA Design Thesis
Charles Waldheim

Independent Design Engineering Project I
Martin Bechthold, Mary Tolikas

Preparation of Doctoral Thesis Proposal
Martin Bechthold, Ann Forsyth, Niall Kirkwood, Ali Malkawi, Erika Naginski, Antoine Picon, Peter Rowe

MArch II Proseminar
Preston Scott Cohen

Urban Design Proseminar
Eve Blau

Proseminar in Urbanism, Landscape, Ecology
Alex Wall

Courses Spring 2019

CORE STUDIOS

Second Semester Architecture Core: SITUATE
Jeffry Burchard, Tomás dePaor, Sean Canty, Michelle Chang, Megan Panzano, Patrick McCafferty

Landscape Architecture II: Second Semester Core Studio
Emily Wettstein, Montserrat Bonvehi Rosich, Craig Douglas, Paola Sturla, Teresa Galí-Izard, Nadir Abdessemed, Eric de Broche des Combes

Second Semester Core Urban Planning Studio
Daniel D'Oca, Brie Hensold, Jennifer Molinsky, Kathy Spiegelman, Richard Peiser

Fourth Semester Architecture Core: RELATE
Jenny French, Jennifer Bonner, Andrew Holder, Sergio Lopez-Pineiro, Oana Stanescu, Elizabeth Whittaker

Landscape Architecture IV: Fourth Semester Core Studio
Jill Desimini, Rosalea Monacella, Danielle Choi, Pablo Pérez-Ramos, Belinda Tato, Alex Wall

Collaborative Design Engineering Studio II
Sawako Kaijima, Jock Herron, Arianna Mazzeo, Peter Stark

OPTION STUDIOS

FAMILY
Mack Scogin

Model as Building—Building as Model
George L. Legendre

Recasting the Outcasts
Jeanne Gang

Setouchi (Seto Inland Sea) Studio
Toshiko Mori

The New Generic
Sharon Johnston

Zero Energy Residential High-Rise
Ali Malkawi, Gordon Gill

A Novel Museum
Johannes Kuehn, Wilfried Kuehn, Simona Malvezzi

How to Live Together . . .
Iñaki Ábalos

American Gothic: Monuments for Small-Town Life
Pier Paolo Tamburelli

The Anamorphic Double: A Bridge for D.C.
Grace La, James Dallman

Tokyo Study Abroad Studio: New Topologies of Our Living Environment
Sou Fujimoto

SUPERBLOOM: Shelter, Drought, and Sculpture in the California Desert
James Lord, Roderick Wyllie

Brexit, Borders, and Imagining a New City-Region for the Irish Northwest
Niall Kirkwood, Gareth Doherty

The Monochrome No-image
Rosetta S. Elkin

Landscape of Trans-Nationality
Jungyoon Kim, Yoon-Jin Park

Build with Life: Transformation and Formation: Landscape and Islamic Culture
Catherine Mosbach

Extreme Urbanism 6: Designing Sanitation Infrastructure, Mahim Koliwada, Mumbai
Rahul Mehrotra

Large-Scale Projects to Create New Centralities in Shanghai: Potentials for the Regular City
Joan Busquets, Dingliang Yang

Designing Atmospheres and Technologies for Social Interaction
Jose Luis Vallejo

Future of Streets in Los Angeles
Andres Sevtsuk

Patterned Justice: Design Languages for a Just Pittsburgh
Toni L. Griffin

Rethinking a Humanist Skyscraper City
Moshe Safdie, Jaron Lubin

VISUAL STUDIES AND COMMUNICATION

Landscape Representation II
Emily Wettstein

Digital Media: Ambience
Allen Sayegh

Digital Media: Writing Form
George L. Legendre

Responsive Environments: Episodes in Experiential Futures
Allen Sayegh, Stefano Andreani

AI and Computer Simulation in Landscape Practice
Paola Sturla

Sections of Every Thing
Jungyoon Kim

The Landscape We Eat
Montserrat Bonvehi Rosich

Drawing for Designers: Human Presence and Appearance in Natural and Built Environments
Ewa Harabasz

Interdisciplinary Art and Design Practices
Malkit Shoshan

DESIGN THEORY

The Nature of Difference: Theories and Practices of Landscape Architecture
Anita Berrizbeitia, Pablo Pérez-Ramos

Designing the American City: Civic Aspirations and Urban Form
Alex Krieger

Design Anthropology: Objects, Landscapes, Cities
Gareth Doherty

Urban Form: Transition as Condition
Eve Blau

Advanced Seminar in City Form: Future of Streets
Andres Sevtsuk

Experiments in Public Freedom
Sergio Lopez-Pineiro

Material, Atmosphere, and Ambience
Toshiko Mori

Place-Based Design Inquiry
Dilip da Cunha

Emergent Urbanizations: Challenges for Theory, Method, and Research
Neil Brenner and Sai Balakrishnan

Factory of the Sensible and the Political* (Equipping Experience)
Catherine Ingraham

Urban Grids: Open Form for City Design 2
Joan Busquets

Tokyo Study Abroad Seminar: Thinning Metropolis—Strategies and Tools for the New Urban Condition
Kayoko Ota

HISTORY AND THEORY

Buildings, Texts, and Contexts II
Erika Naginski, Antoine Picon

Histories of Landscape Architecture II: Design, Representation, and Use
Sonja Dümpelmann

Buildings, Texts, and Contexts III: The Tower and the Sphere: Architecture and Modernity
Amanda Reeser Lawrence, Vittorio Lampugnani

Modernization in the Visual United States Environment, 1890–2035
John R. Stilgoe

Adventure and Fantasy Simulation, 1871–2036
John R. Stilgoe

Modern Architecture and Urbanism in China
Peter Rowe

Making Sacred Space
Christine Smith

Cities, Infrastructures, and Politics: From Renaissance to Smart Technologies
Antoine Picon

Competing Visions of Modernity in Japan
Seng Kuan

Bramante Is Better than Alberti . . .
Jorge Silvetti

Fifteen Things (A Secret History of Italian Design)
Jeffrey Schnapp

Palladio and Raphael: An Innovative Learning Experience
Guido Beltramini, Howard Burns

Forest, Grove, Tree: Planting Urban Landscapes
Sonja Dümpelmann

Architecture and Landscape Before and After Watergate
Edward Eigen

Architecture's Bodies: Agency and Biopolitics
Lisa Haber-Thomson

Power and Place: Culture and Conflict in the Built Environment
George Thomas, Susan Snyder

SOCIOECONOMIC STUDIES

Public and Private Development
Jerold S. Kayden

Urban Politics and Planning (at HKS)
Quinton Mayne

Cities by Design II: Projects, Processes, and Outcomes
Stephen Gray

Advanced Real Estate Finance
Frank Apeseche

Building and Leading Real Estate Enterprises and Entrepreneurship
Frank Apeseche

Theories for Practice in Conflict, Crisis, and Recovery
Marianne Potvin

Housing and Urbanization in Global Cities
Alexander von Hoffman

U.S. Housing Markets, Problems, and Policies
Christopher Herbert

Climate Change Resilience and Adaptation
Jesse M. Keenan

Environment, Economics, and Enterprise
Holly Samuelson, Frank Apeseche

Planning for Climate Change: Scarcity, Abundance, and the Idea of the Future
Abby Spinak

Community Development: Past, Present, and Future
Lily Song

Urban Transportation Planning and Implementation
Frederick Salvucci, Ruth Bonsignore

Urban Design and the Color-Line
Stephen Gray

Making Participation Relevant to Design
Belinda Tato

Developing for Social Impact
Matthew Kiefer

Demographics and Population Processes
Estiri Hossein

Urban Design for Planners
David Gamble

International Humanitarian Response (at HSPH)
Stephanie Kayden

Creating Real Estate Ventures: A Legal Perspective
Michael Haroz

Affordable and Mixed-Income Housing Development, Finance, and Management
Edward Marchant

Market Analysis and Urban Economics
Ray Torto

SCIENCE AND TECHNOLOGY

Building Simulation
Ali Malkawi, Holly Samuelson

Materials
Jonathan Grinham

Ecologies, Techniques, Technologies II
Montserrat Bonvehi Rosich, Karen Janosky, Kirt Rieder

Structural Design 1
Patrick McCafferty

Cases in Contemporary Construction
Eric Höweler

Ecologies, Techniques, Technologies IV
Niall Kirkwood, Alistair McIntosh

Design Survivor: Experiential Lessons in Designing for Desirability (at SEAS)
Beth Altringer

Survey of Energy Technology (at SEAS)
Michael Aziz

Urban and Town Ecology
Richard T. T. Forman

Urban Restoration Ecology
Steven Handel

Interface Design: Integrating Material Perceptions
Sawako Kaijima

Building Human Interaction
Holly Samuelson

Beyond Adaptation and Resiliency: GeoEngineering and Why We Will Need It
Martha Schwartz

Computational Design: Time/Design as Signal
Panagiotis Michalatos

Structures in Landscape Architecture, Joint and Detail
Alistair McIntosh

Mechatronic Optics
Andrew Witt

Planted Form and Re-Formation: Past Futures and Antecedent Inventions
Danielle Choi

Informal Robotics/New Paradigms for Design and Construction
Chuck Hoberman

Tokyo Study Abroad Seminar
Mits Kanada

PROFESSIONAL PRACTICE

Integrative Frameworks for Technology, Environment, and Society II
Nabil Harfoush

Non-Professional Practice
Oana Stanescu

Designing with the Urban Stack: A Practice Course for Designers of the Built Environment
Paul Nakazawa

INTRODUCTORY STUDIES AND ADVANCED RESEARCH

Miami Resilience: Infrastructure
Jesse M. Keenan

Entanglement of Movement and Meaning: The Architect, Spatial Perception, and the Technological Body
Krzysztof Wodiczko, Ani Liu

Thesis Project/Project Thesis
Andrew Holder, Jon Lott, John McMorrough

Independent Thesis in Satisfaction of the Degree MAUD, MLAUD, or MUP

Independent Thesis for the Degree Master in Design Studies

Independent Design Engineering Project II
Martin Bechthold, Mary Tolikas, Peter Stark

Discourse and Methods I
Diane E. Davis, Neil Brenner

Discourse and Research Methods
Martin Bechthold

Fellowships and Prizes

Wheelwright Prize
Aleksandra Jaeschke
(Austin, TX)

2018–2019 LOEB FELLOWS

Stephen Burks
Design Entrepreneurship
New York, NY

Maria Cabildo
Community and Economic Development
Los Angeles, CA

Jeana Dunlap
Community and Economic Development, Urban Planning and Design
Louisville, KY

Washington Fajardo
Urban Planning and Design
Rio de Janeiro, Brazil

Bryna Lipper
Philanthropy
New York, NY

Andrea Reimer
Civic Leadership
Vancouver, Canada

Michael Smith Masis
Architecture
San Jose, Costa Rica

Katie Swenson
Public Interest Design
Boston, MA

Michiel van Iersel
Arts and Culture
Amsterdam, Netherlands

RICHARD ROGERS FELLOWSHIP

Sarosh Anklesaria
Ithaca, NY

Esther Choi
Brooklyn, NY

Peter Christensen
Rochester, NY

Maria Letizia Garzoli
Trecate, Italy

John Paul Rysavy
New York, NY

Michael Waldrep
Berlin, Germany

STUDENT FELLOWSHIPS, PRIZES, AND TRAVEL PROGRAMS

Clifford Wong Prize in Housing Design
Yueyan Li (MArch I AP), Son Truong Vu (MArch I)

Gerald M. McCue Medal
Carrie Bly (MDes HPDM)

Peter Rice Prize
Willem Bogardus (MArch I), Daniel Tish (DDes)

Digital Design Prize
Andrew Bako (MArch I AP)

Plimpton Poorvu Prize
1st Prize: Samuel Craig Adkisson (MAUD), Hiroki Kawashima (MAUD); 2nd Prize: Augustinas Indrasius (MDes REBE), Peteris Lazovskis (MArch I), Thomas Schaperkotter (MArch I)

Frederick Sheldon Traveling Fellowship
Melissa Naranjo (MLA I AP)

The Harvard Joint Center for Housing Studies Prize for the Best Paper on Housing
Charlotte Leib (MLA I, MDes HPDM)

American Institute of Architects Medal
Emily Ashby (MArch I)

Alpha Rho Chi Medal
Julia Roberts (MArch I)

James Templeton Kelley Prize for MArch I
Morgan Starkey (MArch I)

James Templeton Kelley Prize for MArch II
Aimilios Davlantis Lo (MArch II)

Julia Amory Appleton Traveling Fellowship in Architecture
David Solomon (MArch I)

Department of Architecture Faculty Design Award
Khoa Vu (MArch I), Huma Sahin (MArch II)

Kevin V. Kieran Prize
Ningxin Cheng (MArch II)

Charles Eliot Traveling Fellowship in Landscape Architecture
Lane Raffaldini Rubin (MArch I, MLA I AP)

Jacob Weidenmann Prize
Melody Stein (MLA I)

Peter Walker & Partners Fellowship for Landscape Architecture
Matthew Joseph Macchietto (MLA II)

ASLA Certificate of Honor
Malone Matson (MLA I)

ASLA Certificate of Merit
Mariel Collard (MLA I AP, MDes RR), Joshua Stevens (MLA I AP)

Landscape Architecture Foundation Olmsted Scholars
Sarah Diamond (MLA I), Estello Raganit (MLA I)

Norman T. Newton Prize
Ting Liang (MLA I AP, MAUD)

Landscape Architecture Thesis Prize
Emily Hicks (MLA I), Melody Stein (MLA I)

Award for Outstanding Leadership in Urban Planning
Natasha Hicks (MUP, MDes RR)

Award for Outstanding Leadership in Urban Planning
Eamon O'Connor (MUP)

Award for Outstanding Leadership in Urban Design
Steven Austin Ward (MAUD), Boxiang Yu (MLA II, MLAUD)

Award for Academic Excellence in Urban Planning
Mark Bennett (MUP)

Award for Academic Excellence in Urban Design
Evan Shieh (MAUD)

Ferdinand Colloredo-Mansfeld Prize for Superior Achievement in Real Estate Studies
Varzan Patel (MDes REBE)

Druker Traveling Fellowship
Carolyn Angius (MUP)

Urban Planning and Design Thesis Prize in Urban Design
Evan Shieh (MAUD)

Urban Planning and Design Thesis Prize in Urban Planning
Katie Gourley (MUP)

The Award for Excellence in Project-Based Urban Planning
Malika Leiper (MUP)

The Award for Excellence in Urban Design
Evan Shieh (MAUD)

American Institute of Certified Planners (AICP) Outstanding Student Award
Eleni Macrakis (MUP)

American Planning Association's (APA) National Transportation Planning Division Student Paper Competition
Mark Bennett (MUP)

The Design Studies Thesis Prize
Izzy Kornblatt-Stier (MDes CC), Mindy Seu (MDes ADPD), Maggie Tsang (ULE)

Dimitris Pikionis Award
Andrew Scheinman (MDes ADPD)

The Daniel L. Schodek Award for Technology and Sustainability
Pamela Cabrera (MDes EE)

MDE Overall Academic Performance
Terra Moran (MDE)

MDE Outstanding Independent Design Engineering Project
Anesta Iwan (MDE)

MDE Leadership and Community
Jenny Fan (MDE), Vivek Haligeri Veerana (MDE)

Student Groups

STUDENT FORUM 2018–2019

Mena Wasti Ahmed (MArch I, MLA I AP)
President

Andy Lee (MUP, MLA I AP)
Academic Chair

Aditi Agarwal (MDes EE)
Diversity and Inclusion Chair

Malone Matson (MLA I)
Student Groups Chair

Maharshi Bhattacharya (MDes TECH)
Professional Development Chair

Danica Liongson (MLA I, MDes ULE)
Events Chair

Kofi Akakpo (MArch I)
Resources Chair

ORGANIZATIONS

AASU (GSD African-American Student Union)
AfricaGSD
ChinaGSD
Design Research Forum (DRF)
HUPO (Harvard Urban Planning Organization)
Kirkland Gallery
LatinGSD
MEdiNA
Open Letters
Queers in Design
The Real Estate Development (RED) Club
Womxn in Design

CLUBS

AREA (Harvard Asia Real Estate Association & Asia Trek)
Beer and Dogs
Climate Governance Initiative
Community Development Project (CDP)
DDes Conference Committee
Digital Art Collective @GSD
Game!GSD
Greece GSD
GSBees
GSDance
GSD Arts Group
GSD Christian Fellowship
GSD Soccer
GSD West
GSD World Tea Club (GSTea)
GSD Veterans
The Harvard Real Estate Review
Harvard Student Chapter of the American Society of Landscape Architects (ASLA)
Harvard Student East Asia Urban Forum
Harvard Student Urban Planning Forum
Healthy Places
Hong Kong GSD
Japan GSD
JewSD
Korea GSD (KGSD)
MASS ENGAGE
National Organization of Minority Architecture Students (NOMAS)
OpenMDE
ORCA (Organizers for Radical Climate Action)
POP^UP
Rowing Club
South Asia GSD (formerly India GSD)
Southeast Asia GSD (SEA)
Spain GSD
Taiwan GSD
Time Matters
Urban GSD
xDesign
YogaGSD
ZenSD

Research

The Office for Urbanization

Director: Charles Waldheim, John E. Irving Professor of Landscape Architecture

The Office for Urbanization draws upon the School's history of design innovation to address societal and cultural conditions associated with contemporary urbanization. It develops speculative and projective urban scenarios through sponsored design research projects.

RESEARCH CENTERS

Harvard Center for Green Buildings and Cities (CGBC)

Founding Director: Ali Malkawi, Professor of Architectural Technology

The Harvard CGBC aims to transform the building industry through a commitment to design-centric strategy that directly links research outcomes to the development of new processes, systems, and products.

Harvard Joint Center for Housing Studies

Managing Director: Christopher Herbert, Lecturer in Urban Planning and Design

The Harvard Joint Center for Housing Studies advances understanding of housing issues and informs policy through research, education, and public outreach programs.

DESIGN LABS

The Just City Lab

Director: Toni L. Griffin, Professor in Practice of Urban Planning

The Just City Lab investigates the definition of urban justice and the just city, and examines how design and planning contribute to the conditions of justice and injustice in cities, neighborhoods, and the public realm.

Critical Landscapes Design Lab

Director: Gareth Doherty, Associate Professor of Landscape Architecture

The Critical Landscapes Design Lab aims to generate a series of critical design methods and comparative case studies throughout the Islamic and postcolonial worlds.

Computational Geometry Lab

Director: Andrew Witt, Associate Professor in Practice of Architecture

The Computational Geometry Lab studies the intersection of design and science of shape and form, aided by computational tools and design intuition. The lab combines computational, formal, architectural, and historical research into a heterogeneous yet synthetic agenda.

City Form Lab

Director: Andres Sevtsuk, Associate Professor of Urban Planning

The City Form Lab investigates how urban form affects the quality of life in 21st-century cities. It develops new analytic software tools for urban designers and planners and researches the effects of city design decisions on social, economic, and environmental well-being.

Healthy Places Design Lab

Directors: Ann Forsyth, Professor of Urban Planning; Jennifer Molinsky, Lecturer in Urban Planning and Design

The Healthy Places Design Lab asks how health is related to place, and how we can make places healthier—questions of wide current concern in the United States and globally. This lab links faculty and students at the GSD to others within the School and beyond.

Material Processes and Systems Group (MaP+S)

Director: Martin Bechthold, Kumagai Professor of Architectural Technology

MaP+S understands, develops, and deploys innovative technologies in the promotion of design as an agent of change in the quest for a better future.

Responsive Environments & Artifacts Lab (REAL)

Director: Allen Sayegh, Associate Professor in Practice of Architectural Technology

REAL pursues the design of digital, virtual, and physical worlds as an indivisible whole. It recognizes the all-pervasive nature of digital information and interaction in the realms of architectural, urban, and landscape design.

Exhibitions 2018–2019

DRUKER DESIGN GALLERY

The Druker Design Gallery features the work of faculty, students, and researchers and scholars from across the design fields. Located at Gund Hall, the gallery serves as a site for experimentation and explication of ideas and plays a fundamental role in the pedagogical life of the School. The gallery is open to the public, and has a long and rich history of exhibitions that engage the historical and contemporary conditions of design discourse across physical, digital, and spatial media.

Urban Intermedia: City, Archive, Narrative

August 27–October 14, 2018
Curators: Eve Blau, Adjunct Professor of the History and Theory of Urban Form and Design; Robert Pietrusko, Associate Professor of Landscape Architecture
Installation design: Höweler + Yoon Architecture

Urban Intermedia: City, Archive, Narrative, the culmination of a four-year investigation funded by the Andrew W. Mellon Foundation, argues that the complexity of contemporary urban societies and environments makes communication and collaboration across professional boundaries and academic disciplines essential. Four research projects, focused respectively on Berlin, Boston, Istanbul, and Mumbai, use a range of technologies to bring physical and digital media—archival documents, digital data sets, photography, cartography, architectural drawings, graphics, text, animation, film, and video—into dialogue and registration with each other. The media hybridize, exchange properties and techniques, and generate new "intermedia" languages—and, with them, new ways of acquiring and producing knowledge about cities. Projected onto screens, the visual narratives they construct tell their stories through the materials of the research themselves without written or verbal narration, leaving them open to multiple readings and the interactive construction of meaning with viewers of the exhibition.

The Veronica Rudge Green Prize in Urban Design: The High Line

November 1–December 21, 2018
Curators: Stephen Gray, Assistant Professor of Urban Design; Caroline Filice Smith (PhD)

The 13th Veronica Rudge Green Prize in Urban Design recognizes the High Line as exemplar for the complex coordination of creative professionals, philanthropists, and policy makers by deeply committed community advocates. The Green Prize also recognizes Friends of the High Line for their unwavering commitment to improving the public realm through design excellence and for their capacity to continually reinvent the High Line in ways that support more-inclusive public spaces—both in New York and across the globe.

The opening of the High Line in 2009 was neither the park's first nor final achievement. Originally conceived in the early 20th century, the elevated rail was a response to public outcry over rail-related fatalities at street level. Over time, the High Line became increasingly peripheral to New Yorkers, if they noticed it at all, seen more as a decaying behemoth, a platform for vice, and a hindrance to progress than for its potential as a transformative public asset. Nearly 10 years after the first section opened, the High Line's reemergence as a beloved and celebrated public space has not only transformed a neighborhood, it has also influenced how we approach and understand urban design on a global scale.

The Veronica Rudge Green Prize in Urban Design: The High Line.

Mountains and the Rise of Landscape

January 22–March 10, 2019

Curators: Pablo Pérez-Ramos, Assistant Professor of Landscape Architecture; Edward Eigen, Senior Lecturer in the History of Landscape and Architecture; Michael Jakob; Anita Berrizbeitia, Professor of Landscape Architecture and Chair of the Department of Landscape Architecture

To ask when we started looking at mountains is by no means the same as asking when we started to see them. Rather, it is to question what sorts of aesthetic and moral responses, what kinds of creative and reflective impulses, our newfound regard for them prompted. It is evident enough that in a more or less recent geological time frame mountains have always just been there. It is possible that mountains, like the sea, best provide pleasure, visual and otherwise, when experienced from a (safe) physical and psychical distance. But it might also be the case that the pleasures mountains hold in store are of a learned and acquired sort.

Which is also to say that mountains themselves, for all their unforgivingthereness, are themselves the products of unwitnessed Neptunian and Vulcanian tumults or divine judgment. For the late 17th-century theologian and cosmogonist Thomas Burnet, mountains were "nothing but great ruins." A dawning appreciation of these wastelands appeared in the critical writings of John Dennis. Satirized as "Sir Tremendous Longinus" for his rehabilitation of the antique aesthetic category of the sublime, Dennis expressed the complex concept of "delightful horror." Mountain gloom was ready to become mixed with mountain glory. More work was still to be done on the literary and philosophical front before the Romantic breakthrough, one high vantage point being the essayist Joseph Addison's dream of finding himself in the Alps, "astonished at the discovery of such a Paradise amidst the wildness of those cold hoary landscapes."

But a kindred innovation in seeing and feeling was called for in the formation of mountains and the rise of landscape. Mountains, among other earth forms, are both the medium and the outcome of still-evolving habits of experiencing, making, and imagining. Architects and landscape architects, mutually occupied with the horizontal surface, have had a touch equally as searching as that of mountaineers and poets in sensing the terrain. *Mountains and the Rise of Landscape* is the culmination of a curatorial project and a research seminar conducted at the Harvard GSD, the latter focusing on the question, How do you model a mountain? The installation collects diverse objects and scientific instruments, drawings, photographs, and motion pictures of built and imagined projects and presents invitingly challenging modes of seeing (and hearing!) mountains of varied definition. Allied with the work of artists, visionaries, and interpreters of natural and cultural meaning, they propose new and foregone possibilities of perception and form-making in the acts of leveling and grading, cutting and filling, shaping and contouring, mapping and modeling, of reimagining "matter out of place," and finally of stacking the odds and mounting the possibilities.

Mountains and the Rise of Landscape.

Platform 11: Setting the Table

March 25–May 17, 2019
Curators: Esther Mira Bang (MArch '18); Lane Raffaldini Rubin (MArch, MLA '19); Enrique Aureng Silva (MDes '18)

The table hosts a diverse body of topics from the witty banter of a first date to the weighty gravitas of a negotiation. Its materiality and temperament range from the cold sterility of a dissection to the adrenaline-pumping anxiety of an interrogation. Some guests are offered a seat at the table, some burst onto the scene uninvited, while still others must fight for their place.

The table is reimagined as a new setting, an active volume within the GSD, entangled within the very structure of the building, recasting projects upon a single shared datum. After reading through hundreds of syllabi, event transcripts, project descriptions, research abstracts, and theses, the editors cut up these materials and collaged words and phrases that have special resonance for each table—shuffling them, reconfiguring them, juxtaposing them—ending up with a poetic construct: a table of contents that draws out the true art of setting the table.

Platform 11: Setting the Table.

Dazibao

August 28–October 14, 2018
Curator: George L. Legendre, Associate Professor in Practice of Architecture

Dazibao (大字报; Chinese: *big character report*) proposes a selection of 360 student drawings spanning a decade of GSD option studios taught by George L. Legendre. Themes include the legacy of high modernism ("Mies Immersion II," 2009), form vs. function ("Real and Imaginary Variables: Art Spaces," 2012), architectural typology ("Block Blob Mat Slab Slat," 2015) and modes of material production ("Building as Model–Model as Building," 2018). The selection is curated in the form of a giant Dazibao, referring to public mural newspapers of the Chinese Cultural Revolution (1966–1976).

How to See Architecture: Bruno Zevi (MArch '42)

November 1–December 20, 2018
Curator: K. Michael Hays, Eliot Noyes Professor of Architectural Theory and Associate Dean for Academic Affairs

This exhibition begins with a 1941 student memo to the GSD, entitled "An Opinion on Architecture." In this memo, Bruno Zevi, along with other student authors, states the importance of discourse in architecture in general, specifically calling upon GSD students to create their own publication. To evidence the importance of his position, we have created a bifurcated timeline: on the top are the suite of books authored by Zevi throughout his lifetime, and running along the bottom are the multiple GSD student publications created since "An Opinion on Architecture," culminating in the eleventh volume of *Platform*, a new turn on the yearly series that has shifted the editorial role from faculty to students.

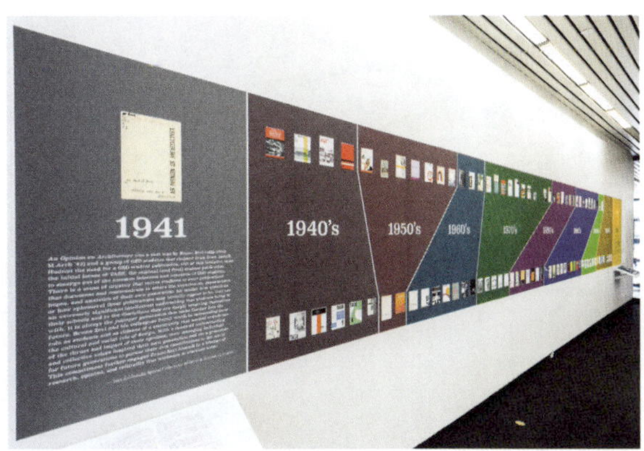

How to See Architecture: Bruno Zevi (MArch '42).

How to Model a Mountain

January 28–March 17, 2019
Curator: Edward Eigen, Senior Lecturer in the History of Landscape and Architecture;

A complement to *Mountains and the Rise of Landscape*, an exhibition concurrently displayed in the Druker Design Gallery.

Multiple Miamis

April 1–May 17, 2019
Curators: Chris Reed, Professor in Practice of Landscape Architecture; Sean Canty, Assistant Professor of Architecture

The *Multiple Miamis* exhibition encompasses research and studio work undertaken by students studying landscape architecture, urban design, and architecture at the Harvard GSD. Directed by Chris Reed and Sean Canty under the Future of the American City Initiative, the eponymous Fall 2018 option studio examined the Overtown neighborhood near downtown Miami, and looked to imagine new and diverse urban strategies that recognized a multiplicity of environmental, social, cultural, and economic starting points that redefine what an inclusive and civically minded urbanism could be.

As a whole, the interdisciplinary studio tackled pressing contemporary urban challenges facing many American cities, including accessibility and mobility, housing and affordability, race and cultural identity, climate change and adaptation, and struggles for a more inclusive and diverse public realm.

Drawing by Hiroki Kawashima (MAUD) and Samuel Adkisson (MAUD), produced in the "Multiple Miamis" option studio.

DEAN'S OFFICE

Inside Architecture

August 31–October 14, 2018
Curators: Luisa Lambri with Mark Lee, Chair of the Department of Architecture and Professor in Practice of Architecture

Based on a workshop conducted by artist Luisa Lambri in January 2018, this exhibition features students' photographs of the interior of Harvard University's Carpenter Center for Visual Arts designed by Le Corbusier. The project explores the relationship between the students and their experiences within the spaces and interiors of the Carpenter Center, which offers a canvas for the student's/photographer's own personal and artistic expression. The focus is not so much a classic representation of Corbusier's building, but rather a highly subjective approach to how an iconic structure can be explored beyond its historical significance in the canon of architectural history and photography.

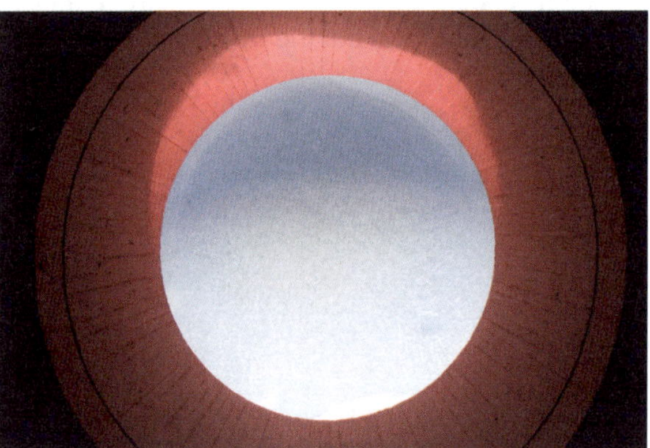

Photograph by Boxiang Yu (MLA I, MLAUD), produced in the "Inside Architecture" J-Term workshop.

New Student Fellowships

November 1–December 20, 2018

Through the Grounded Visionaries campaign, the GSD endowed 25 new fellowships—an increase of 60 percent. We are very grateful to the many individuals, corporations, and foundations that have stepped up to support financial aid for students. These fellowships help broaden the diversity of the student body and enable many of our graduates to make career choices rooted in their passions, rather than their obligations to repay student loans. All of this contributes to a robust range of ideas that our students bring to the School and to the disciplines.

Death, Divorce, Down-Sizing, Dislocation, and (Now) Display: A Self-Storage Center for a More Exhibitionist Future

January 28–March 17, 2019
Author: Hyojin Kwon (MArch '18)

The self-storage center for a near future presents collectors with many options for storage and display, both physical and digital, accommodating a wide range of storage formats under one roof. Public exhibition of personal possessions achieves an institutional character for the self-storage center, in which objects gain an architectural importance. Constant curation of objects resists hoarder culture, instead asking what belongs in storage when the previously dark and hidden becomes bright and showcased. As the new self-storage center takes on museological presentation and develops a distinct form, it acts as a monument to collections of the tangible and intangible within its urban context. Can such an establishment blur the distinctions between storage space, personal collection, and cultural museum?

Death, Divorce, Down-Sizing, Dislocation, and (Now) Display: A Self-Storage Center for a More Exhibitionist Future.

Now Arriving: A Transit Landscape for Manhattan

April 1–May 17, 2019
Curator: Gary Hilderbrand, Peter Louis Hornbeck Professor in Practice of Landscape Architecture

This exhibition presents the work of the eponymous Fall 2018 option studio led by Gary Hilderbrand—the third in a series examining technological, operational, and spatial changes to mobility and public realm patterns in Manhattan. This studio and exhibition suggest that New York's central transit hub—today's dreaded Penn Station—could be reimagined as the city's largest civic plaza.

EXPERIMENTS WALL

Names, Things, Cities: Divine Comedy

August 28–October 14, 2018
Curator: Francesca Benedetto, Design Critic in Landscape Architecture

Nomi, Cose, Città. Divina Commedia. The exhibition deconstructs the *Divina Commedia* in singular elements that are part of specific categories, and creates a visual archive of one of the most famous long narrative poems in the world. Every illustrated image refers to main characters as well as objects, atmospheric agents, architectures, cities, landscapes, animals, and so on.

Names, Things, Cities: Divine Comedy.

Outside the Lines: Across Disciplines with Harvard's Design Engineers

November 1–December 20, 2018
Curator: Andrew Witt, Assistant Professor in Practice of Architecture

Harvard's recently launched Master in Design Engineering program is a first-of-its-kind synthesis of future-oriented strategic design, cross-scalar imagination, and rigorous engineering. In this exhibit, we reveal some methods and products of this unique experiment in systemic solutions that cross fields and address issues ranging from food networks to human aging and mobility.

enGENDERing Urban Equity: Inclusive Design Strategies in Argentina

January 28–March 17, 2019
Curator: Chelina Odbert (MUP '07), Design Critic in Urban Planning and Design

How can participatory planning and design morph cities into places that genuinely work for all genders? The product of Chelina Odbert's Fall 2018 option studio, "Gendering Urban Development," this exhibition showcases the output of a collaborative and participatory planning and design process where partner outcomes are just as important as learning outcomes, where process is just as important as product.

Representation First (!!!), Then Architecture

April 1–May 17, 2019
Curator: Jennifer Bonner, Associate Professor of Architecture
Installation design: Mindy Seu (MDes ADPD); Edward Wang (MArch I)

Current tendencies in the discipline suggest a split between two opposing architectural projects: the easy project versus the difficult project. Primarily related to architecture's form, this oversimplification of the divide might also be used to identify developments in representation: cheap and fast one-point perspectives with minimal material changes as opposed to laborious photo-realistic renderings oozing tactile interiors. The hourly "swipe"—up/down/left/right—and the way architectural images are posted, pinned, shared, and liked moments after they are created places a further immediacy on the making of representation and the naming of an agenda. Rather than question the easy over the difficult, might we readjust our focus towards the conceptualization of representation first, as a way of conceiving of architecture?

Thing Tank: 18 Design Fictions

May 29–August 4, 2019
Curators: Renee Tapp, Lecturer in Urban Planning and Design; Jeffrey Schnapp, Carl A. Pescosolido Professor of Romance Languages and Literatures and of Comparative Literature

The world of things is more than the body of everyday equipment that accompanies our lives: It is a laboratory where the intentions of makers and marketers collide with unstable scenarios of past, present, and future use. *The Thing Tank* explores this terrain of contact and collision in the form of 18 student projects that engage in a dialogue with some of the defining works of 20th-century Italian design, from Carlo Bugatti's 1902 Cobra Chair to the Olivetti calculators of the 1980s.

KIRKLAND GALLERY

Kirkland Gallery is a student organization dedicated to supporting the Harvard GSD community and its emerging artists and designers.

2018–2019 Curators: Kathryn Abarbanel (MDes ADPD), Inés Benítez (MDes ADPD), Eric Moed (MDes ADPD), Sampath Pediredla (MArch II), Mindy Seu (MDes ADPD), Alicia Valencia (MDes ADPD)

Object of Memory

Isabel Chun (MArch I), Marc Dessauvage (MArch I)

Observer / What I Like About This Building

Henrik Ilvesmäki (MArch II, MDes HPDM), Bijan Thornycroft (MArch I)

Sugar Thief

Je Sung Lee (MDes ADPD)

mirror/MIRUS

Caleb Marhoover (MArch I), LEENA

Dinner Party

Ciara Stein (MLA I); Womxn in Design

Breaths, Touching Slowly

Daniel Shieh (MDes ADPD)

A quien corresponda:

Edgar Rodriguez (MArch II), Inés Benitez (MDes ADPD)

Publications 2018–2019

HARVARD DESIGN MAGAZINE

Harvard Design Magazine 46: “No Sweat.” Edited by Jennifer Sigler and Leah Whitman-Salkin. Fall/Winter 2018.

Harvard Design Magazine 47: “Inside Scoop.” Edited by Jennifer Sigler and Leah Whitman-Salkin. Spring/Summer 2019.

THE INCIDENTS

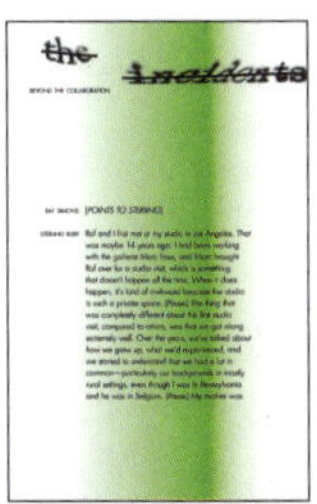

Sterling Ruby and Raf Simons. *Beyond the Collaboration.* Copublished with Sternberg Press, 2018.

PLATFORM

Platform 11: *Setting the Table*. Edited by Esther Mira Bang (MArch '18), Lane Raffaldini Rubin (MArch I, MLA I AP), Enrique Aureng Silva (MDes '18). Copublished with Actar, 2018.

STUDIO REPORTS

Rok Oman, David Rubin, Špela Videčnik. *Manila: Future Habitations.* 2018.

Marina Tabassum. *$2000 Home.* 2019.

Toyo Ito and Jun Yanagisawa. *Transforming Omishima.* 2019.

Teresa Galí-Izard. *Regenerative Empathy.* 2019. Available in French.

Iwan Baan and Tatiana Bilbao. *The House: The Waken Desire.* 2019.

NEW GEOGRAPHIES

New Geographies 10: “Fallow.” Edited by Michael Chieffalo (DDes), Julia Smachylo (DDes). Copublished with Actar, 2019.

COPUBLICATIONS

Andrew Witt and Christopher Reznich. *The Natural Forces Laboratory: Ralph Knowles and the Instrumentalized Studio.* Copublished with the Canadian Centre for Architecture, 2018.

Andrew Witt and Eliza Pertigkiozoglou. *Computation as Design: Ron Resch and the New Media of Geometry.* Copublished with the Canadian Centre for Architecture, 2019.

STUDENT PUBLICATIONS

Harvard Real Estate Review 7: “Disruption and Resilience.” Edited by Malia Teske (MUP), with Diana Guo (MLA I), Dixi Wu (MArch I, MDes REBE), George Zhang (MArch I), Edward Madigan (MDes REBE), Winston Chang (MDes REBE).

Open Letters, issue nos. 65–74. Edited by Audrey Chan, Jessica Lim (MArch I), Milos Mladenovic (MArch I), Edward Wang (MArch I AP), Adrian Wong (MArch II).

Public Programs 2018–2019

Eve Blau, Laura Kurgan, Lev Manovich, Robert Pietrusko, and Jeffrey Schnapp
"Urban Intermedia: City, Archive, Narrative"
September 5, 2018

Pezo von Ellrichshausen
"Deciduous Plan"
September 7, 2018

Anna Puigjaner
"Kitchen Stories"
Wheelwright Prize Lecture
September 11, 2018

Meet the Loeb Fellows
2018–2019 Fellows: Stephen Burks, Maria Cabildo, Jeana Dunlap, Washington Fajardo, Bryna Lipper, Michael Smith Masis, Katie Swenson, and Michiel van Iersel
September 11–18, 2018

Kees Christiaanse
"Inversion and Subtraction in Urban Design"
September 14, 2018

Alison Brooks
"Model Building Model: Making Oxford's New Collegiate Architecture"
September 17, 2018

Alison Brooks.

Francesca Benedetto
"Names, Things, Cities: Divine Comedy"
September 18, 2018

Michael Hays, Tim Benton, Lisa Haber-Thomson, John May, and Mirko Zardini
"The Open University's Course A305 and the Future of Architecture Education"
September 19, 2018

Ranjani Mazumdar
"The Cinematic Slum"
September 20, 2018

Ranjani Mazumdar.

Nora Akawi
"Traversing Territories"
Aga Khan Program Lecture
October 1, 2018

Carla Juaçaba
"Empty Space"
October 2, 2018

Hannah Beachler with Jacqueline Stewart
Rouse Visiting Artist Lecture
October 4, 2018

Mohammad al-Asad
"The Center for the Study of the Built Environment (CSBE): A 20-Year Journey"
Aga Khan Program Lecture
October 5, 2018

Christopher Hawthorne
October 9, 2018

Sou Fujimoto
"Between Nature and Architecture"
October 11, 2018

"PRACTICE: Outside In | Inside Out"
Symposium participants: Mack Scogin, Mark Lee, Aaron Cayer, Neena Verma, Jesse Keenan, Alison Brooks, Grace La, Eduard Sancho Pou, Sawako Kaijima, Randy Deutsch, and Robert Pietrusko
October 12, 2018

Bruno Latour
"A Tale of Seven Planets – An Exercise in Gaiapolitics"
Senior Loeb Scholar Lecture
October 16, 2018

José Esparza Chong Cuy
"Building Cycles"
October 18, 2018

Marty Poirier
"The Creativity Continuum | How I learned about the place of art and design in culture"
October 22, 2018

Fritz Haeg, Nils Norman, and Julieta González
Rouse Visiting Artist Lecture
October 23, 2018

Michael Van Valkenburgh
"New Parks"
Frederick Law Olmsted Lecture
October 25, 2018

Pippo Ciorra, Jean-Louis Cohen, Michael Hays, Alicia Imperiale, Jorge Francisco Liernur, Daria Ricchi, and Tamar Zinguer
"How to See Architecture: Bruno Zevi (MArch '42)"
October 26, 2018

Elisa Silva
"Territorial Inequality and the Urban Cassandras of Our Times"
October 29, 2018

Irma Boom
Open House Lecture
November 1, 2018

Irma Boom's tiny books.

Jan Boelen
"Design as Learning"
Margaret McCurry Lectureship in the Design Arts
November 7, 2018

Thomas Woltz
"Threatened Landscapes: Designed Countermeasures of Nelson Byrd Woltz Landscape Architects"
November 8, 2018

Anna Heringer
"Architecture as a Tool to Improve Lives"
Aga Khan Program Lecture
November 13, 2018

Diane E. Davis, Stephen Gray, Elizabeth Diller, Ric Scofidio, James Corner, Liza Tziona Switkin, Robert Hammond, and Joshua David
"The Veronica Rudge Green Prize in Urban Design: The High Line"
November 14, 2018

John Alschuler, Joshua David, Robert Hammond, Belinda Tato, and Diane E. Davis
"The High Line: A Debate"
November 15, 2018

Stanislaus Fung
"Recent Projects in Rural China"
November 15, 2018

Yara Sharif
"The Not So Ordinary: Capturing Possibilities Through The Gaps"
Aga Khan Program Lecture
November 19, 2018

Shirin Neshat
November 27, 2018

HHF (Tilo Herlach, Simon Hartmann, and Simon Frommenwiler)
November 29, 2018

Hans Ulrich Obrist
Rouse Visiting Artist Lecture
November 30, 2018

Michael Jakob, Edward Eigen, Anita Berrizbeitia, Pablo Perez-Ramos, and Martino Pedrozzi
"On Mountains"
Panel Discussion and Exhibition Opening Reception
January 29, 2019

Pablo Perez-Ramos (left) and Martino Pedrozzi.

Beate Holmebakk
"Constructions on Sites and Paper"
February 4, 2019

Norman Kelley
"Things not as they are"
Margaret McCurry Lectureship in the Design Arts
February 5, 2019

Dilip Da Cunha
"The Invention of Rivers"
Daniel Urban Kiley Lecture
February 19, 2019

Dilip Da Cunha.

HECTOR
February 21, 2019

Kuehn Malvezzi
"A HOUSE BETWEEN"
February 22, 2019

David Hartt
"Urban Futures of the Recent Past"
Rouse Visiting Artist Lecture
February 26, 2019

Loreta Castro Reguera
February 28, 2019

Loreta Castro Reguera.

Rania Ghosn
Aga Khan Program Lecture
March 4, 2019

Demita Frazier
"Aesthetic Apartheid: Gender, Race, and Socioeconomic Class, and the Impact on Perception, Engagement, and Experience"
International Womxn's Day Lecture
March 7, 2019

Kenneth Helphand
"Lawrence Halprin"
March 11, 2019

Rosi Braidotti
"Posthuman Knowledge"
March 12, 2019

Sahel Al Hiyari
Aga Khan Program Lecture
March 14, 2019

Kimberly Dowdell
"Diverse City: How Equitable Design and Development Will Shape Urban Futures"
John T. Dunlop Lecture
March 26, 2019

Janette Sadik-Khan
"Streetfight: Handbook for an Urban Revolution"
March 28, 2019

Janette Sadik-Khan.

Monserrat Bonvehi Rosich
Kiley Fellow Lecture
April 1, 2019

"Cambridge Talks: Other Histories of the Digital"
Keynote by Michael Osman, "The Augmented Architect"; Participants: Brandon Finn, Demetra Vogiatzaki, Jacobé Huet, Matthew Allen, Olga Touloumi, Theodora Vardouli, John May, Andrew Holder, Sean Keller, Andrew Witt, Daniel Cardoso Llach, and Antoine Picon
April 1–2, 2019

"Final Revue: Celebrating Mohsen Mostafavi's 11 Years as Dean"
With Michael Hays, Homi Bhabha, Kathleen McCartney, Carrie Bly, Isabella Caterina Frontado, Jihyun Ro, Santiago Mota, Natasha Hicks, Dana McKinney, Jaline McPherson, Daisha Martin, Vijay Iyer, Yosvany Terry, Cynthia Deng, Lindsey Krug, Julia Roberts, Marisa Villarreal, Adelle York, Gabriel Ramos, Ken Stewart, Youngjin Song, Ani Liu, Lins Derry, and Boya Guo
April 2, 2019

Marc and Matthias Armengaud
"Of Monsters and Territorial Reconfiguration: Stories by Marc Armengaud and Matthias Armengaud"
Open House Lecture
April 4, 2019

Rip Rapson, Maurice Cox, and Toni Griffin
"Designing Detroit: A Decade of Change and Transformation"
April 11, 2019

Preston Scott Cohen, James Dallman, Jeanne Gang, Gary Hilderbrand, Eric Höweler, Grace La, Mack Scogin, and Georgeen Theodore
"First Projects: An Unplugged Conversation"
April 12, 2019

Romy Hecht
"The Green Ideal: Botanical Practices and the Creation of Santiago's Civic Landscape"
April 18, 2019

Krzysztof Wodiczko, Ani Liu, and Debra McCall
"Space, Movement, and the Technological Body: A Tribute to the Bauhaus"
April 24, 2019

Performance developed in collaboration with the course "Entanglement of Movement and Meaning: The Architect, Spatial Imagination, and the Technological Body."

Ted'A
April 29, 2019

Teju Cole
Class Day Lecture
May 29, 2019

Credits

The editors derived most question headers throughout the project pages either directly from project submissions and course syllabi or through editorial interpretation of the content. Special cases are found on pages 23, 32, 37, 40, and 44, where the editors propose original questions for the purpose of conceptual grouping.

IMAGE CREDITS

Page 23: Images courtesy Carrie Bly (MDes HPDM) and Jonathan Ng (MArch I); Pages 52–53: Image courtesy Syed Ali (MUP); Page 34: Images courtesy Yashada Wagle (MDes HPDM) and Alexandra Sanyal (MDes CC); Page 49: Images courtesy Yaxuan Liu (MArch I); Page 74: Credits for source photos: (A) Tonika Lewis Johnson, (B) Tracie Hall; Page 75: Credits for source photos, (C) Rae Chardonnay, © Michaela Quan, (D) Isis Ferguson, (E) Maya Bird-Murphy, (F) Jacqueline Stewart, and (D) © Nathan Keay; Page 82: Archival photos courtesy the Boston Public Library; Pages 84–85: Images courtesy Arvind Talati, © CEPT Archives; Page 182: Image courtesy Isabella Caterina Frontado (MLA I, MDes ADPD)

Acknowledgments

We would like to thank Jennifer Sigler for the opportunity to take on this project and the encouragement to make it our own. This book's emphasis on student perspectives would have been an impossible project without her support of student editors taking the reins of the *Platform* series. We thank Marielle Suba, who was with us throughout this editorial journey and guided us without fail—we are grateful for her insights and advice.

We had the privilege to work with Dean Mohsen Mostafavi and three faculty advisors, Gareth Doherty, Jenny French, Abby Spinak, who helped ground our work with thoughtful engagement and direction. Immeasurable support also came from the Harvard GSD Communications Department and Frances Loeb Library: Ken Stewart, for facilitating this project with grace and style; Meg Sandberg, David Zimmerman-Stuart, Maggie Janik, Kevin Lau, Janina Mueller, and Ann Whiteside, for helping us navigate our roles as collectors and documentors of student work. We'd especially like to thank Ines Zalduendo and her insights into the School's institutional history and student publications, without which we could not have realized this project.

Special thanks to graphic designers Neil Donnelly and Ben Fehrman-Lee for their creative collaboration. We also thank photographer Adam DeTour for his creative input and excitement in developing and capturing our concluding photo essays; and thanks too to Dan Borelli, for providing resources both physical and conceptual for these photographs.

Lastly, we were energized and inspired by the students, faculty, and staff who brought their whole selves to the work of design. Many of them have shaped our careers as students, and we are grateful for the conversations.

Published by the Harvard University Graduate School of Design and Actar.

Printed in Germany by PIEREG Berlin

ISBN 978-1-948765-36-7

Library of Congress Control Number: 2019950505

This book is typeset in Simonici Garamond, Akzidenz Grotesk Old Face, and Nimbus Monospace.

The Harvard University Graduate School of Design educates leaders in design, research, and scholarship to make a resilient, just, and beautiful world.

Every attempt was made to acknowledge the source of all images.

Actar
440 Park Avenue South
17th Floor
New York, NY 10016
actar.com

Harvard University
Graduate School of Design
48 Quincy Street
Cambridge, MA 02138
gsd.harvard.edu